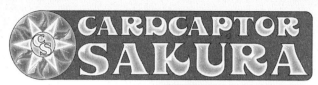

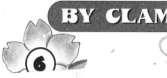

CARDCAPTOR SAKURA

BY CLAMP

TOKYOPOP

TOKYOPOP® Presents
Cardcaptor Sakura 6 by CLAMP
TOKYOPOP is a registered trademark
of Mixx Entertainment, Inc.
ISBN: 1-892213-74-5
First Printing March 2002

10 9 8 7 6 5 4 3 2 1

This volume contains the Cardcaptor Sakura installments from
TOKYOPOP Manga comics No. 23 through No. 26 in their entirety.

Translator-Anita Sengupta. Retouch Artist-Bernard San Juan III.
Graphic Assistant-Anna Kernbaum. Graphic Designer-Akemi Imafuku.
Associate Editor-Stephanie Donnelly. Editor-Robert Coyner.
Senior Editor-Jake Forbes. Production Manager-Fred Lui. Art Director-Matt Alford.
Brand Manager-Kimberly Bird. VP of Production-Ron Klamert.
Publisher-Stuart Levy.

Email: editor@press.TOKYOPOP.com
Come visit us at www.TOKYOPOP.com

TOKYOPOP®
Los Angeles - Tokyo

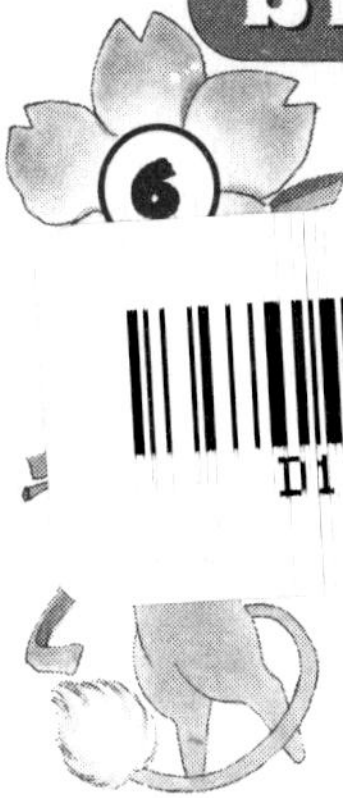

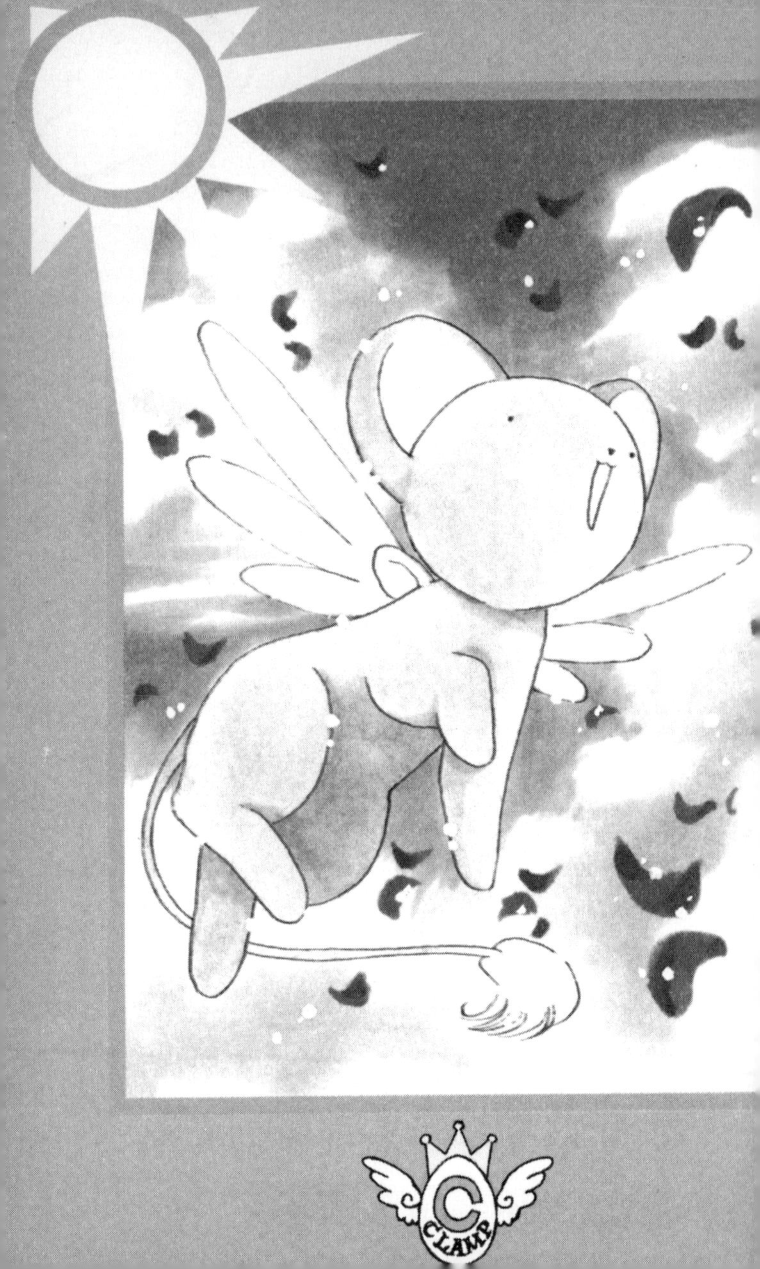

CLOW CARD

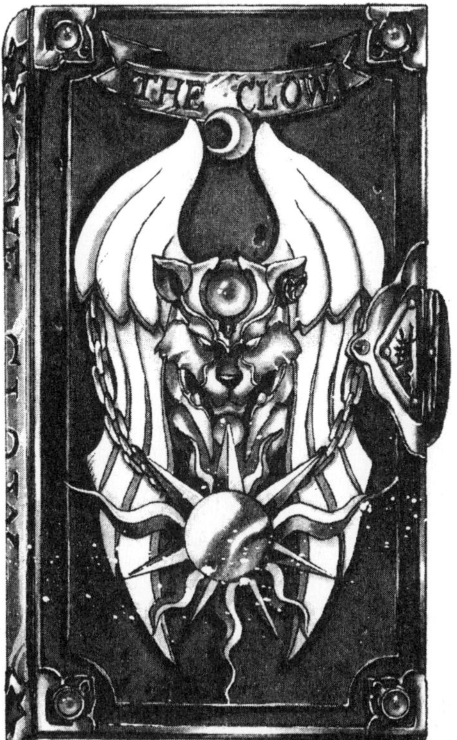
THE CLOW

When the seal is broken...

Evil will befall this world...

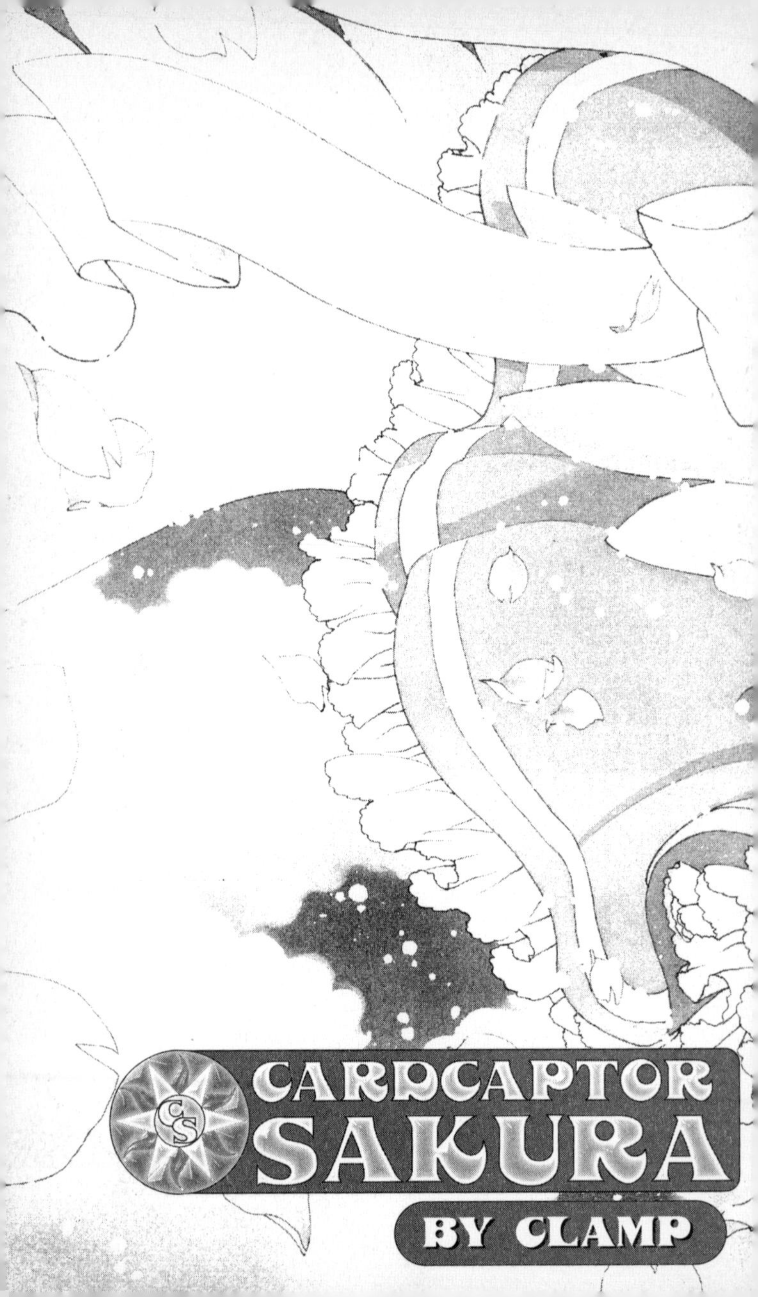

CARDCAPTOR SAKURA

BY CLAMP

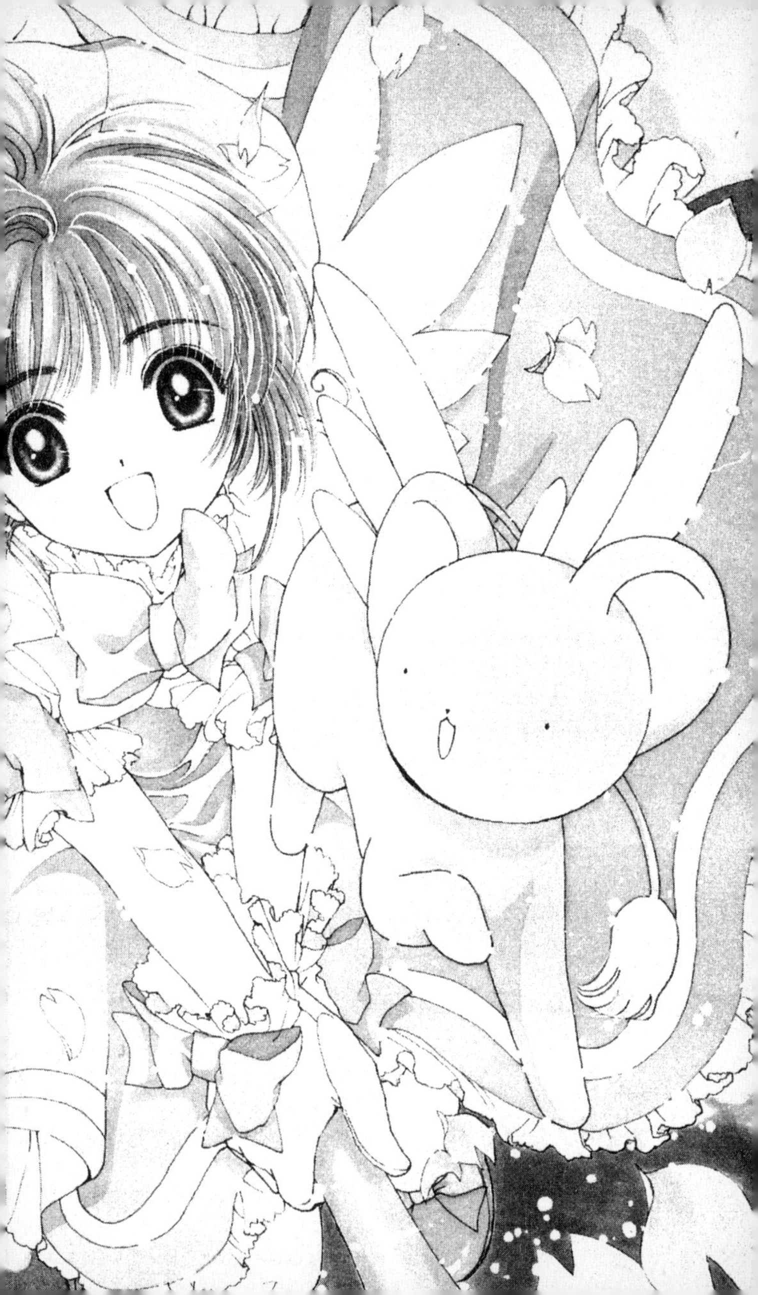

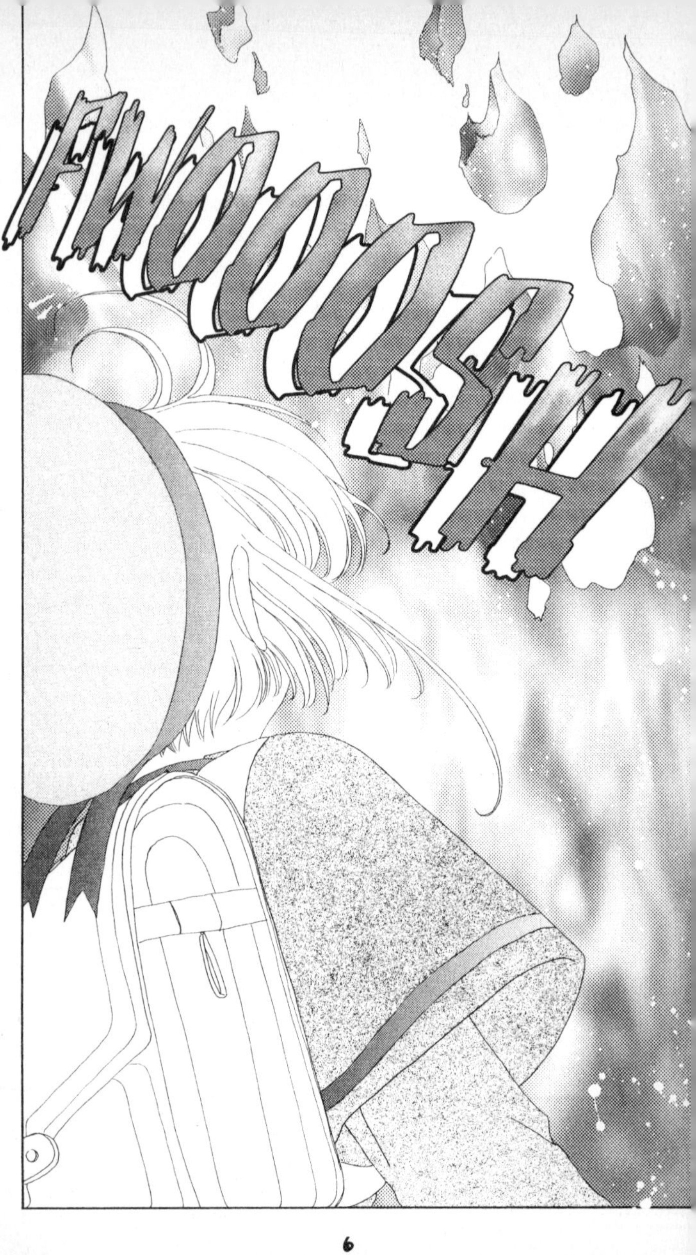
FWOOOSH

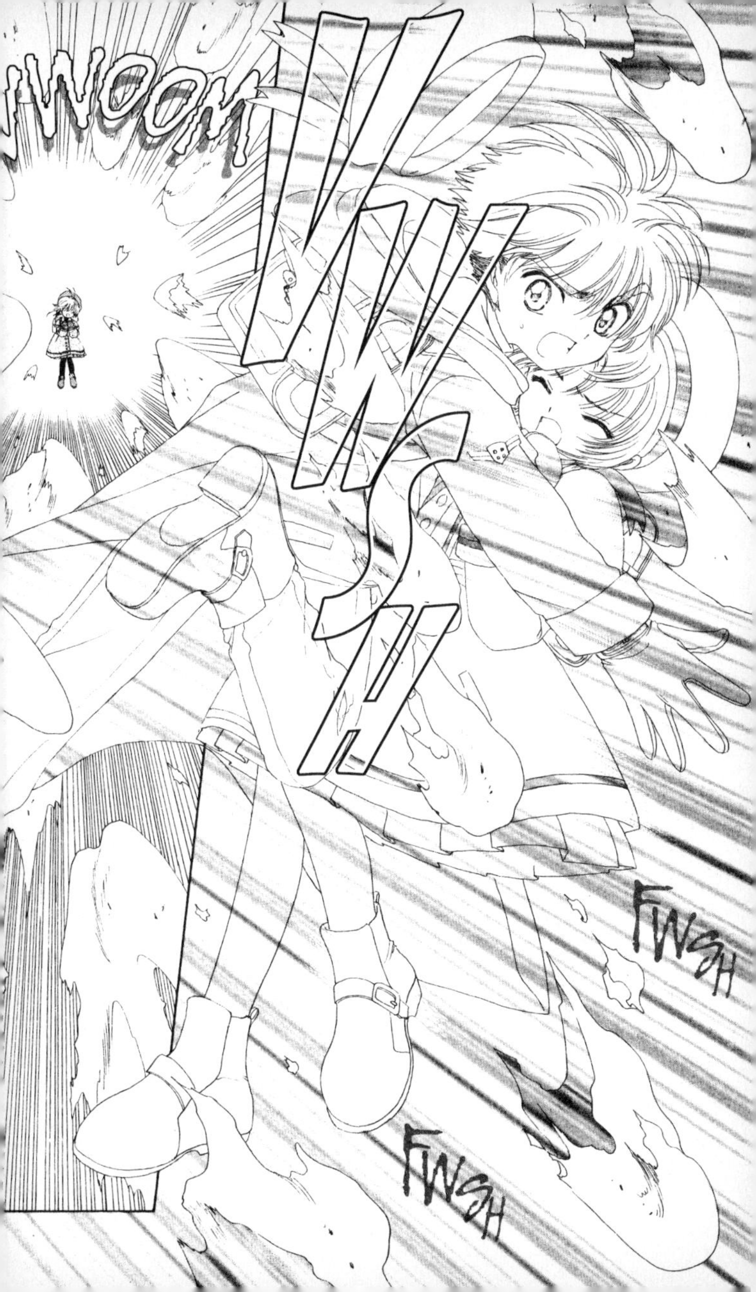
WOOM
VWWSH
FWSH
FWSH

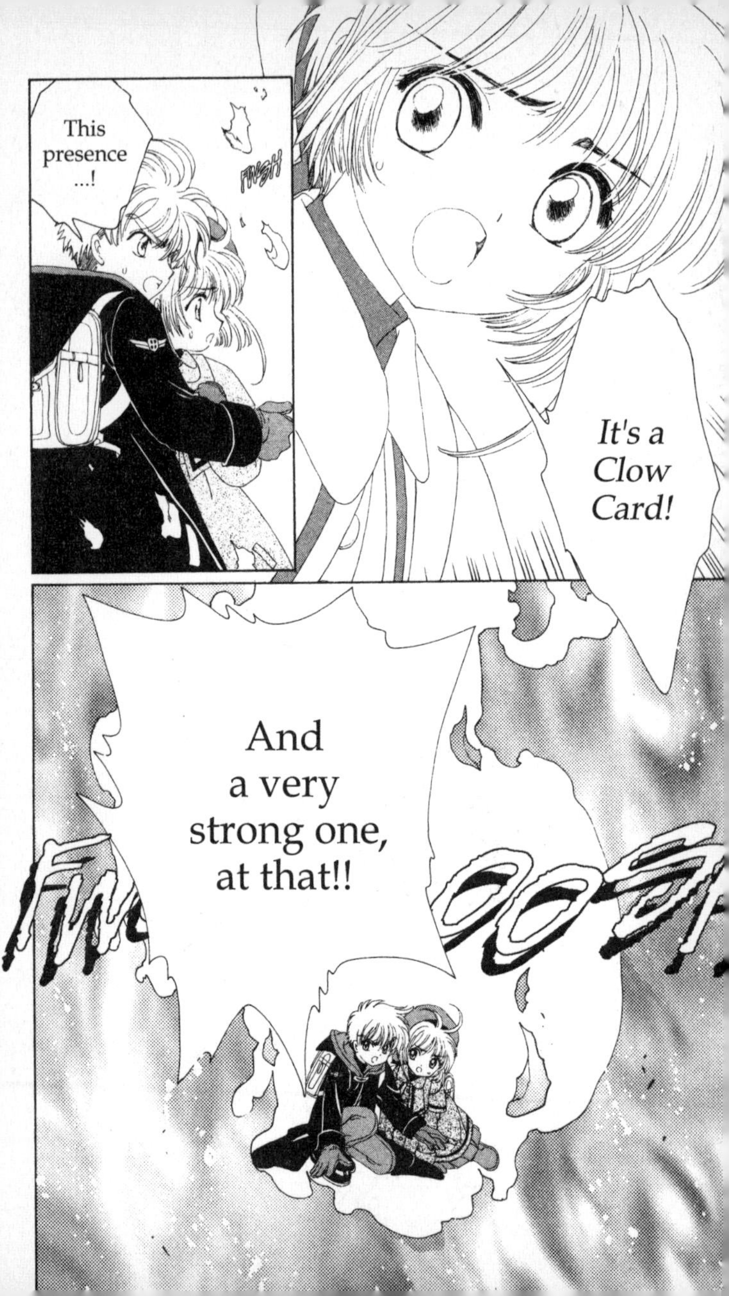
This presence ...!
FWSH
It's a Clow Card!
And a very strong one, at that!!

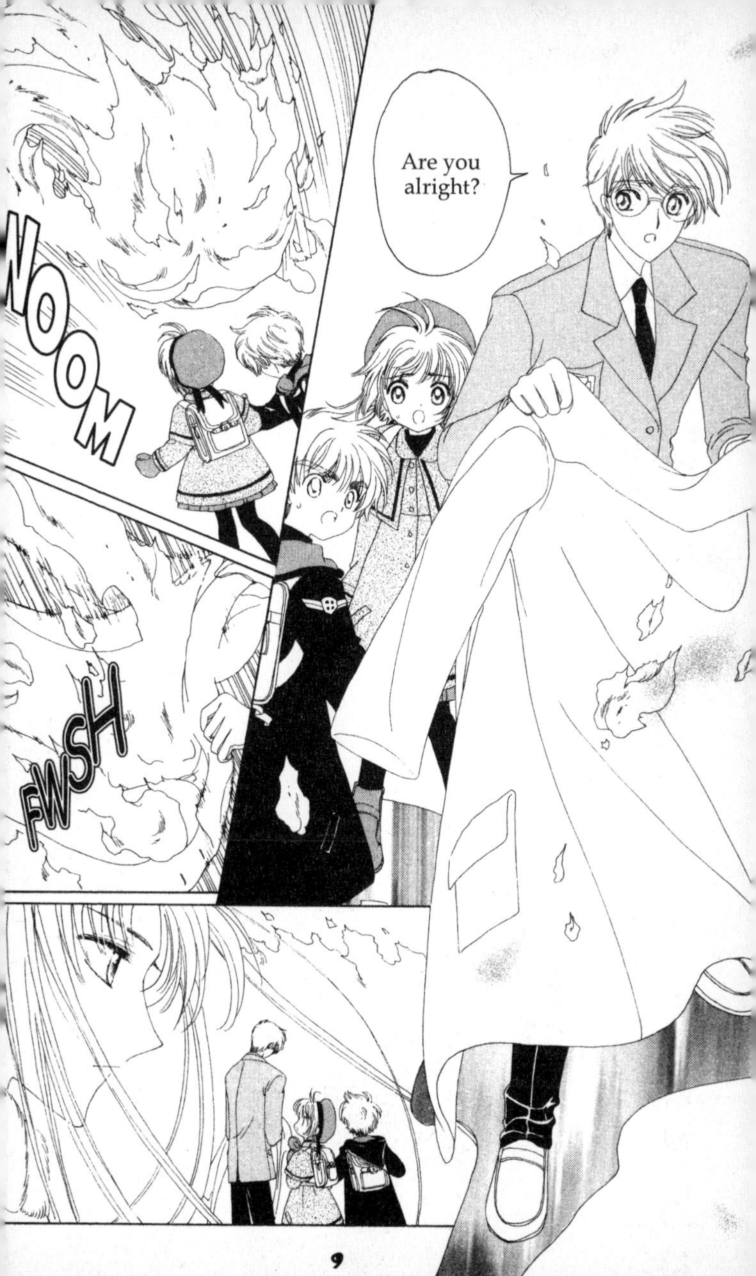
Are you alright?
WOOM
FWSH

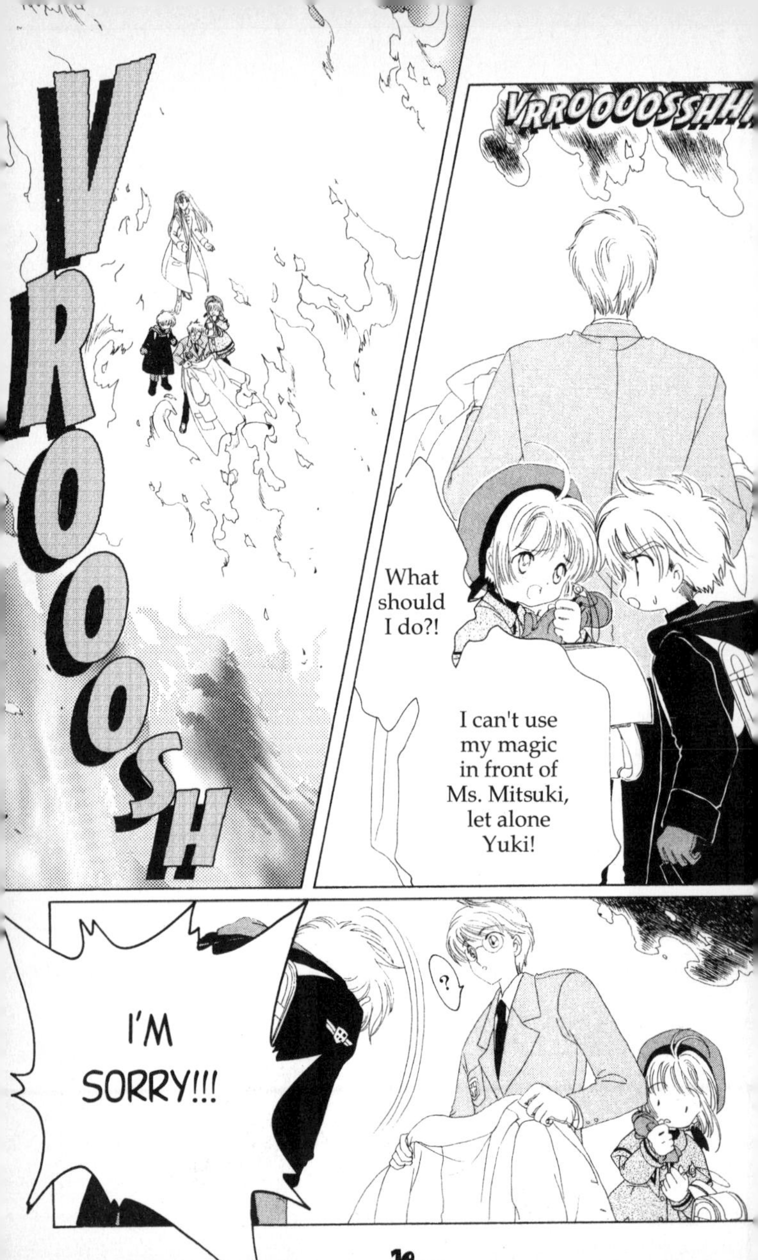
VRROOOOSSHH
What should I do?!
I can't use my magic in front of Ms. Mitsuki, let alone Yuki!
VROOOOSH
?
I'M SORRY!!!

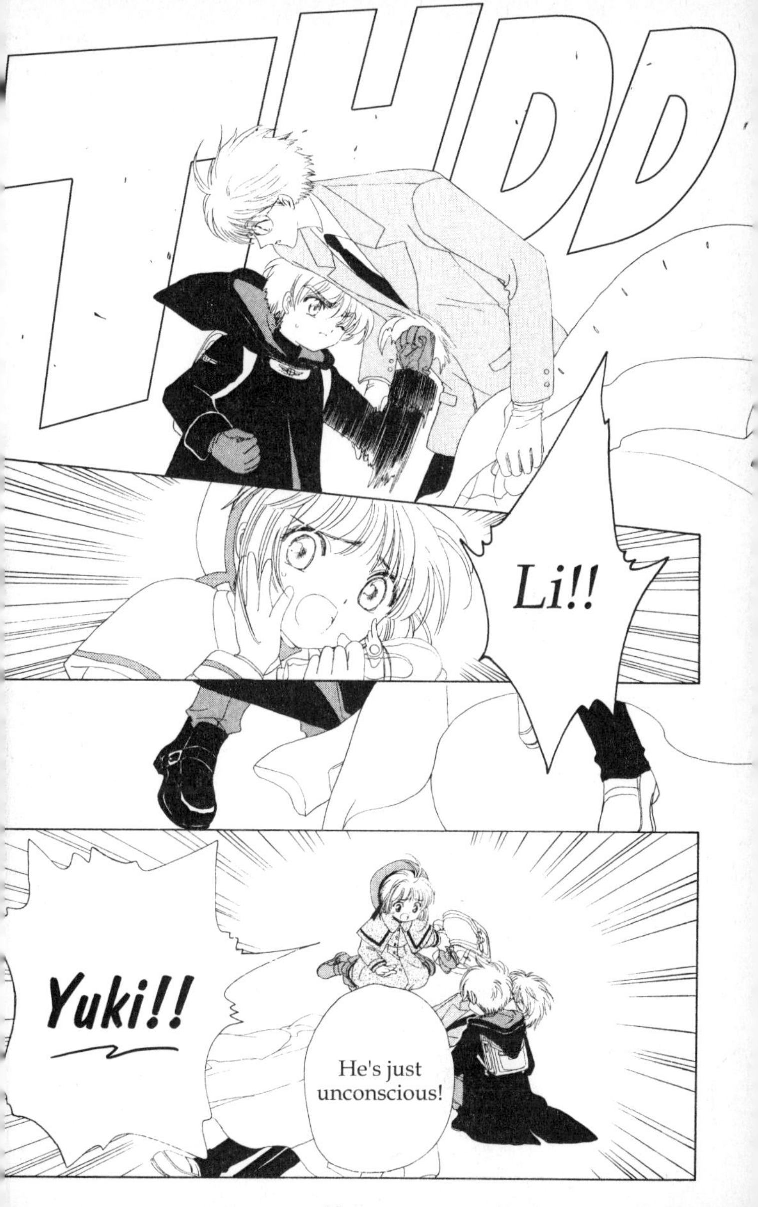
THDD
Li!!
Yuki!!
He's just unconscious!

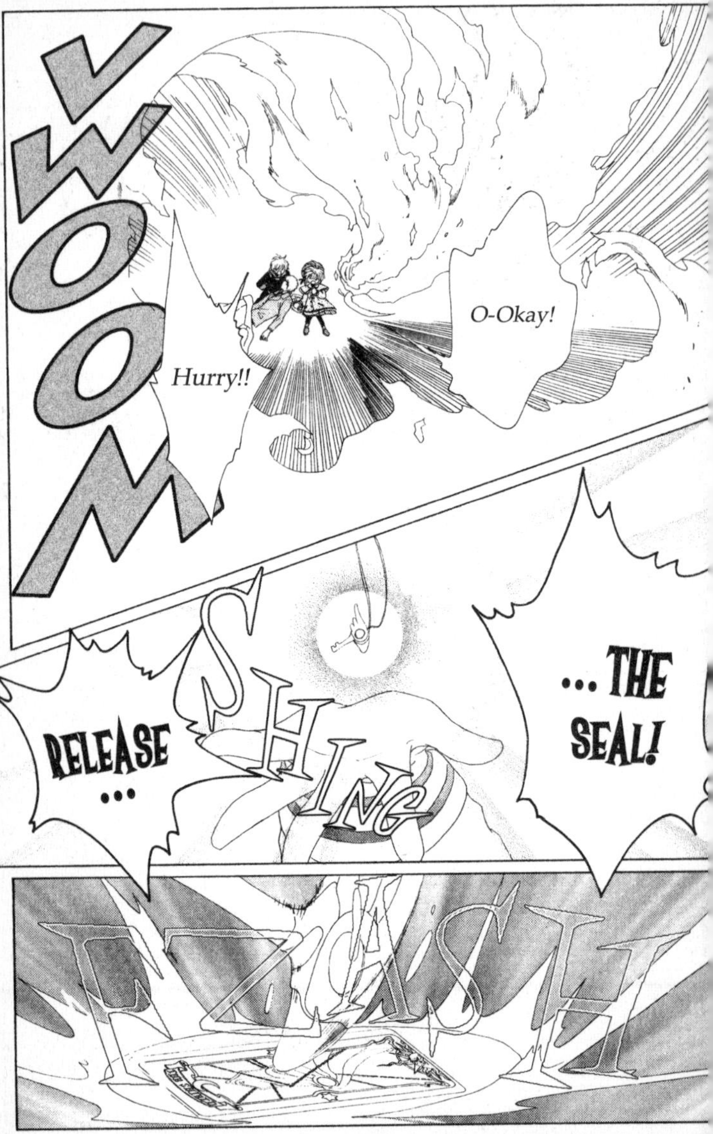
VWOOM
Hurry!!
O-Okay!
RELEASE ...
SHING
... THE SEAL!

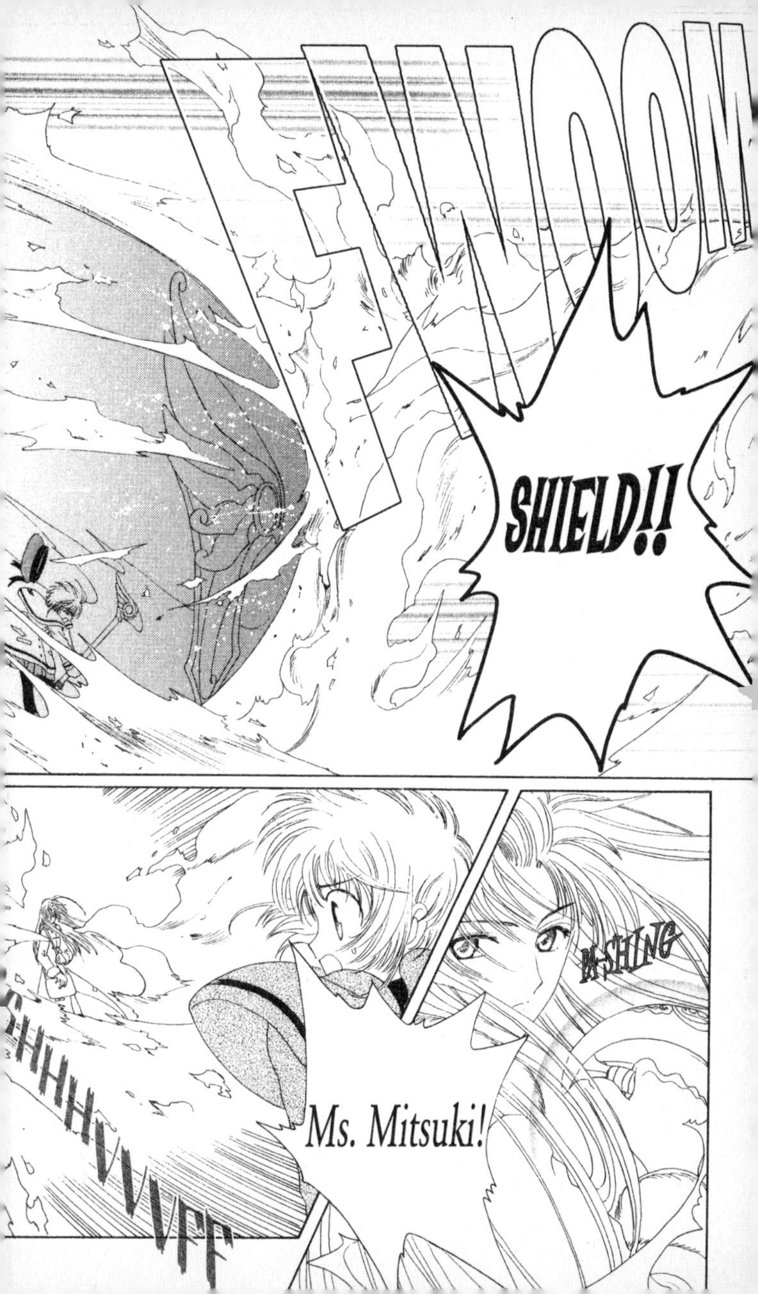
FWOOM
SHIELD!!
PA-SHING
Ms. Mitsuki!
HHHVVVFF

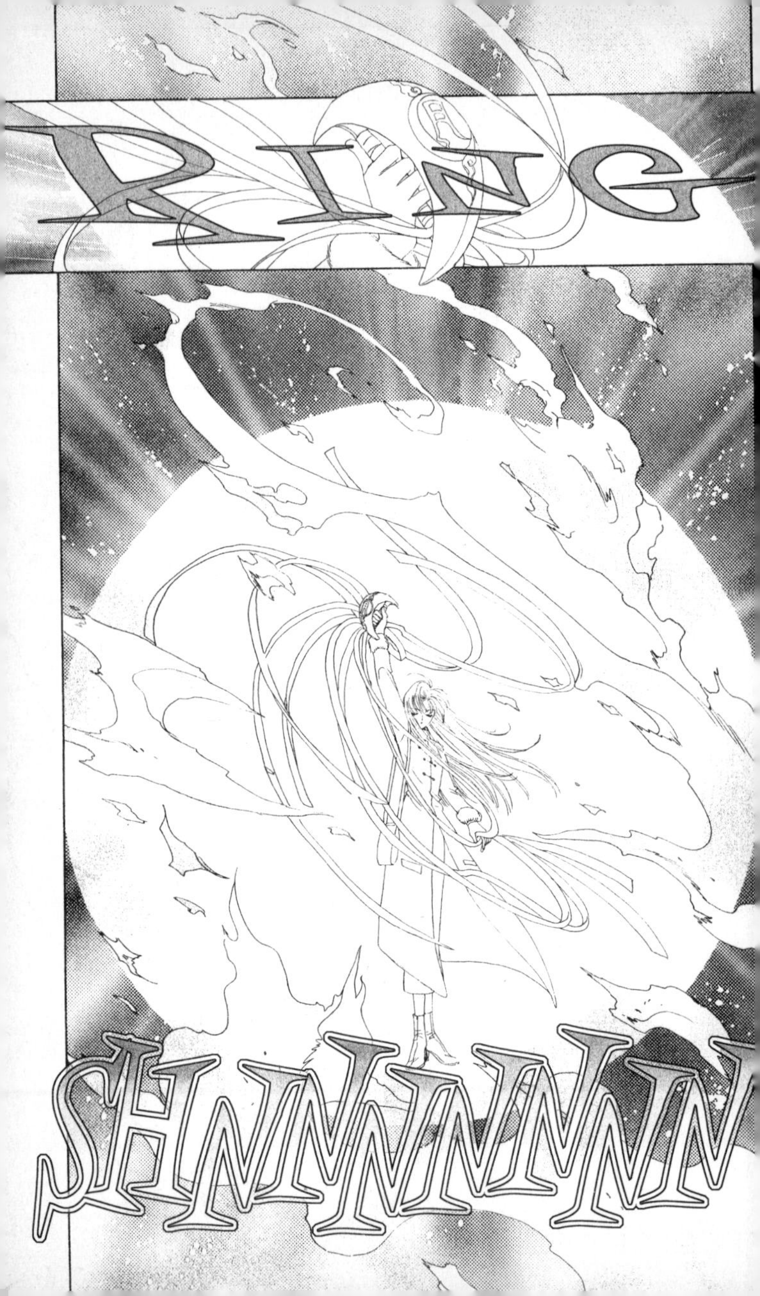
RING
SHINNNNN

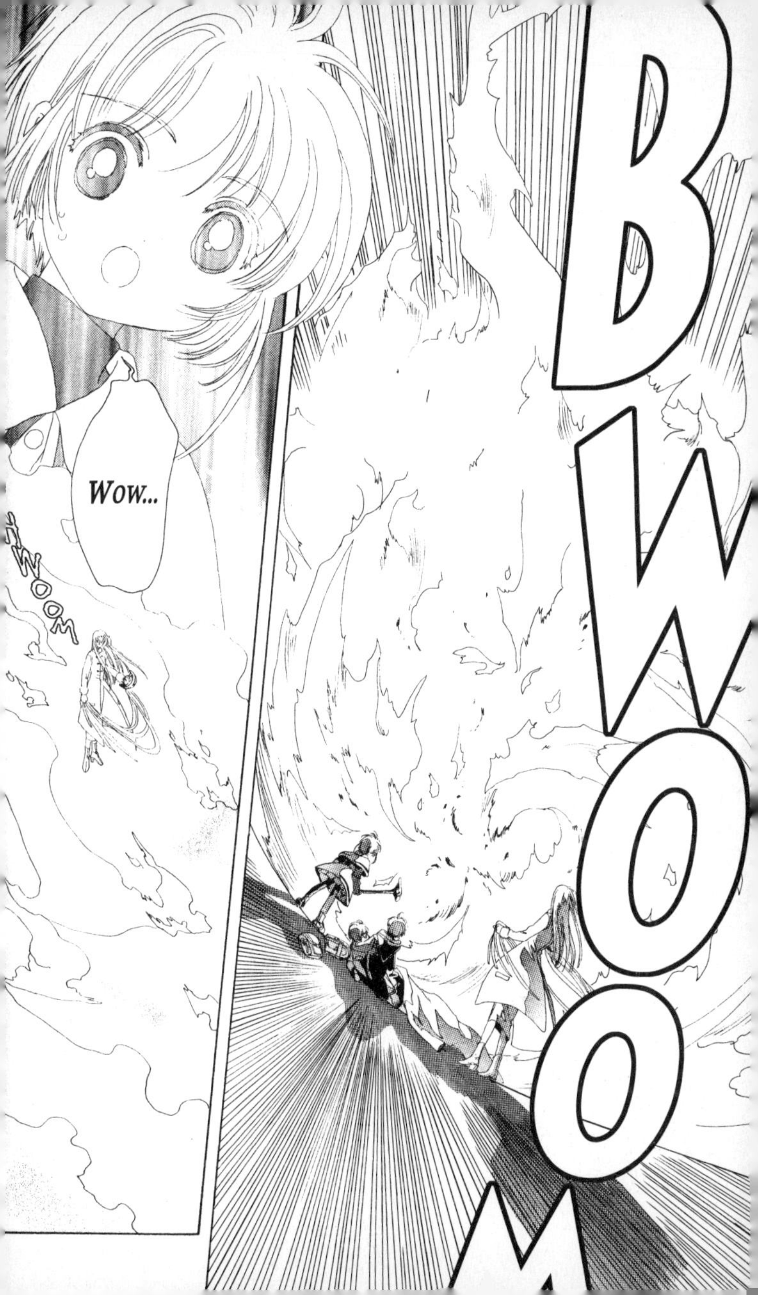
BWOOM
Wow...

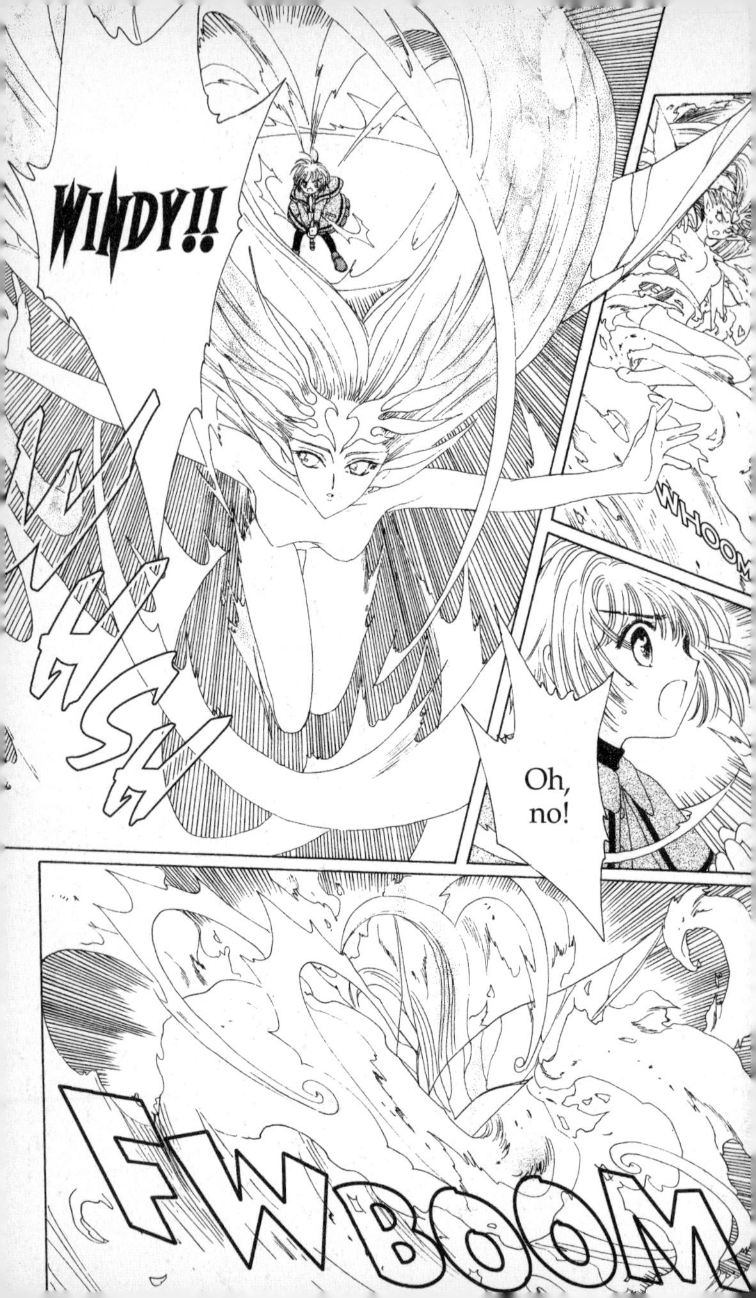
WHOOM
Oh, no!
WINDY!!
WHSH
FWBOOM

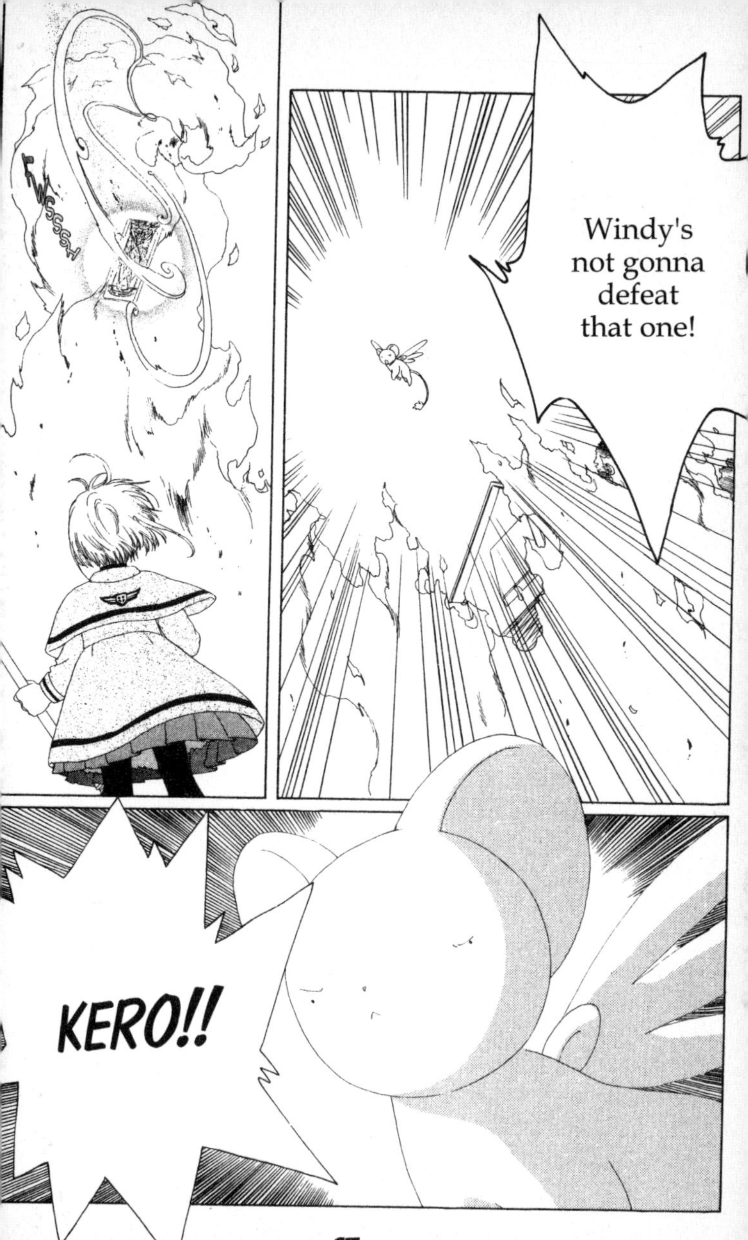
Windy's not gonna defeat that one!
FWSSSSH
KERO!!

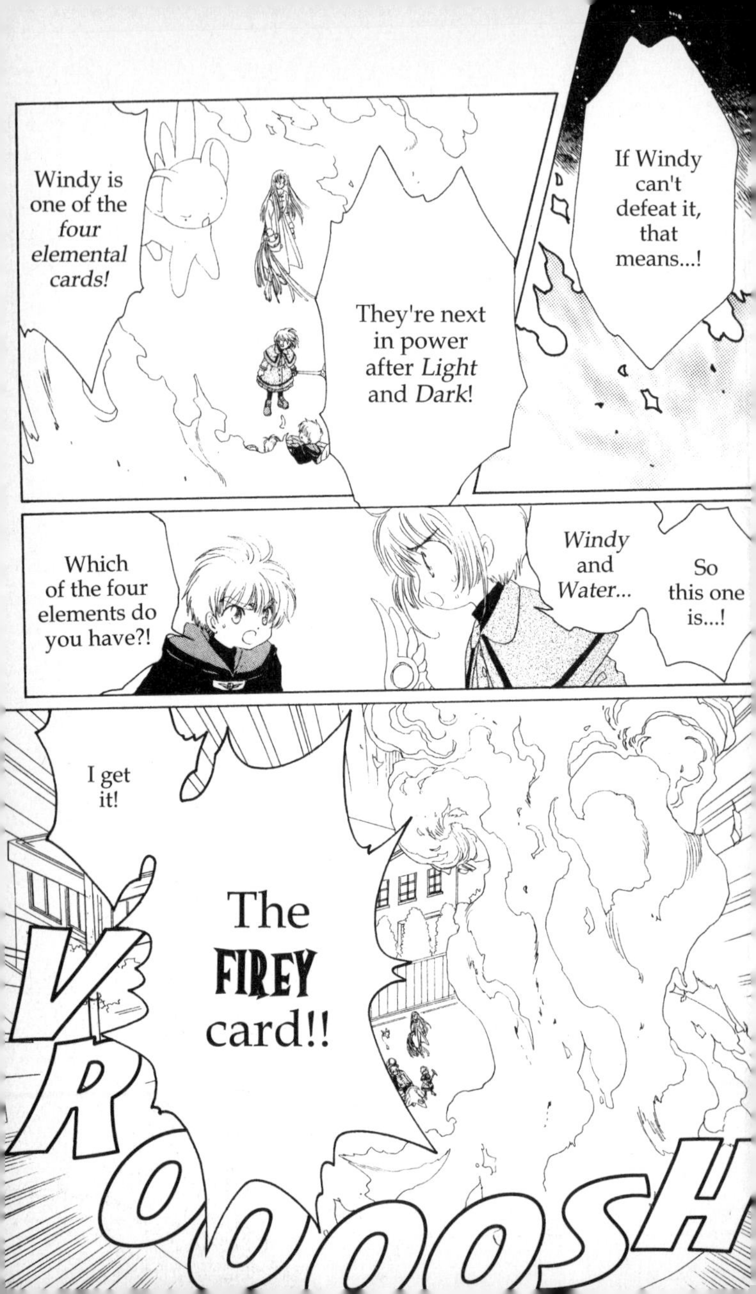
Windy is one of the *four elemental cards!*
They're next in power after *Light* and *Dark*!
If Windy can't defeat it, that means...!
Which of the four elements do you have?!
Windy and *Water*...
So this one is...!
I get it!
The **FIREY** card!!
VROOOOSH

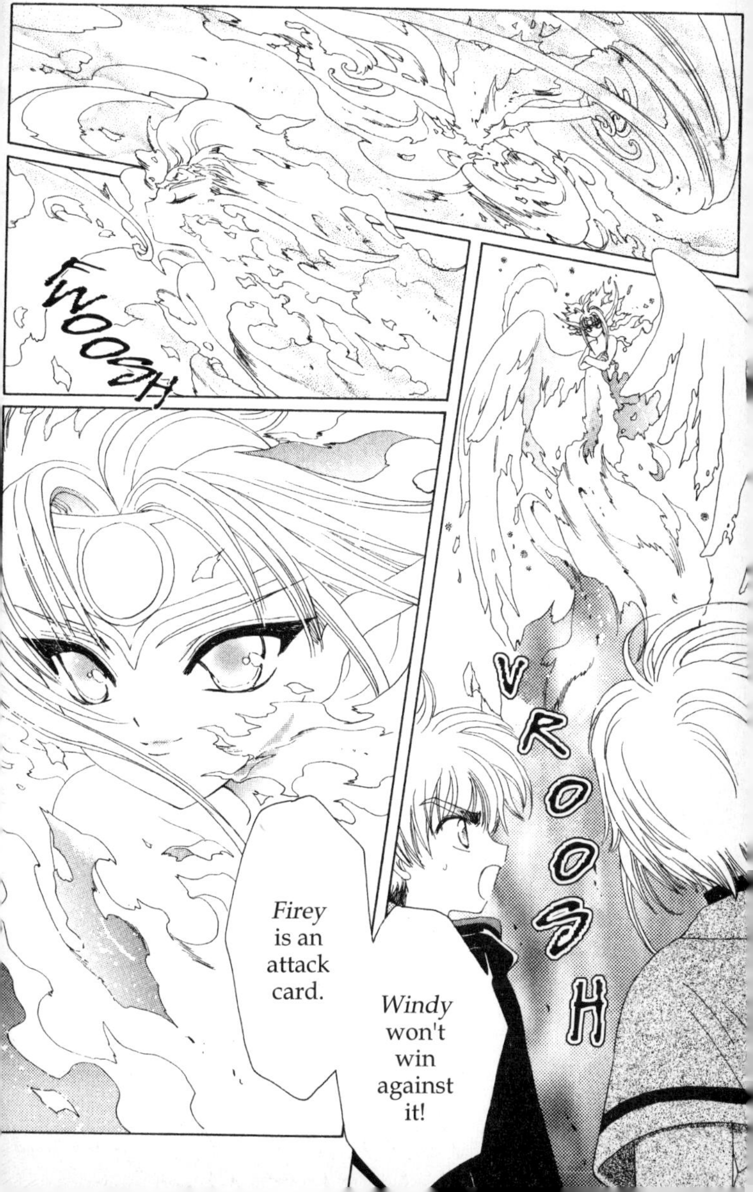

WOOSH
VROOOSH
Firey is an attack card.
Windy won't win against it!

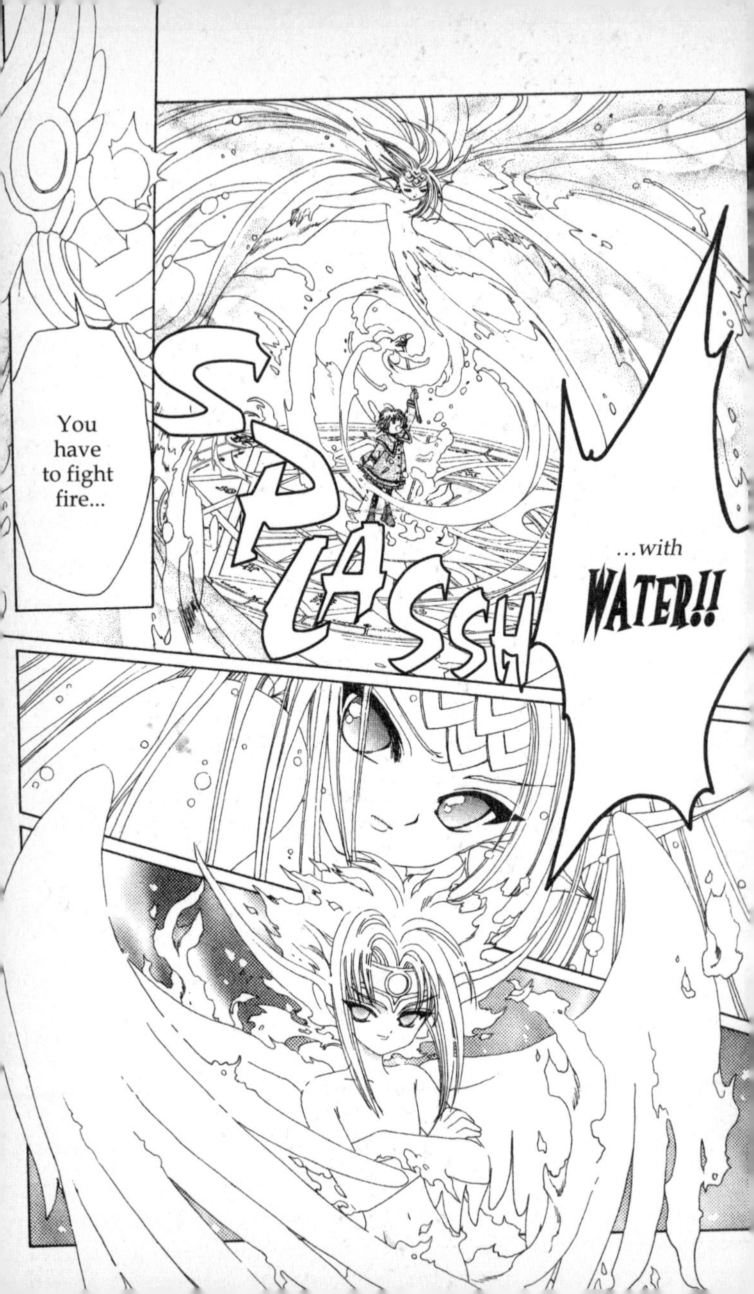
You have to fight fire...
SPLASSH
...with WATER!!

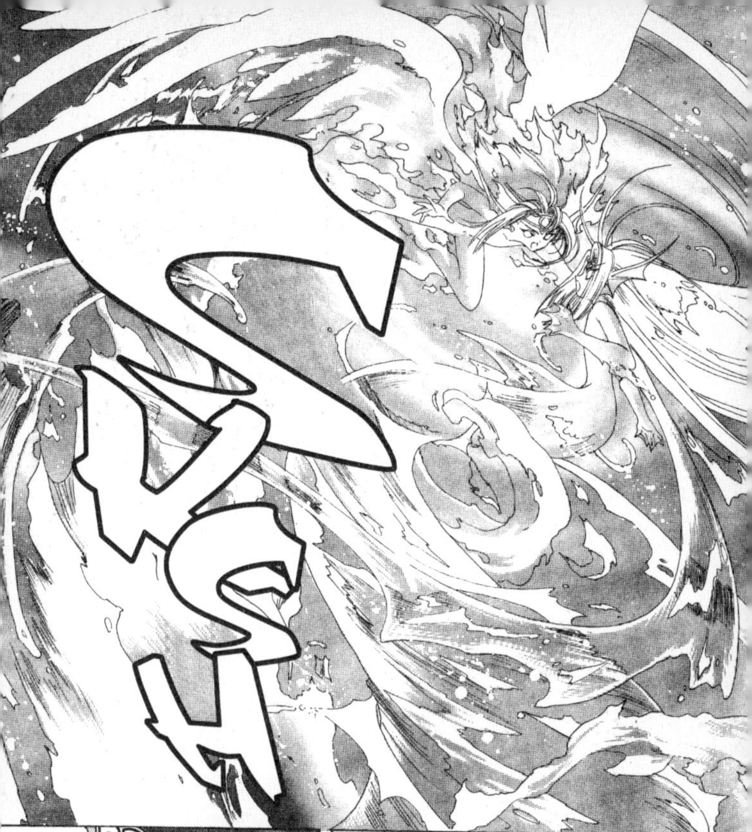

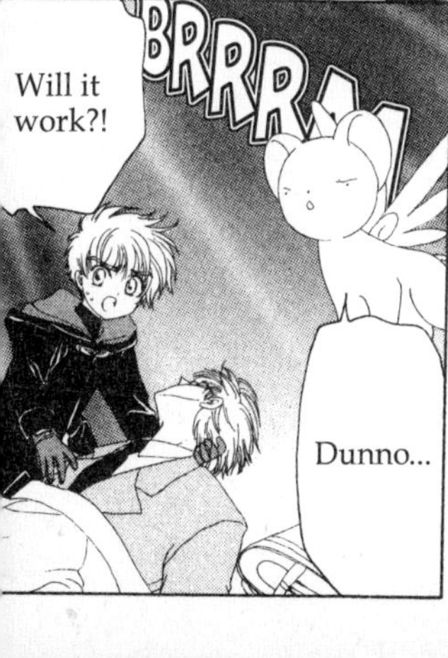
Will it work?!
Dunno...

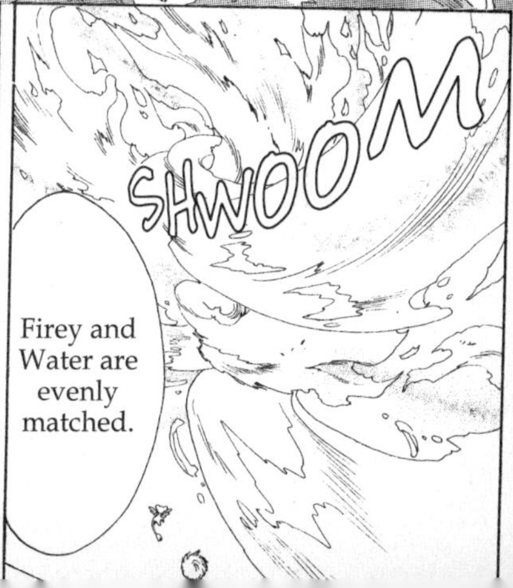
SHWOOM
Firey and Water are evenly matched.

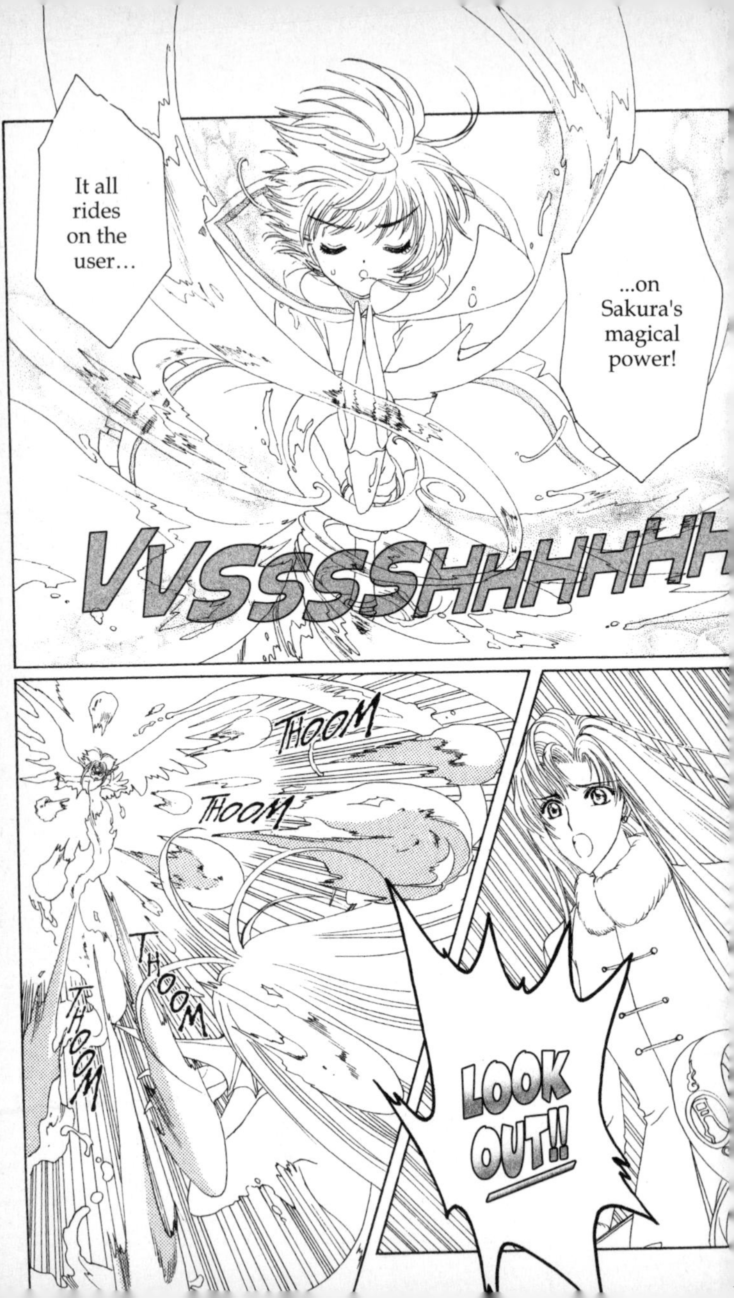
It all rides on the user…
...on Sakura's magical power!
VVSSSSHHHHHH
LOOK OUT!!
THOOM
THOOM
THOOM
THOOM

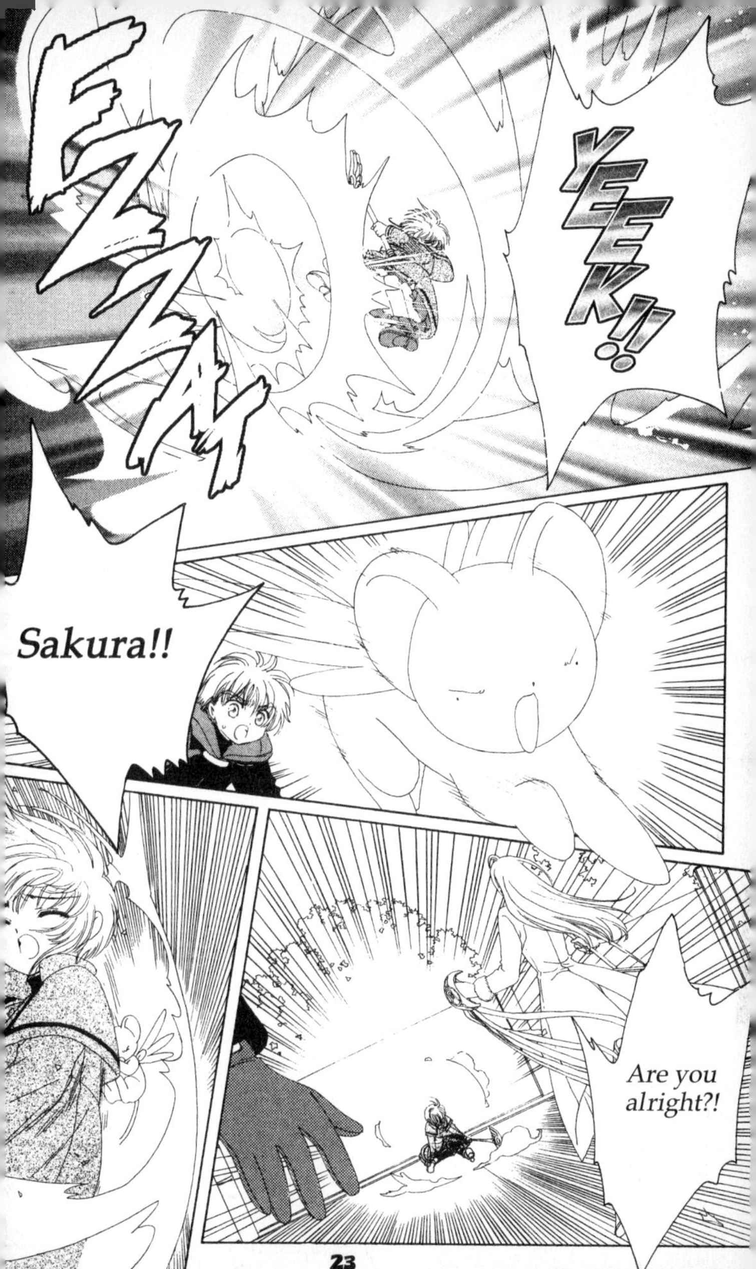
YEEK!!
EZZAY
Sakura!!
Are you alright?!

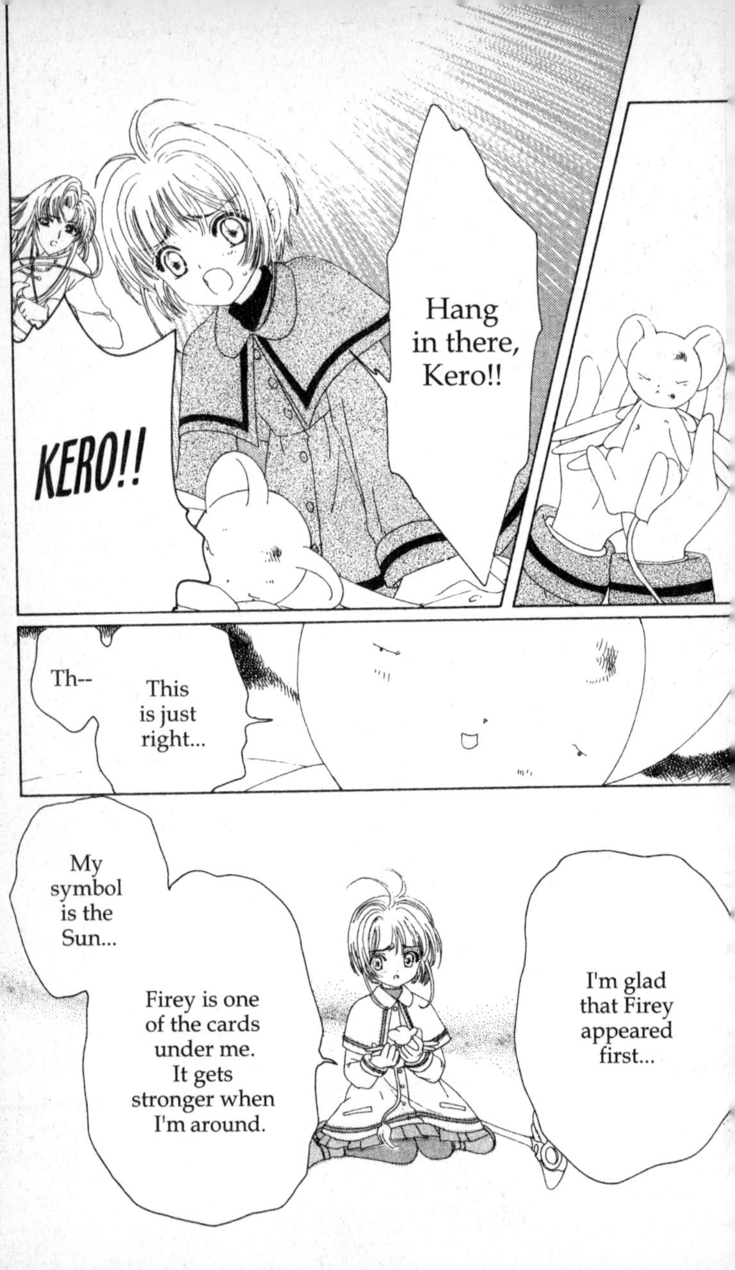

Hang in there, Kero!!
KERO!!
Th--
This is just right...
I'm glad that Firey appeared first...
My symbol is the Sun...
Firey is one of the cards under me. It gets stronger when I'm around.

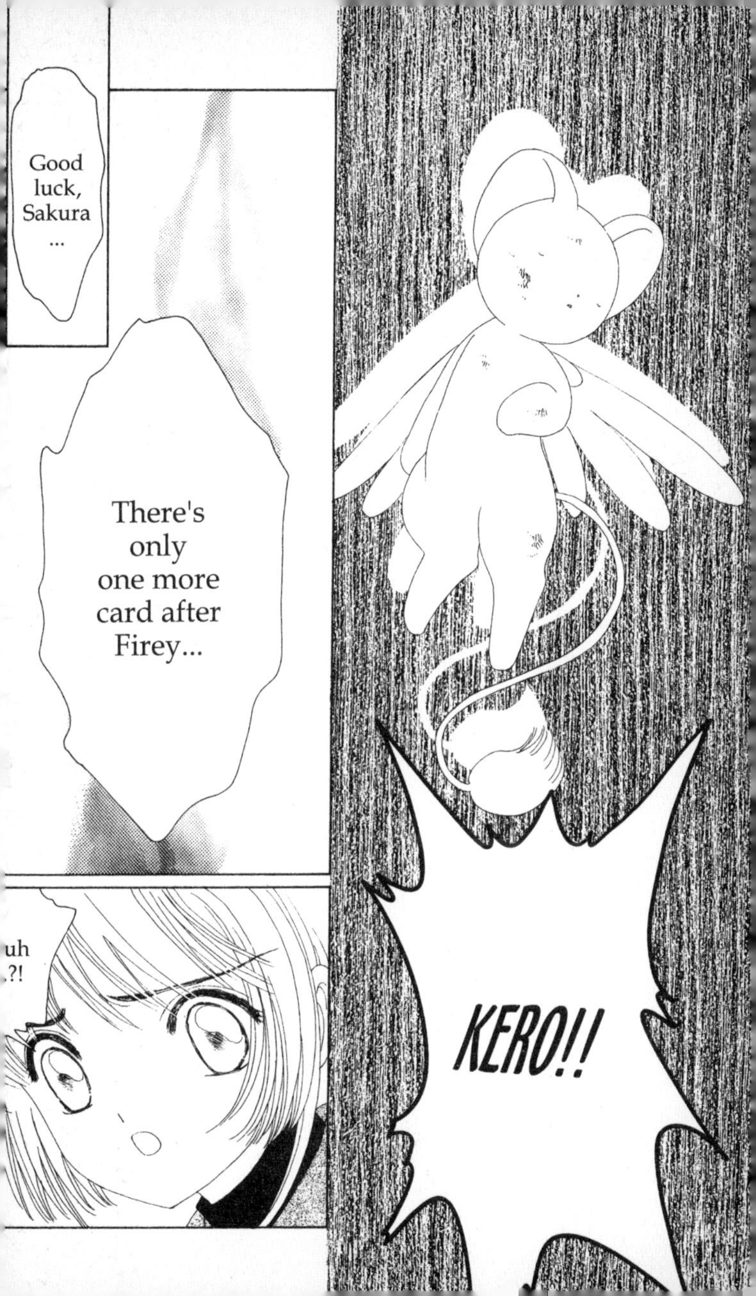
KERO!!
Good luck, Sakura ...
There's only one more card after Firey...
uh ...?!

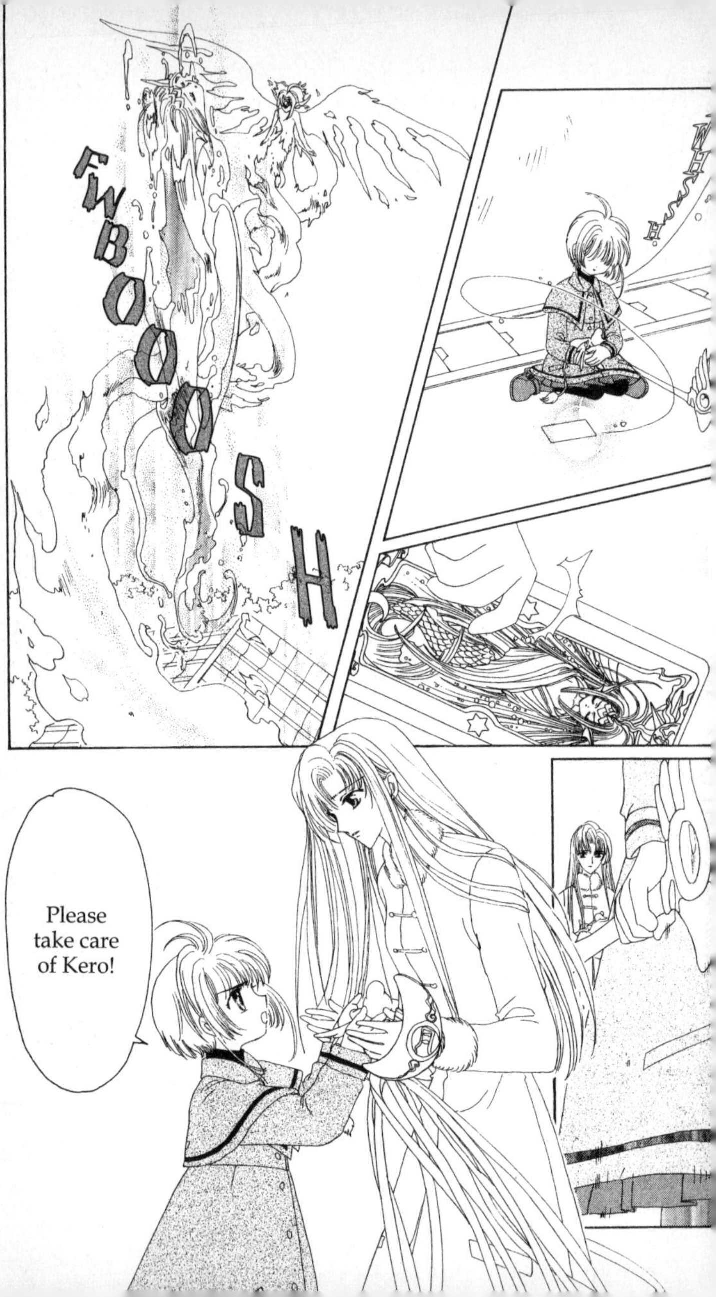
WHSSSH
FWBOOOSH
Please take care of Kero!

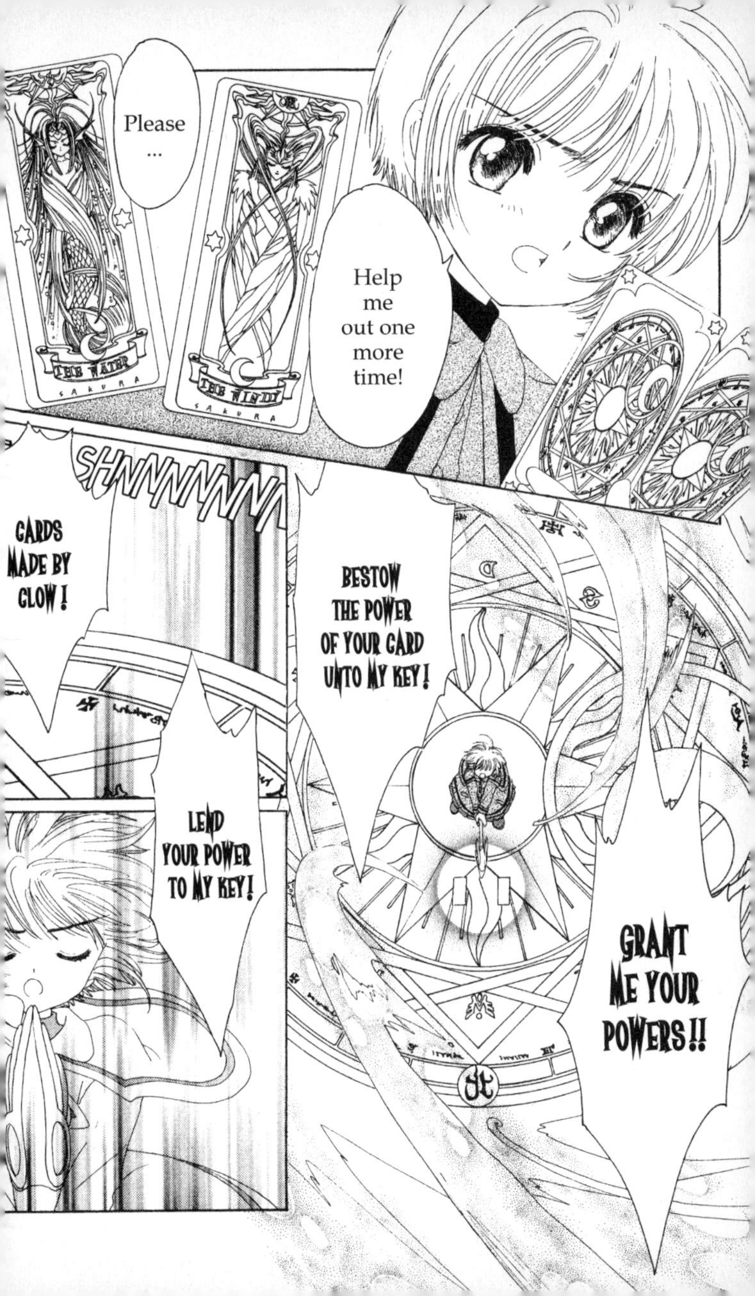
Please ...
Help me out one more time!
THE WATER
SAKURA
THE WINDY
SAKURA
SHNNNNNNN
CARDS MADE BY CLOW!
BESTOW THE POWER OF YOUR CARD UNTO MY KEY!
LEND YOUR POWER TO MY KEY!
GRANT ME YOUR POWERS!!

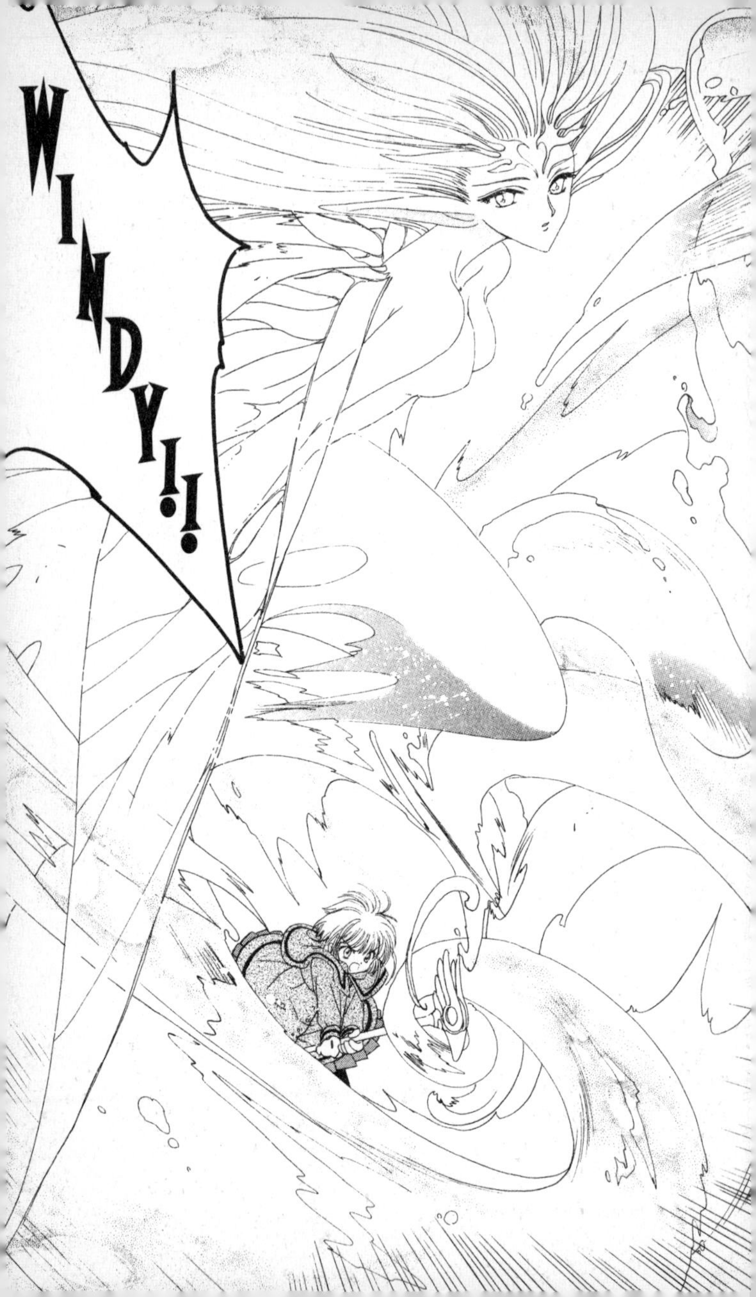
WINDY!!

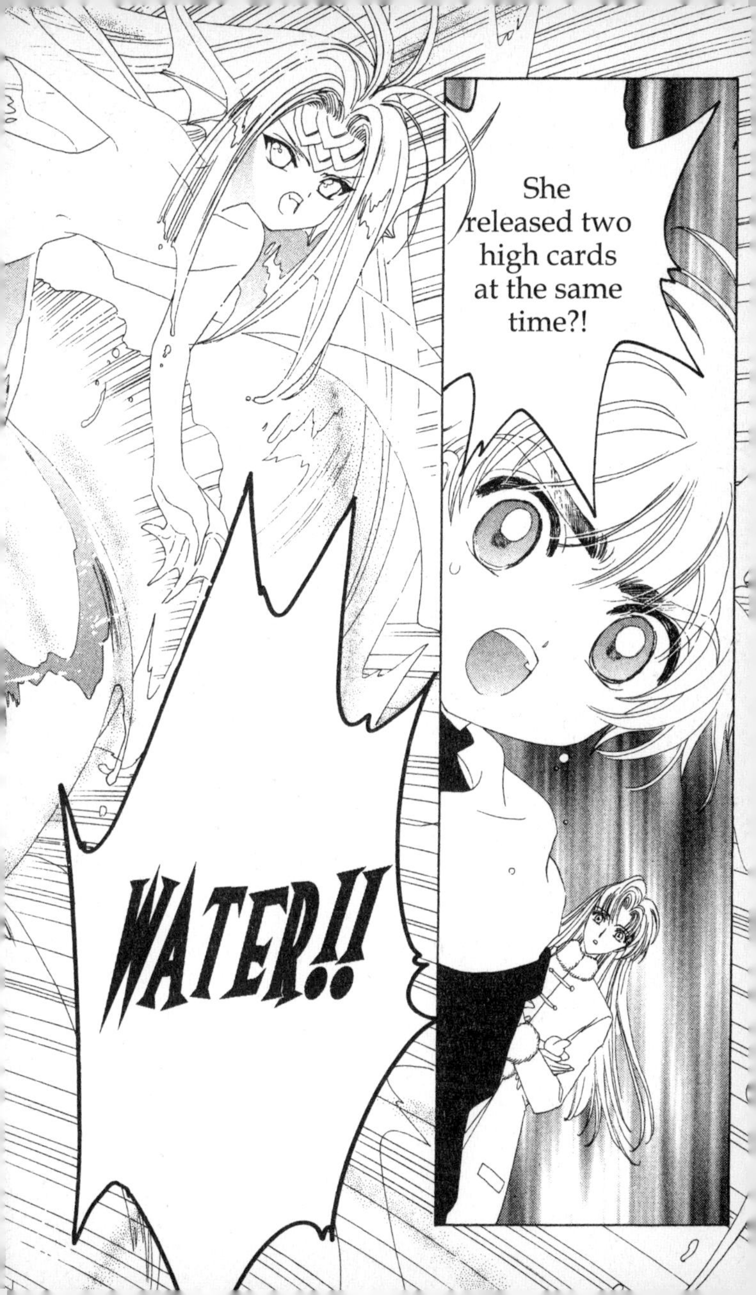
She released two high cards at the same time?!
WATER!!

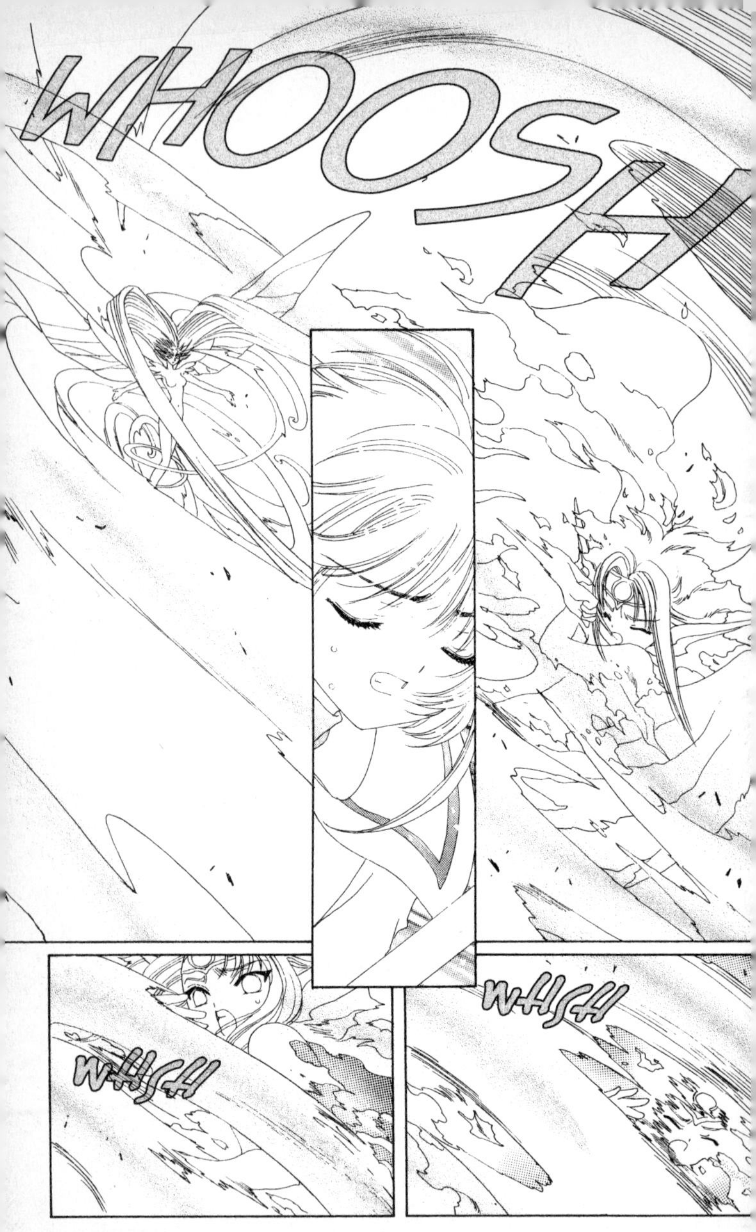
WHOOSH
WHISH
WHISH

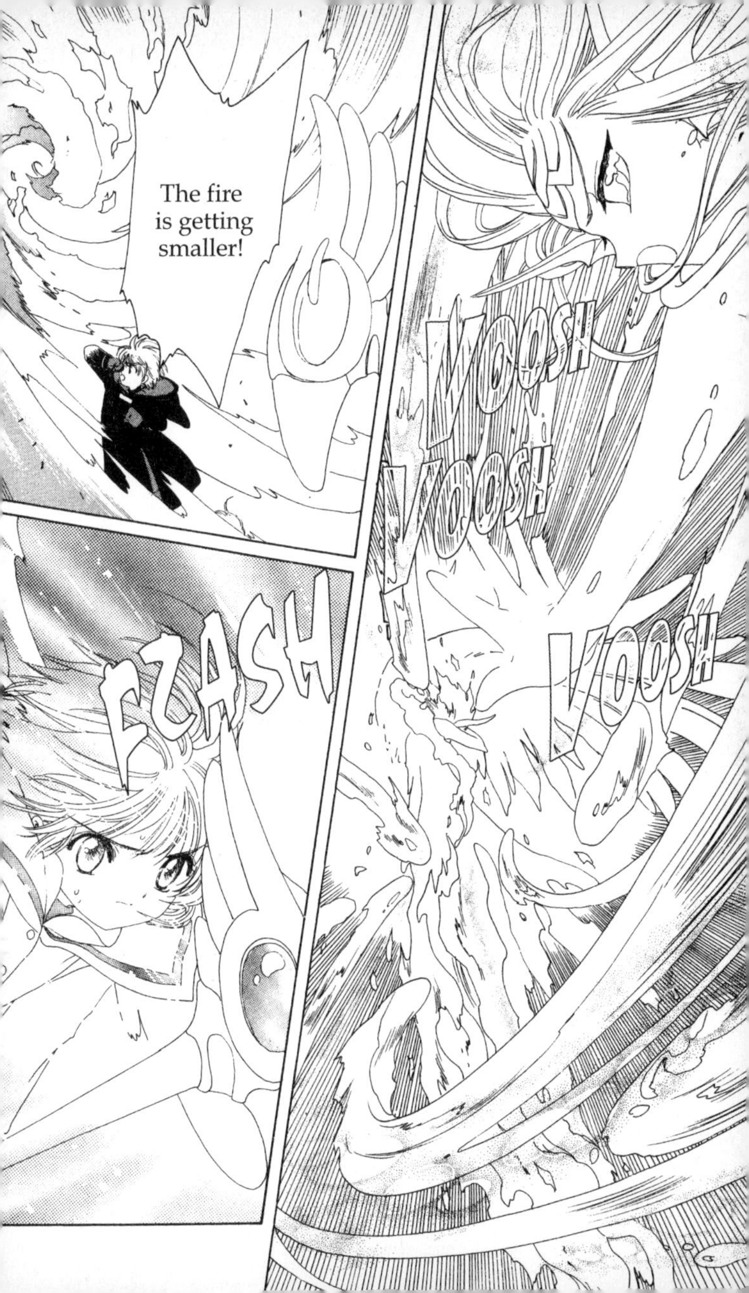
VOOSH
VOOSH
VOOSH
The fire is getting smaller!
FLASH

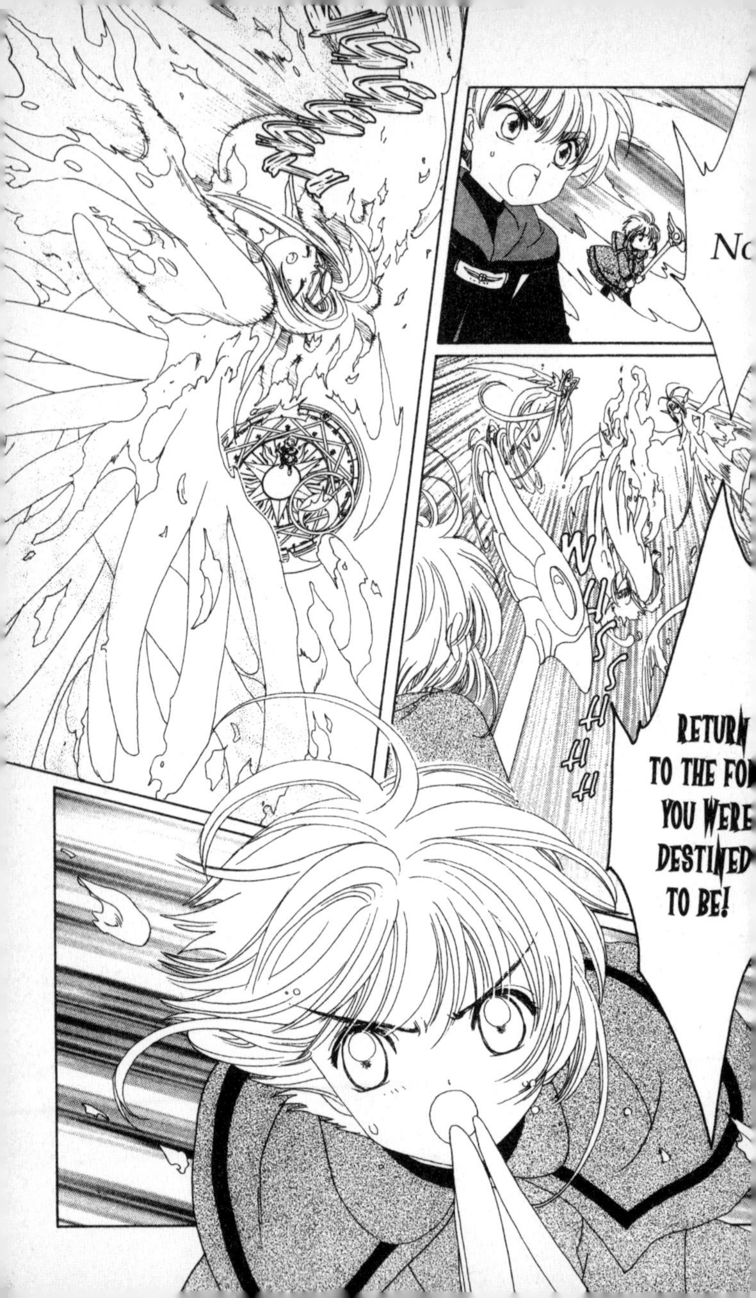
No
RETURN
TO THE FO
YOU WERE
DESTINED
TO BE!

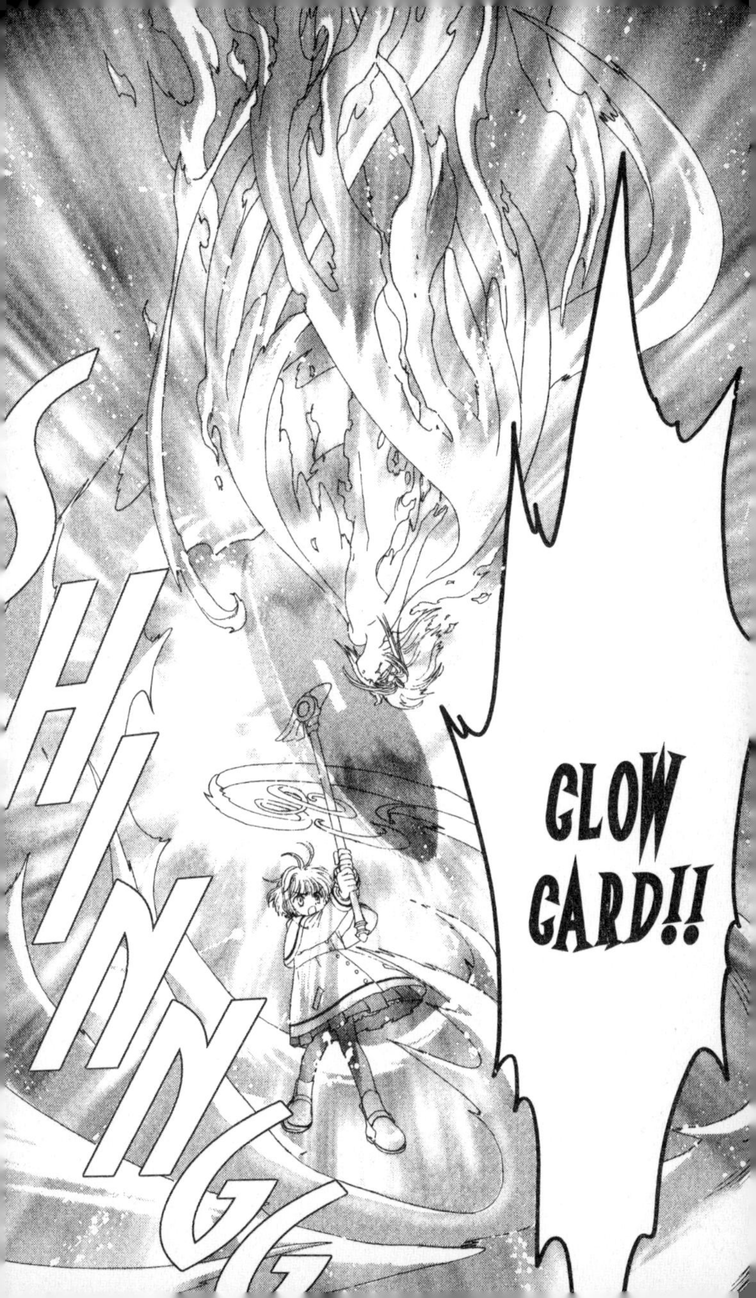
GLOW CARD!!
SHINING

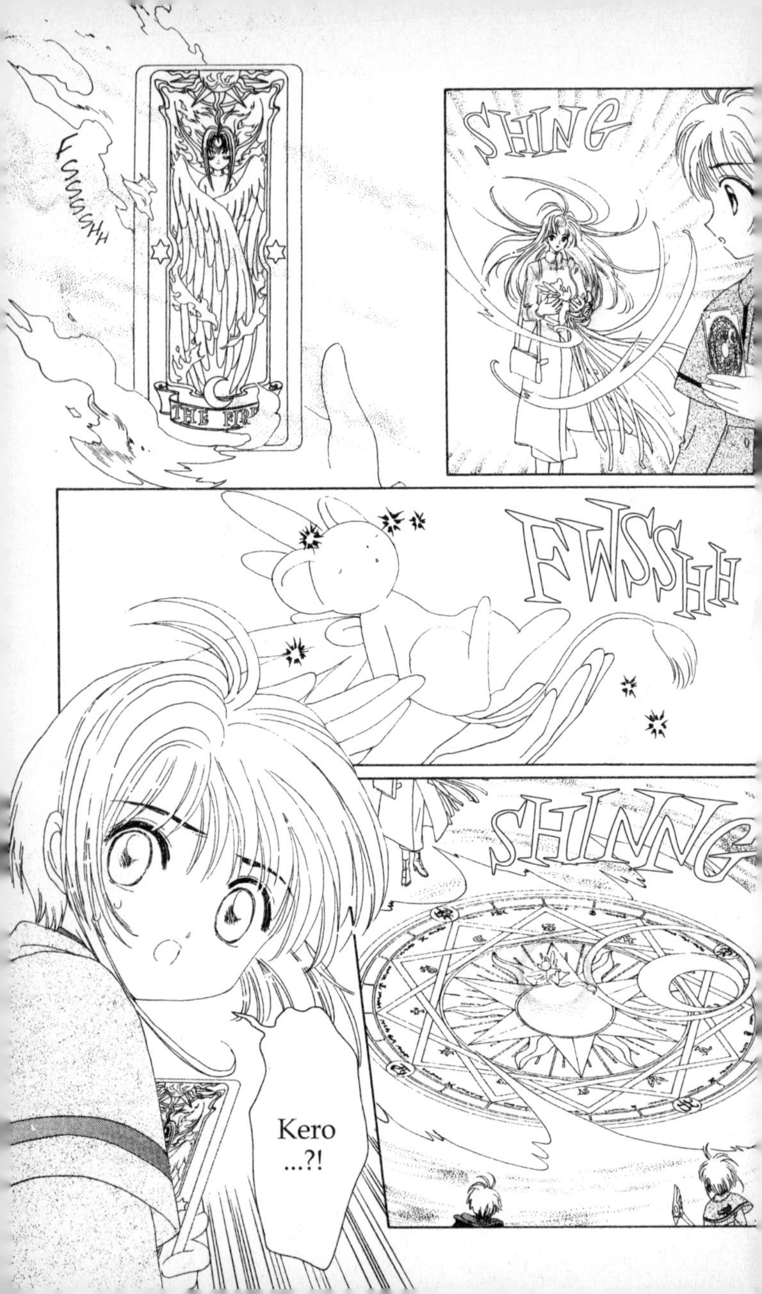
SHING
FWSSHH
SHINNG
Kero
...?!

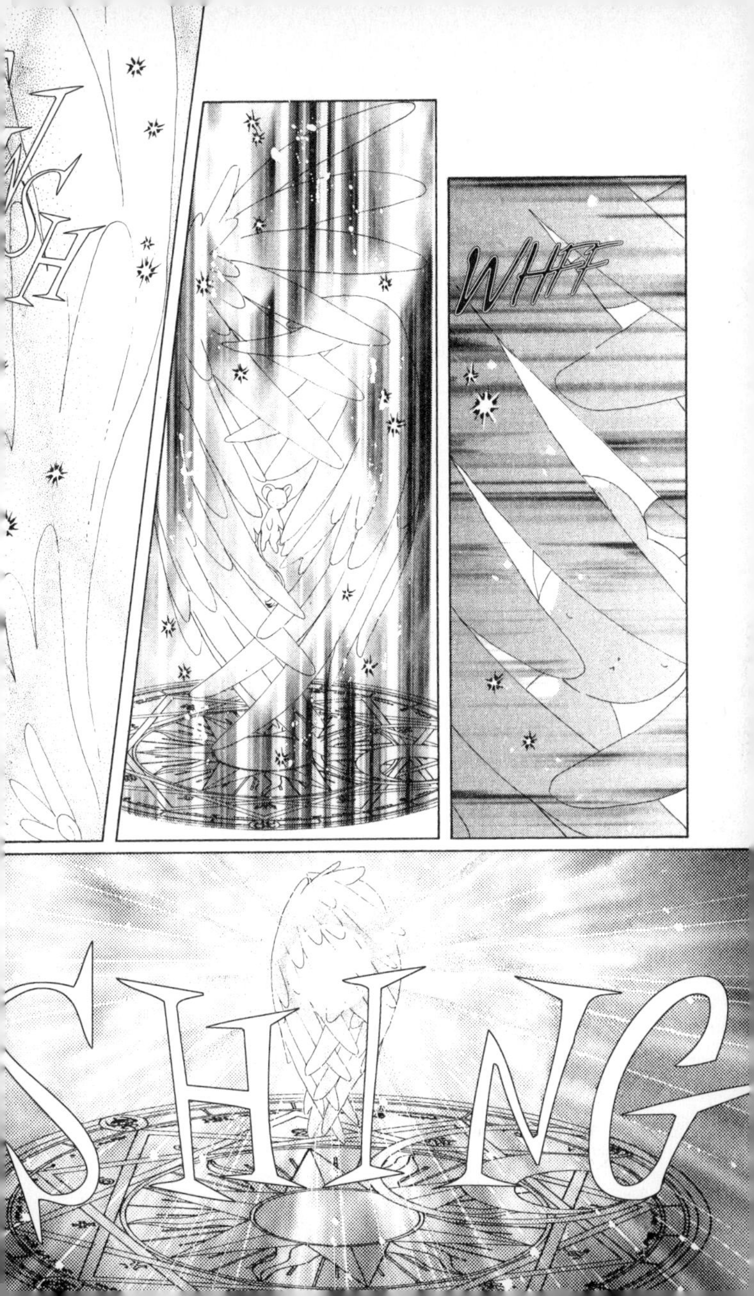
WHFF
WSH
SHING

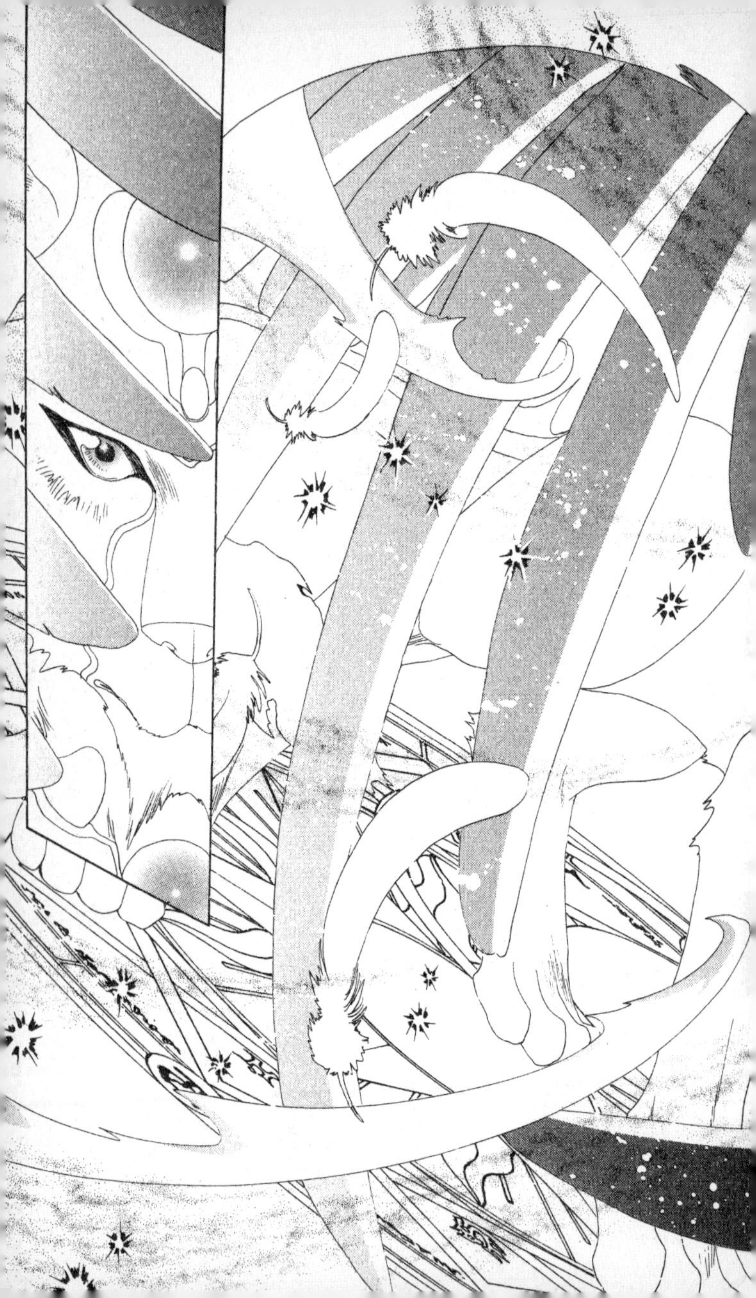

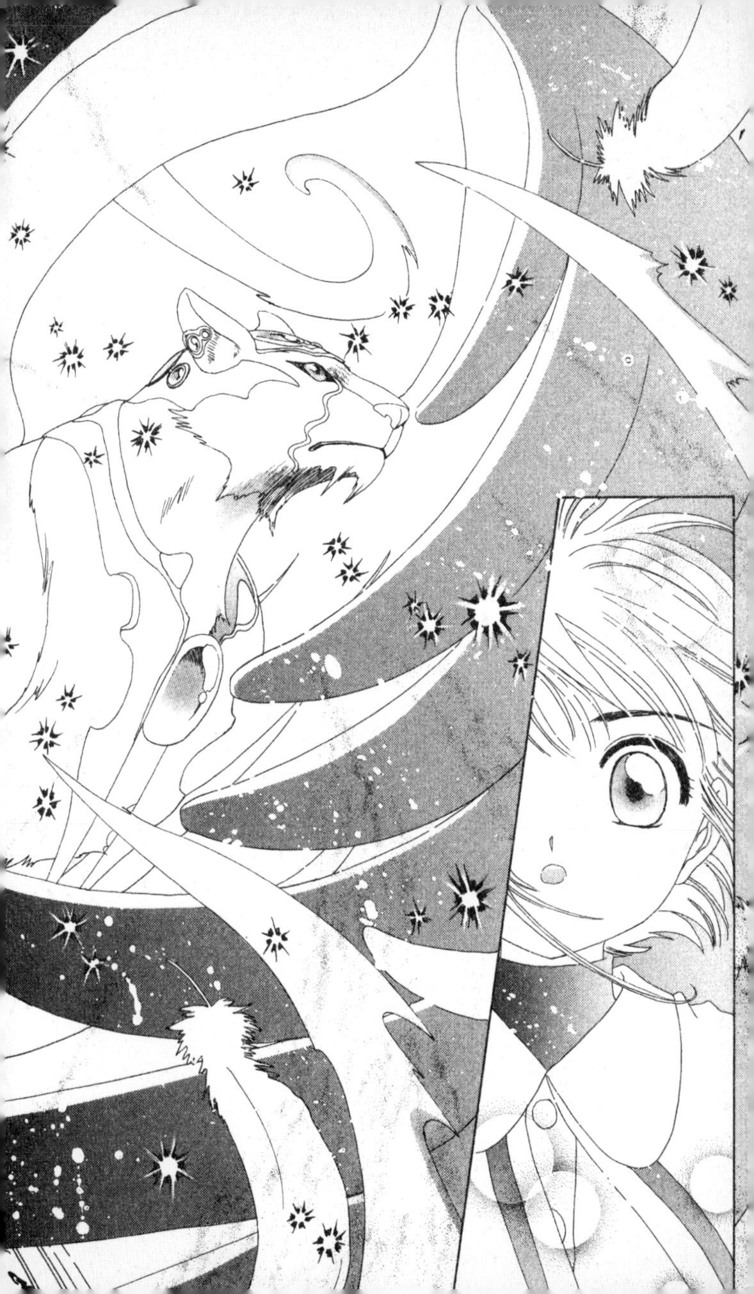

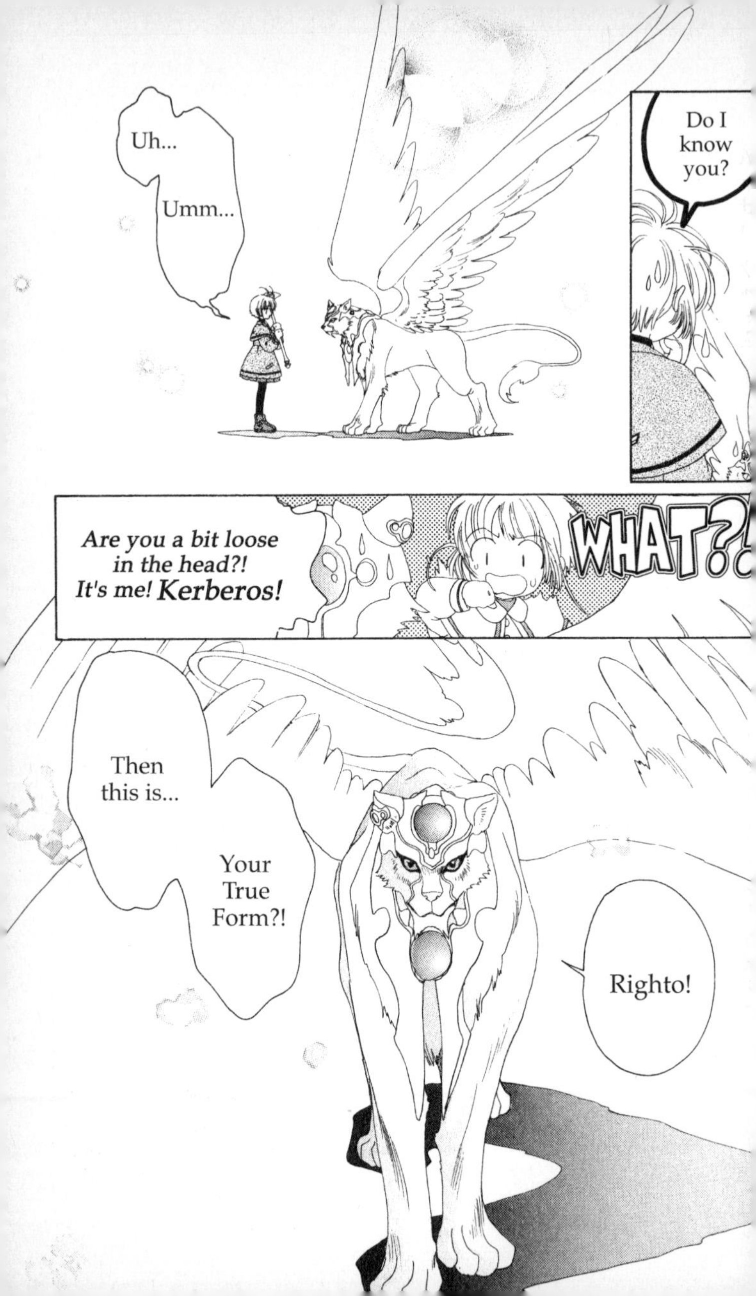
Uh... Umm...
Do I know you?
Are you a bit loose in the head?! It's me! Kerberos!
WHAT?!
Then this is... Your True Form?!
Righto!

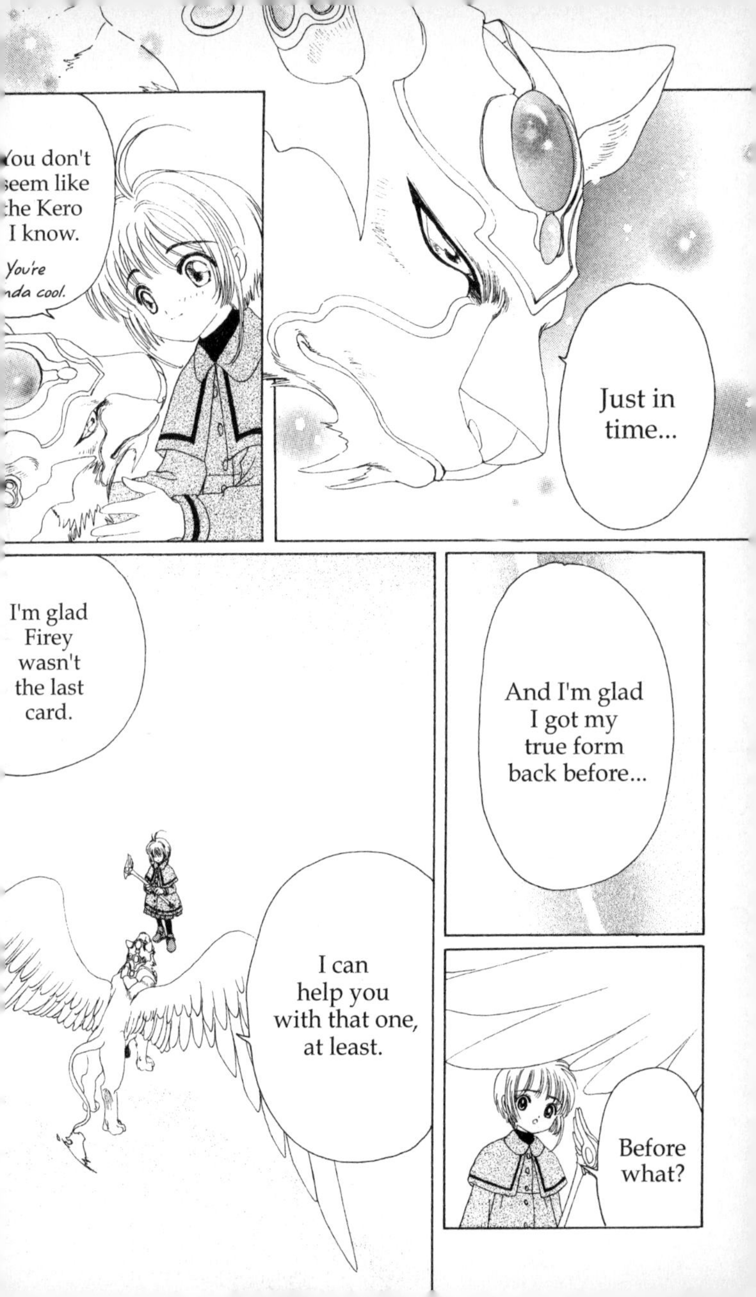
You don't seem like the Kero I know.
You're nda cool.
Just in time...
I'm glad Firey wasn't the last card.
I can help you with that one, at least.
And I'm glad I got my true form back before...
Before what?

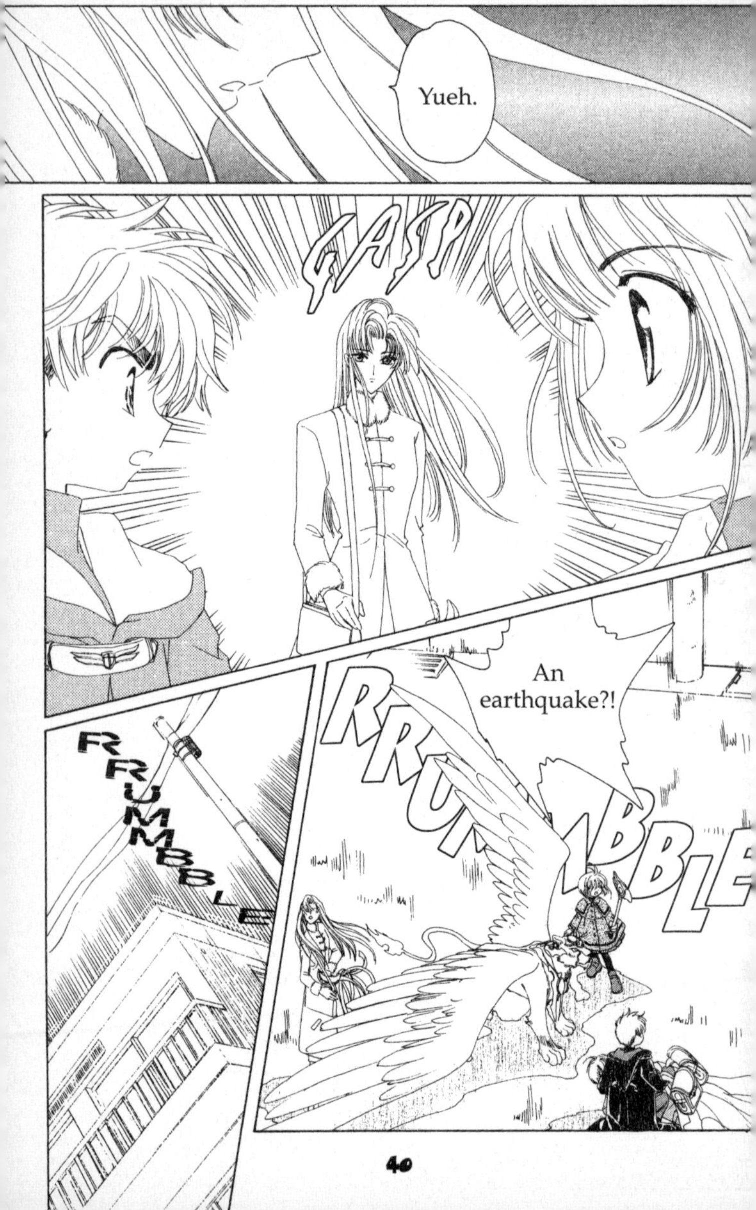
Yueh.
GASP
An earthquake?!
RRUMBBLE
RRUMMBBLE

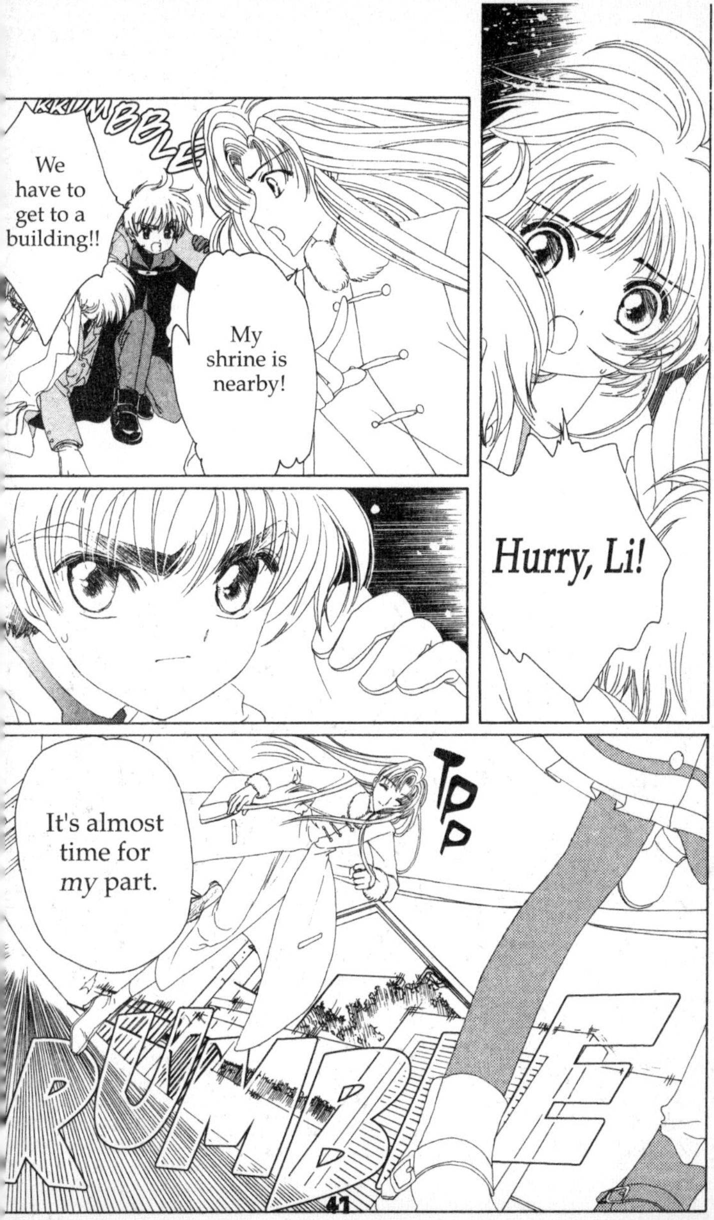
Hurry, Li!
KRUMBBLE
We have to get to a building!!
My shrine is nearby!
TPP
It's almost time for *my* part.
RUMBLE

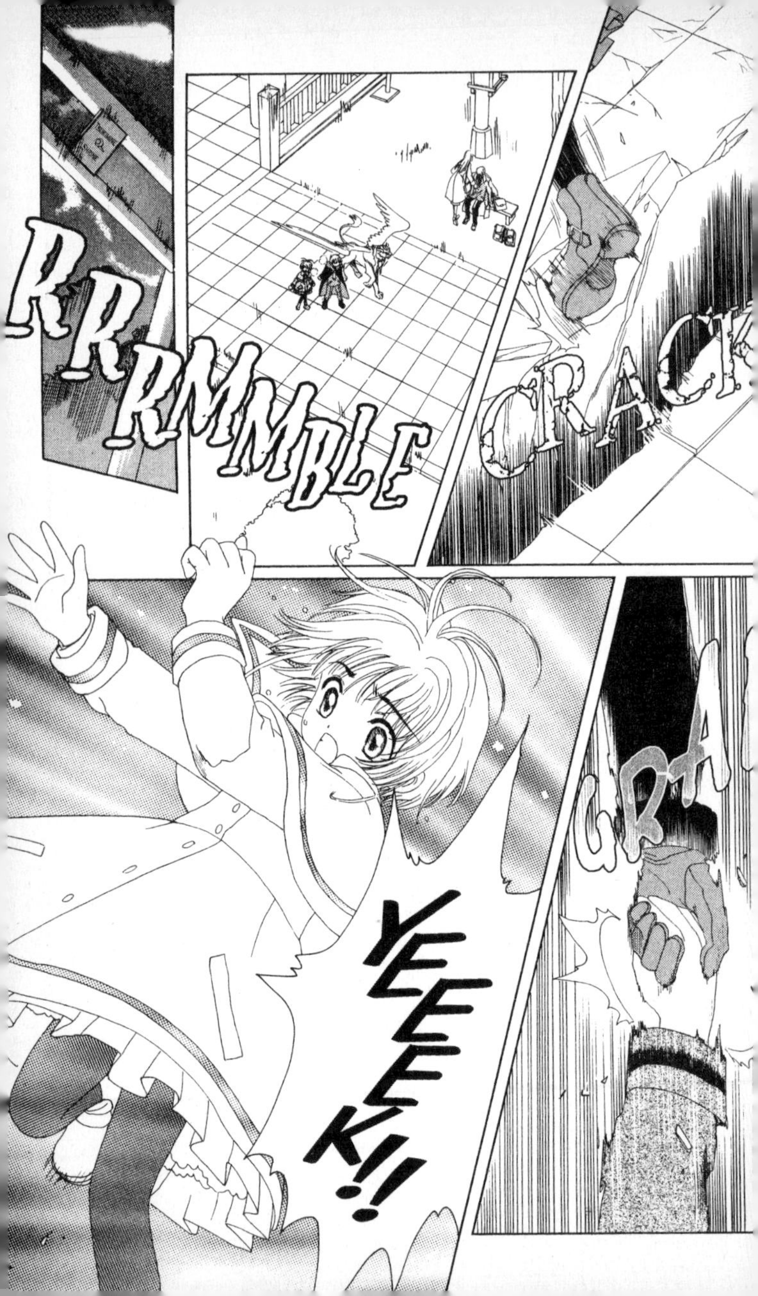
CRACK
RRRMMMBLE
CRA
YEEEEK!!

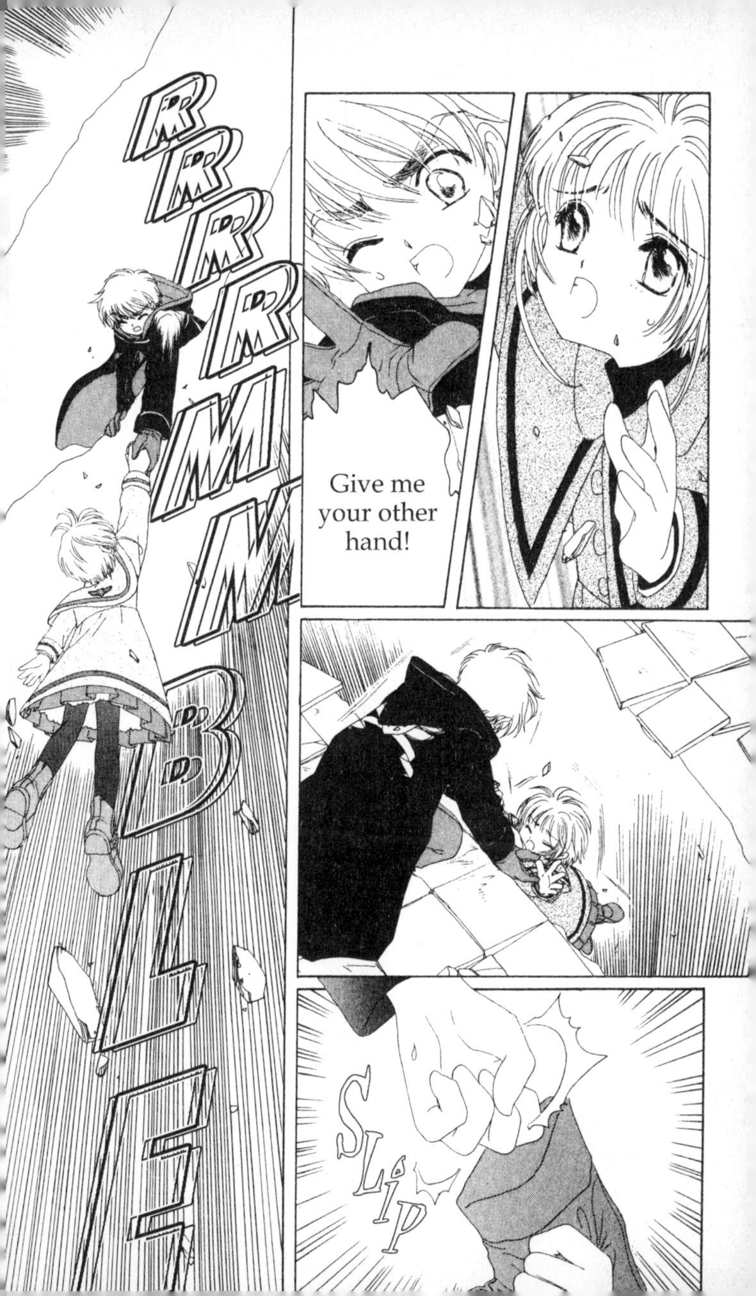
Give me your other hand!
SLIP
RRRRMMMBLE

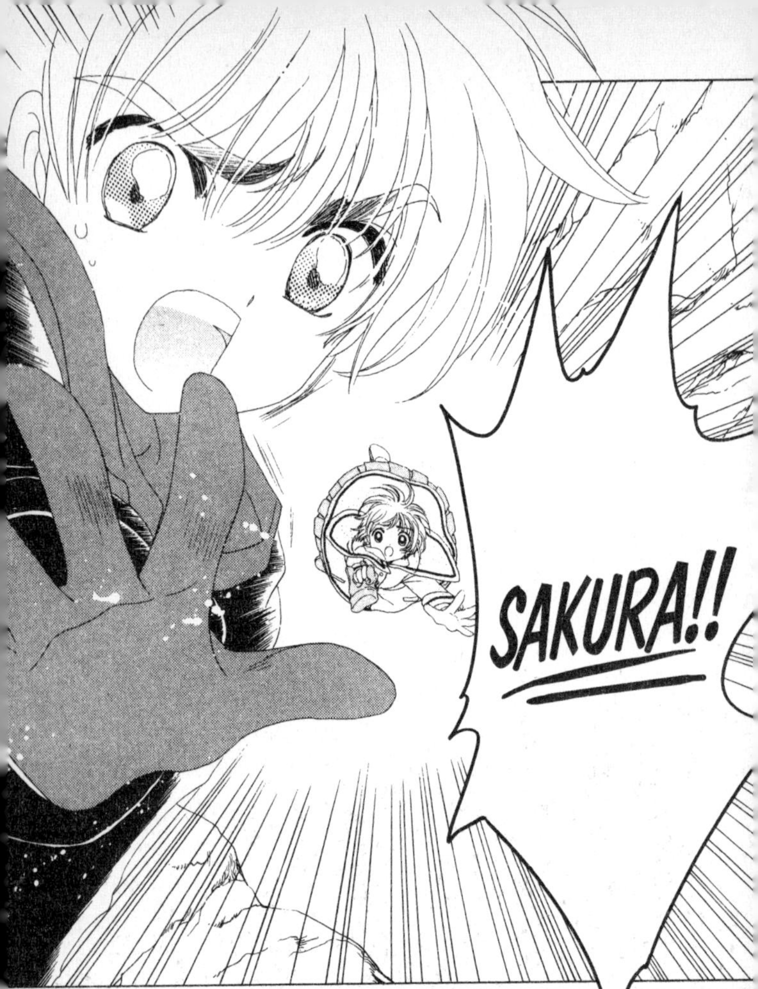
SAKURA!!

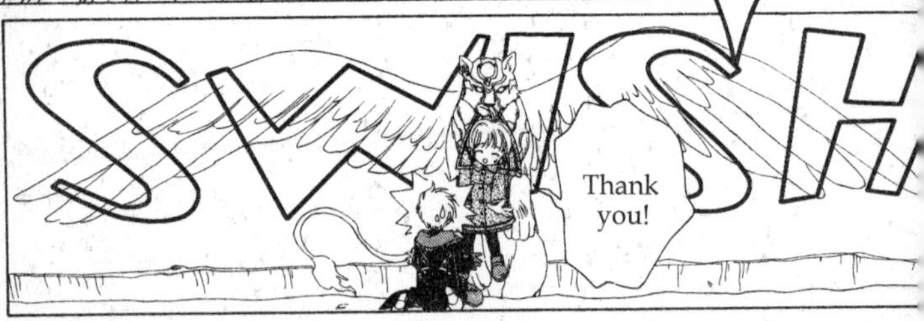
SWISH
Thank you!

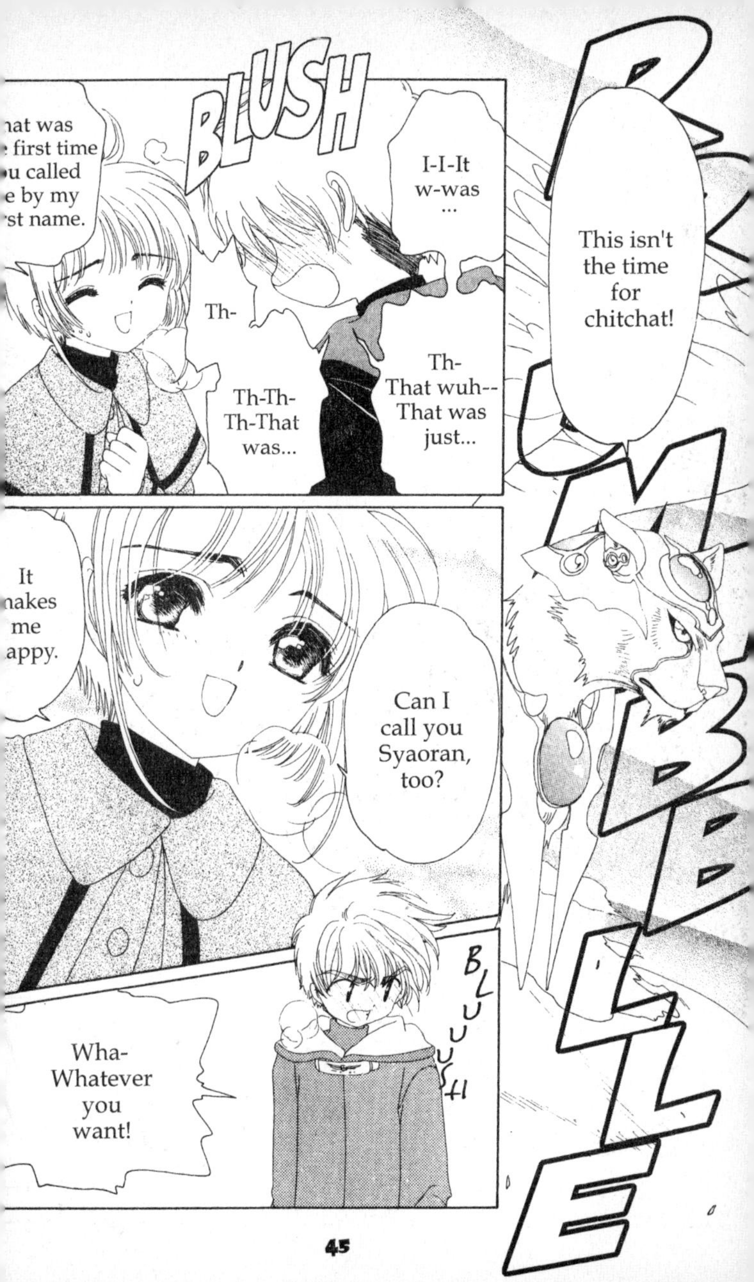
at was
first time
u called
e by my
st name.
BLUSH
I-I-It w-was ...
Th-
Th- That wuh-- That was just...
Th-Th- Th-That was...
It
akes
me
appy.
Can I call you Syaoran, too?
Wha- Whatever you want!
BLUUUSH
This isn't the time for chitchat!
RUMBLE

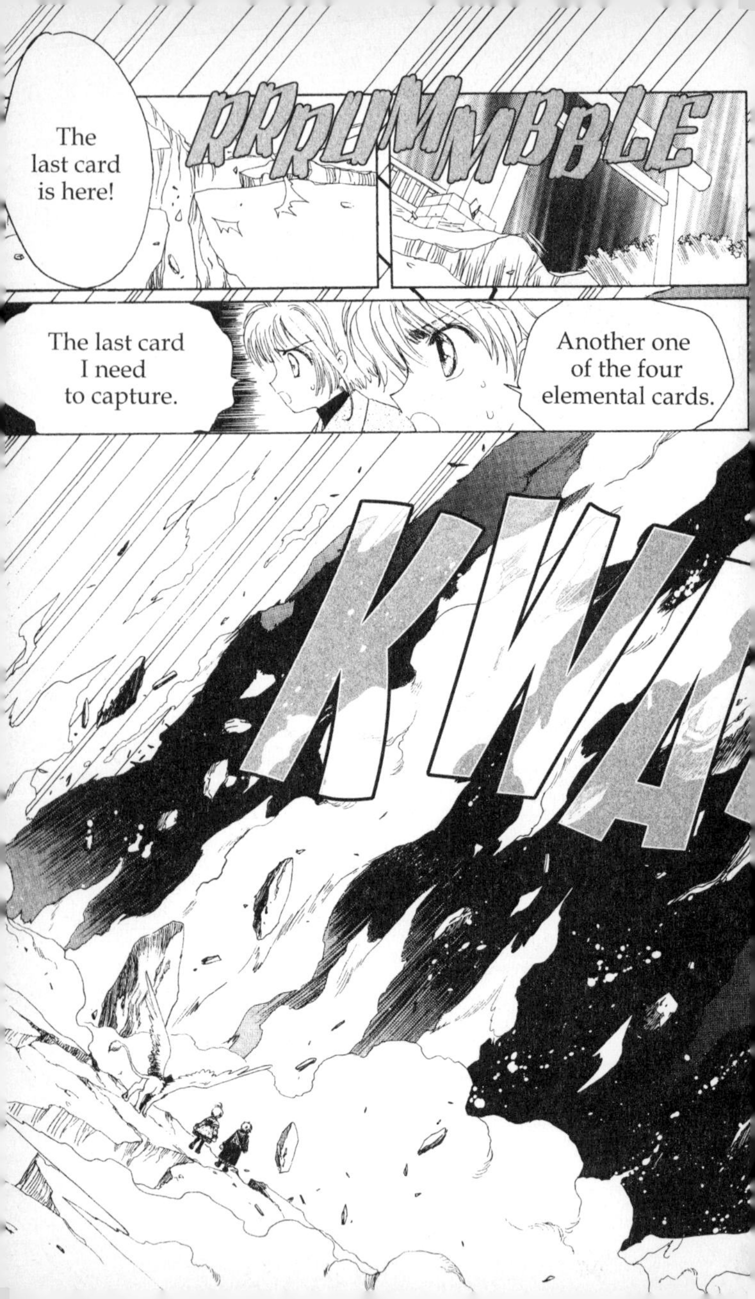
RRRUMMBBLE
The last card is here!
Another one of the four elemental cards.
The last card I need to capture.
KWA

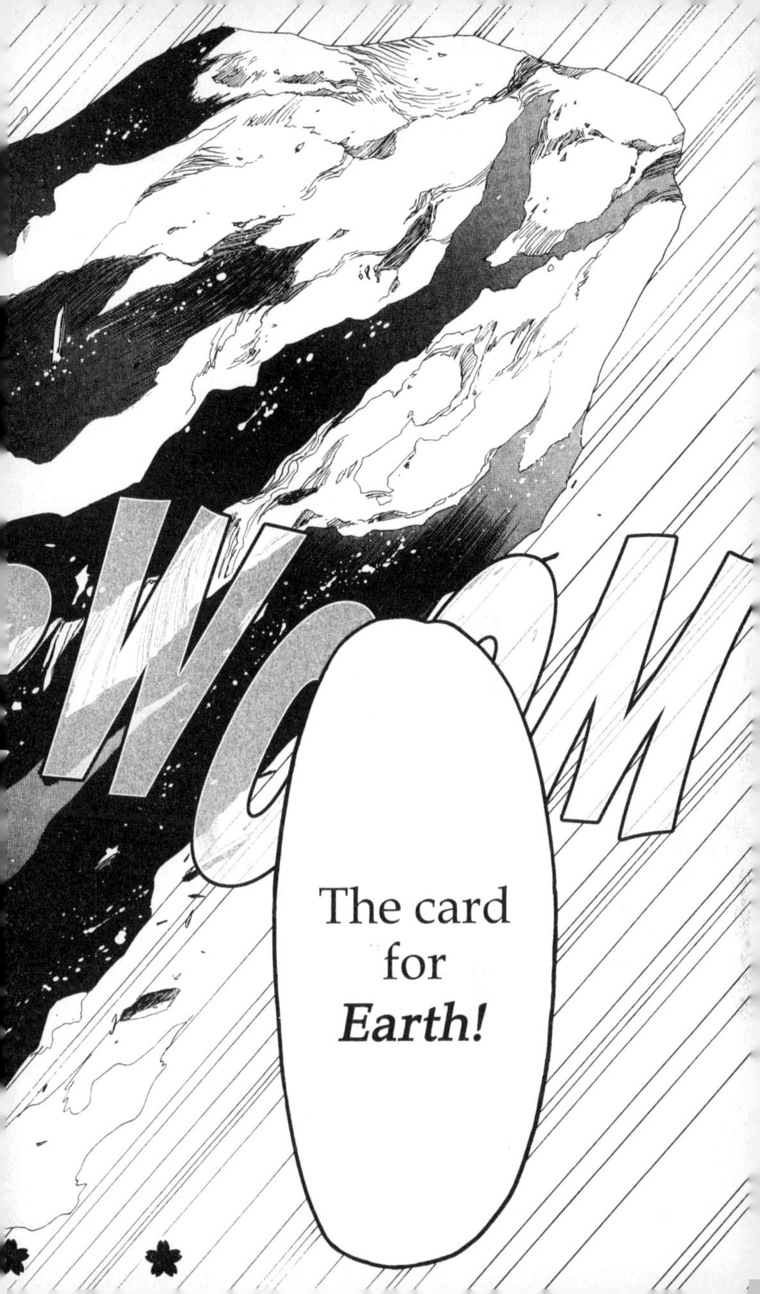
The card for *Earth!*

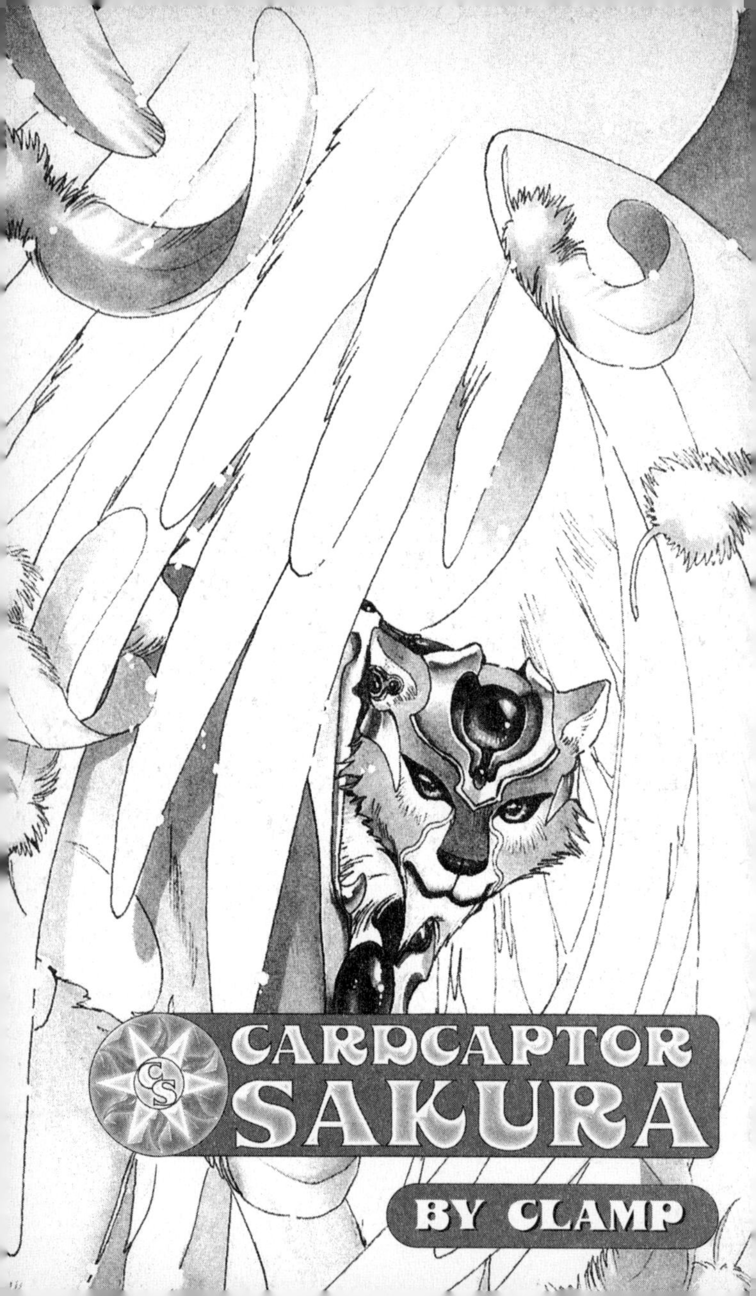
CARDCAPTOR SAKURA
BY CLAMP

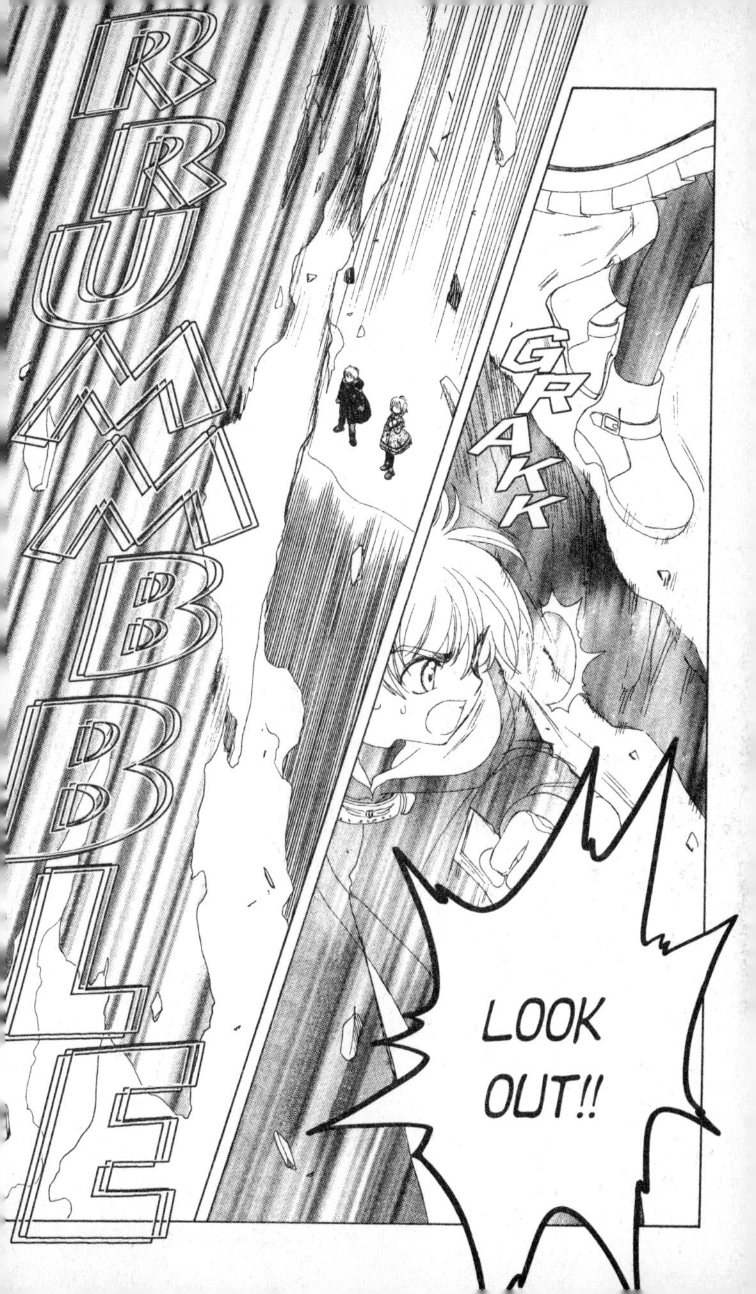
GRAKK
RRUMMMBBLE
LOOK OUT!!

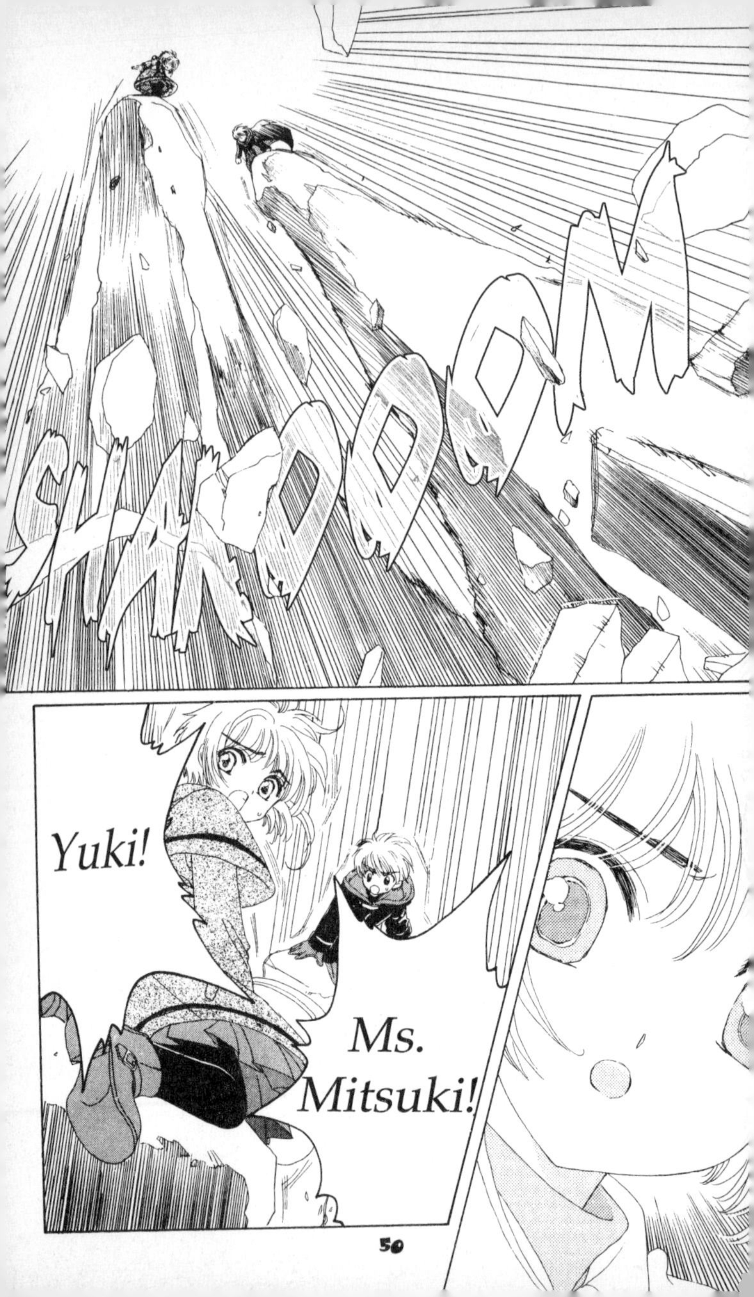
SHAKOOOOM
Yuki!
Ms. Mitsuki!

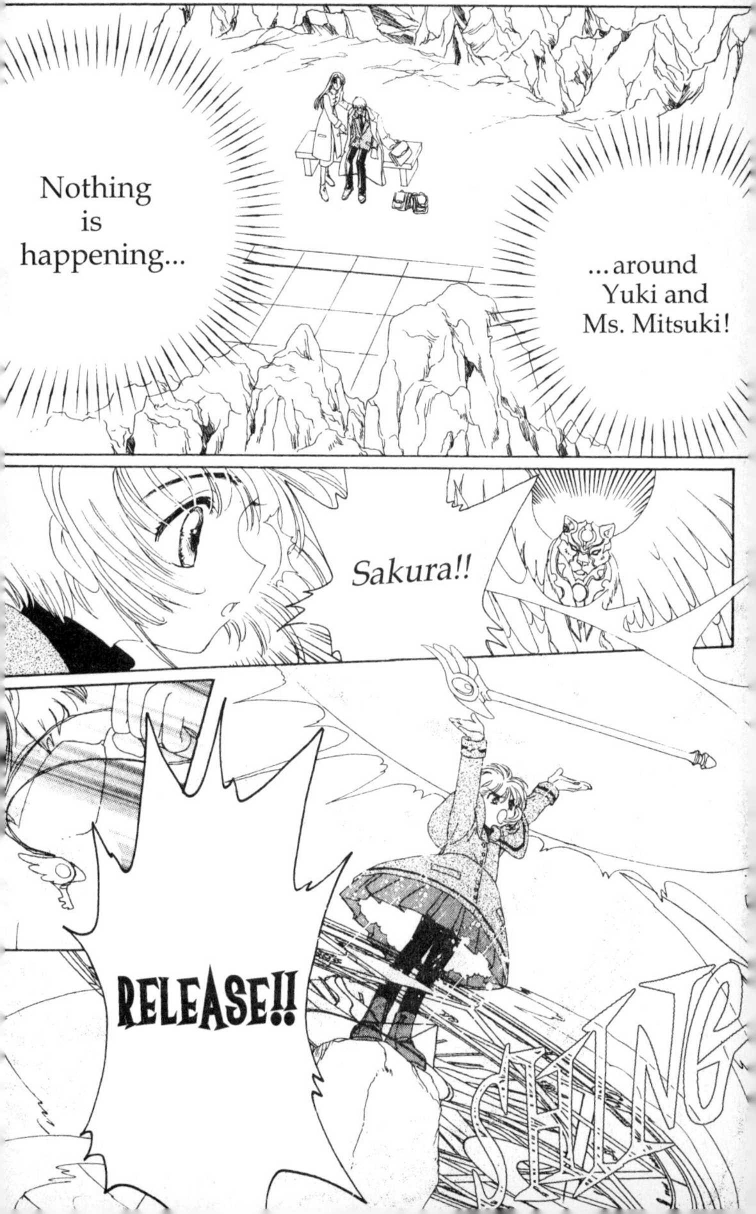
Nothing is happening...
...around Yuki and Ms. Mitsuki!
Sakura!!
RELEASE!!
SHING

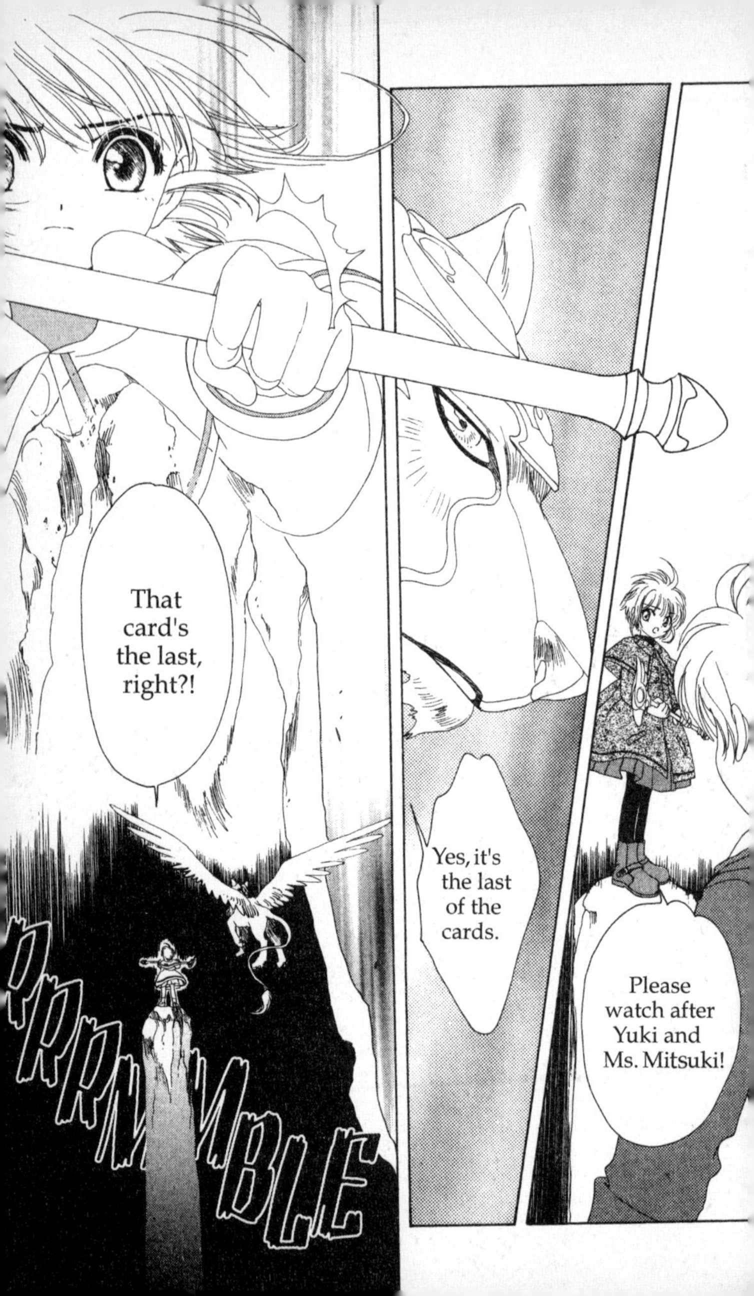
That card's the last, right?!
Yes, it's the last of the cards.
Please watch after Yuki and Ms. Mitsuki!

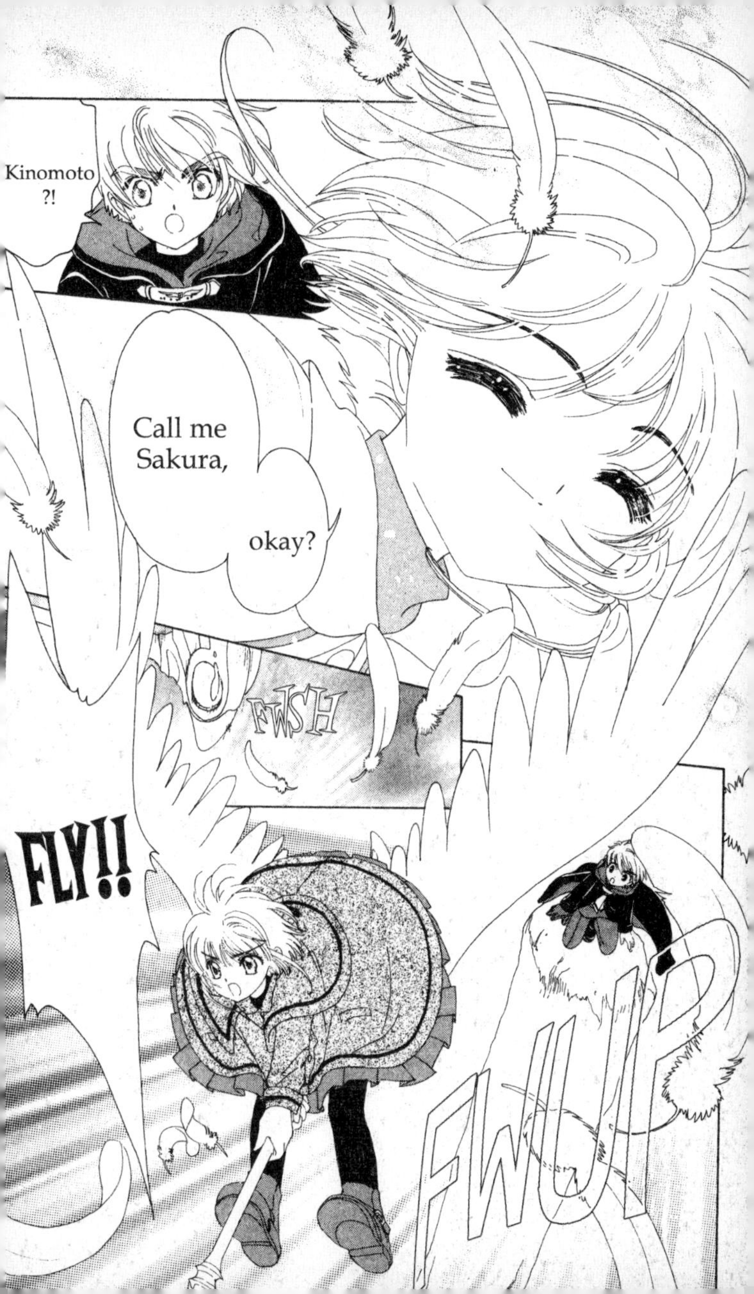
Kinomoto ?!
Call me Sakura, okay?
FWSH
FLY!!
FWUP

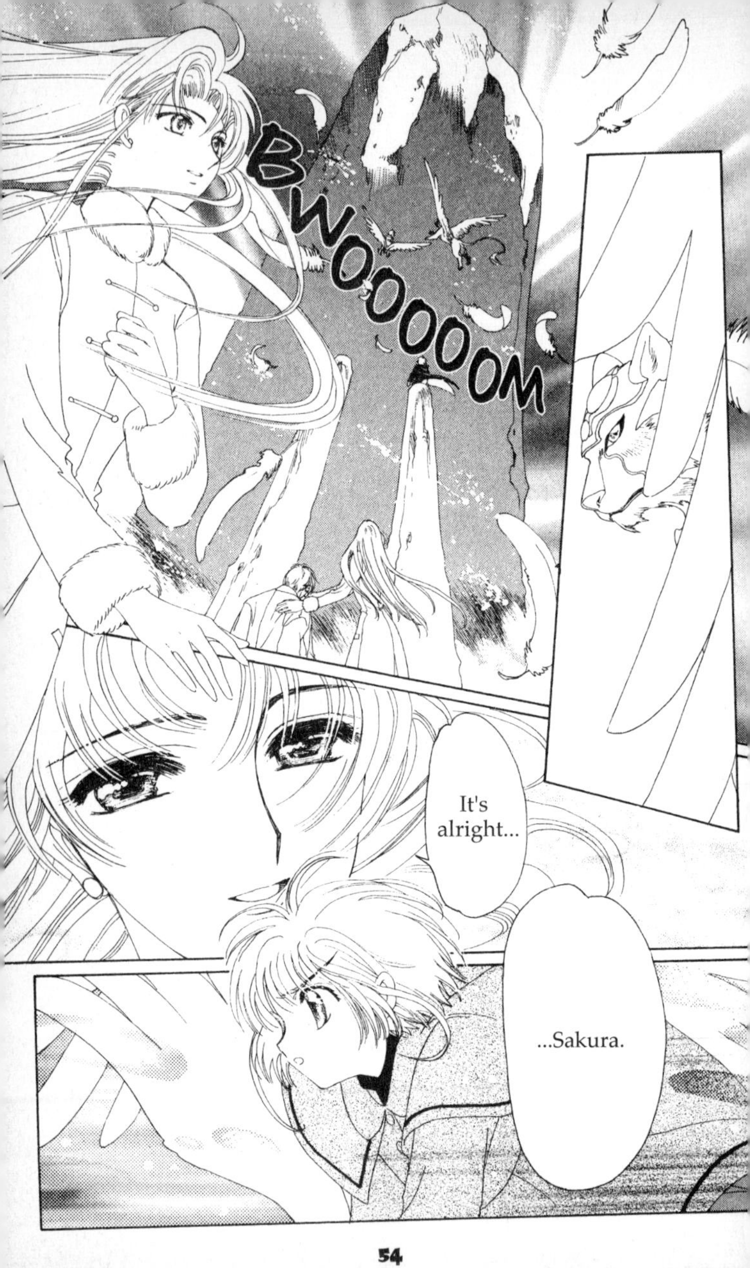
BWOOOOOM
It's alright...
...Sakura.

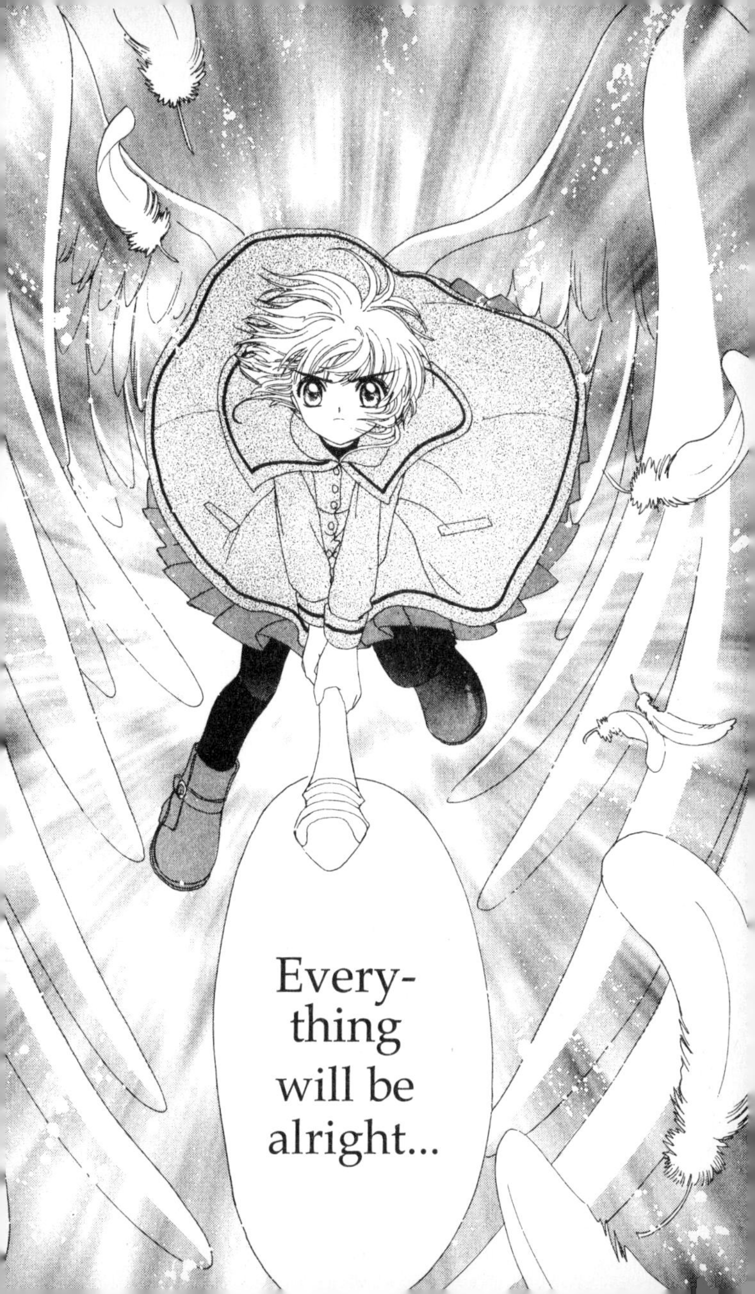
Every-thing will be alright...

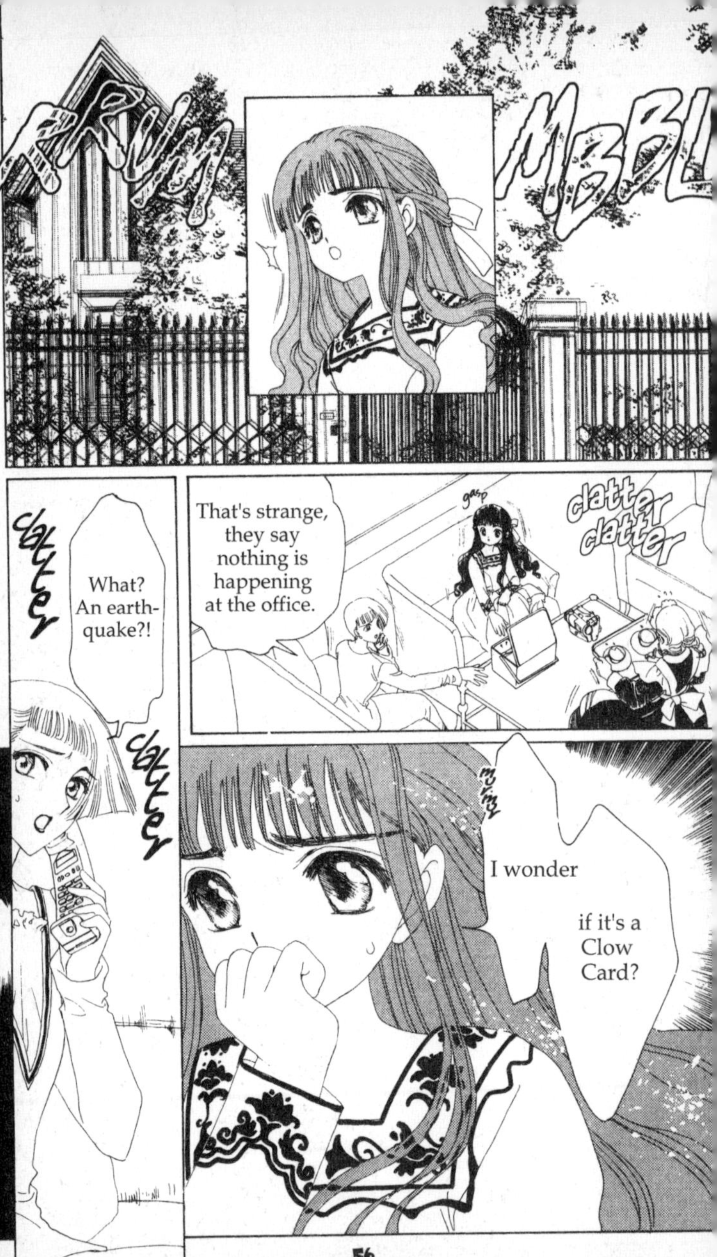
RRUM
MBBL
clatter clatter
gasp
That's strange, they say nothing is happening at the office.
murmur
I wonder
if it's a Clow Card?
clatter
What? An earth-quake?!
clatter

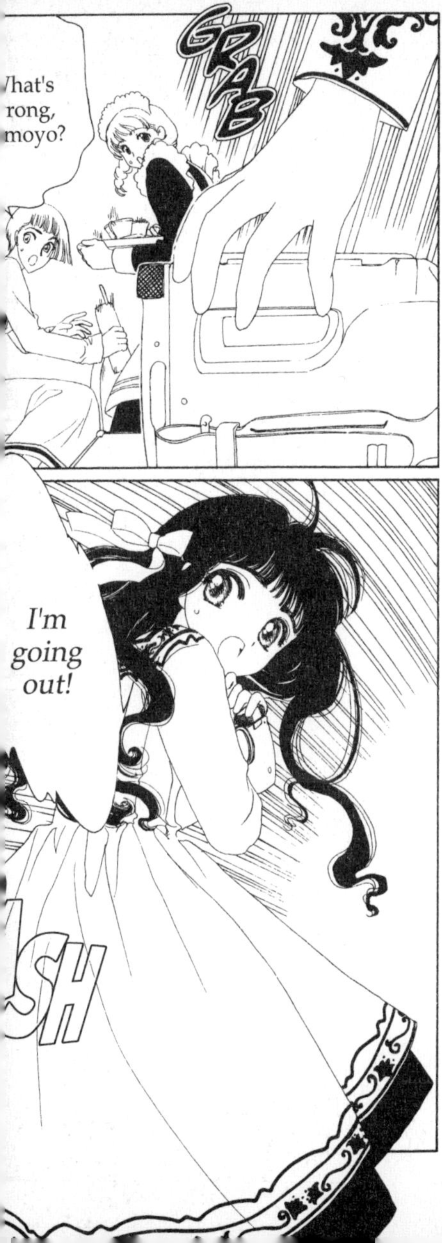
GRAB
hat's rong, moyo?
I'm going out!
SH

17

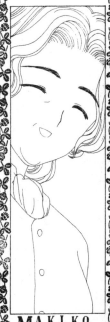

Makiko Midori

Birthdate:
November 19
Job:
Elementary School Teacher
Favorite Food:
Pickled Vegetables
Least Favorite Food:
Noodles
Favorite Thing:
Cleaning
Favorite Color:
Purple
Favorite Flower:
Chinese Bellflower
Favorite Recipe:
Japanese Cooking
Achilles Heel:
Can't stay up late
Hobby:
Ikebana (Flower Arranging)
Special Talent:
Japanese Dressmaking

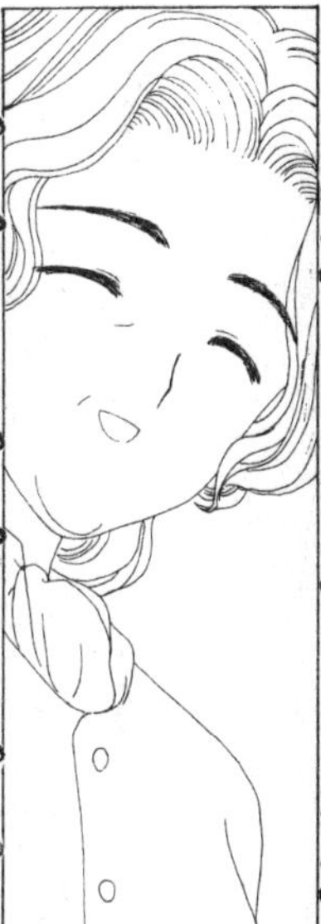

MAKIKO MIDORI

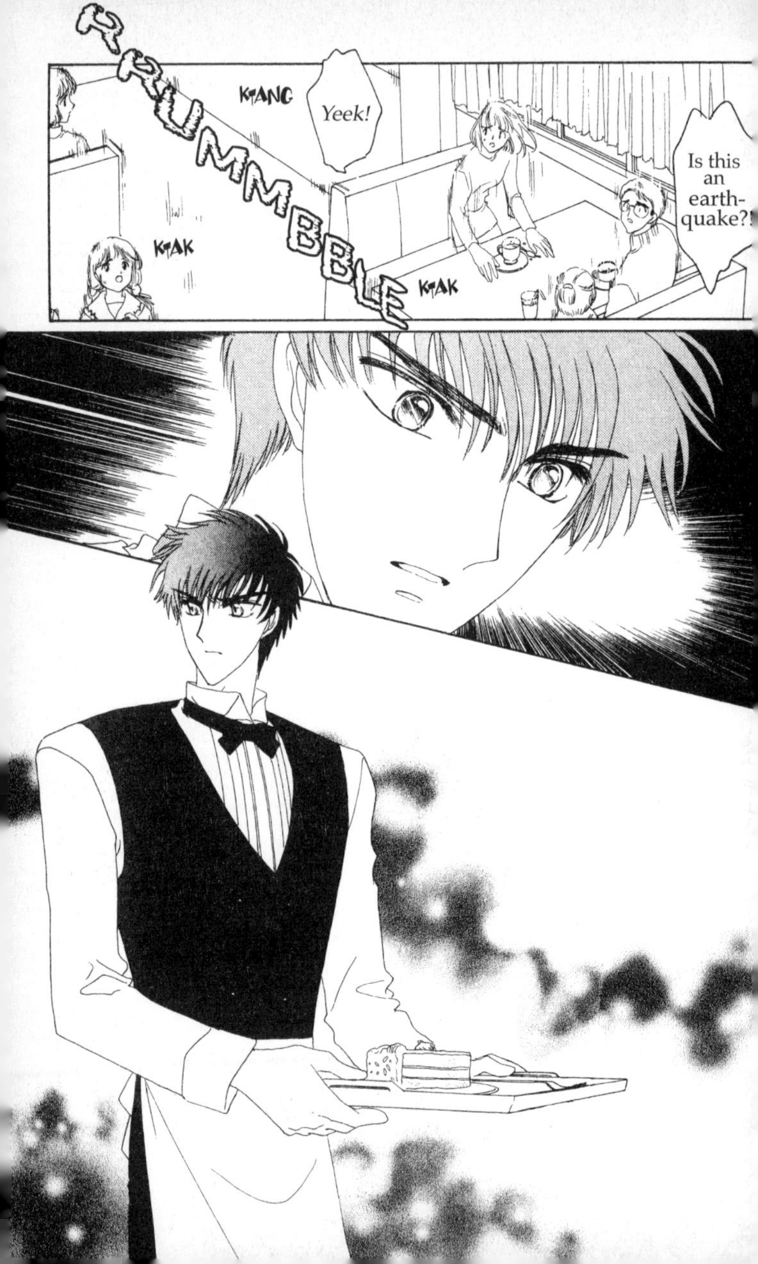
Is this an earthquake?!
Yeek!
KTANG
TRUMMBBLE
KTAK
KTAK

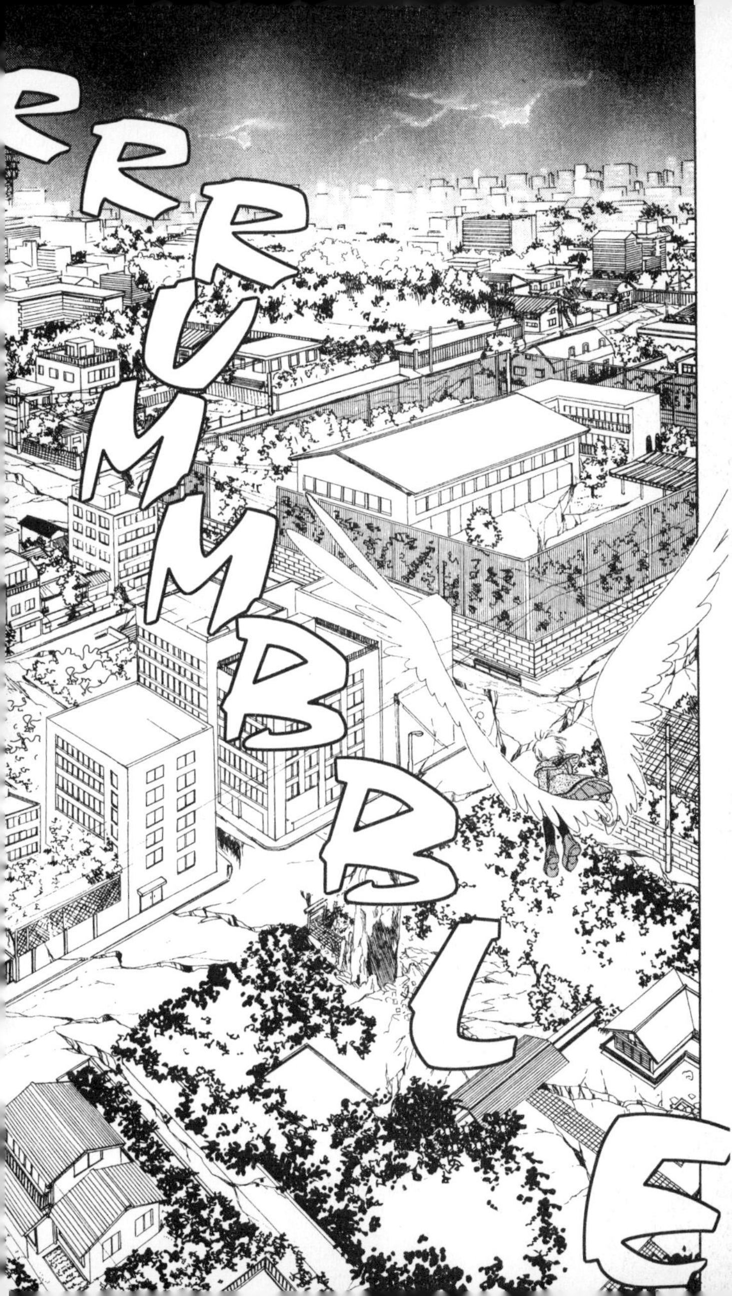
RRUMMBBLE

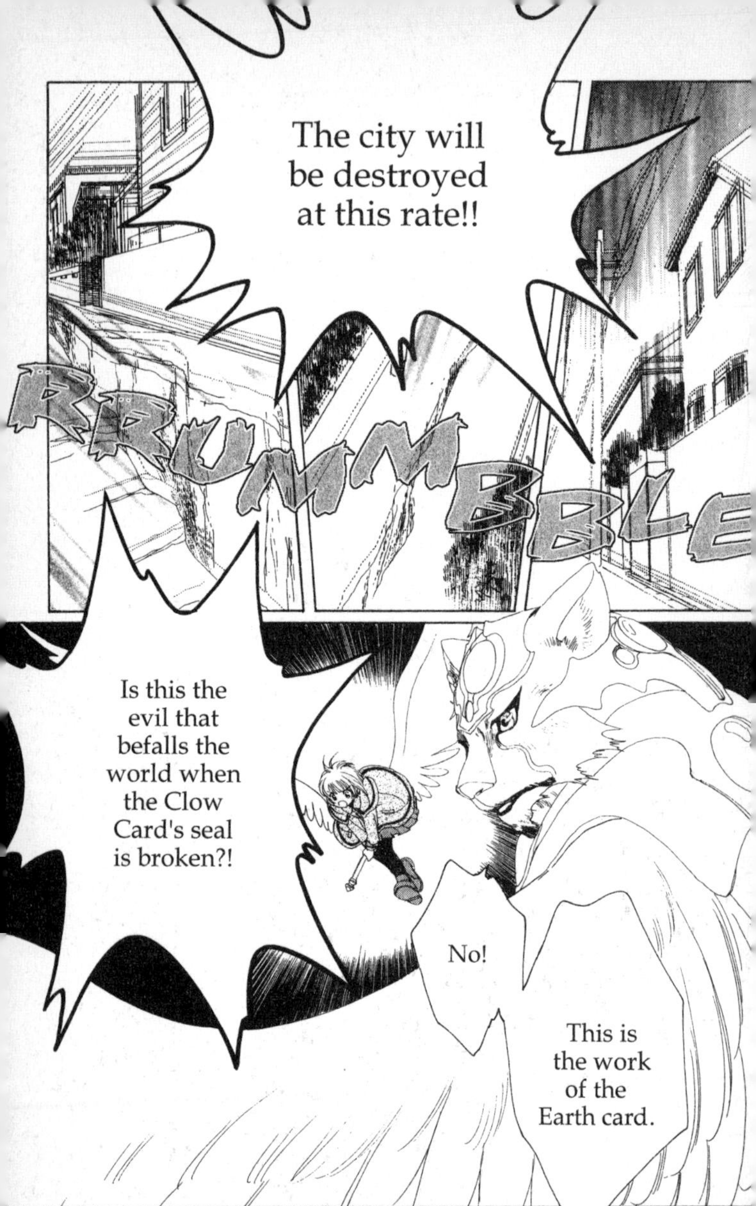
The city will be destroyed at this rate!!
RRUMMBBLE
Is this the evil that befalls the world when the Clow Card's seal is broken?!
No!
This is the work of the Earth card.

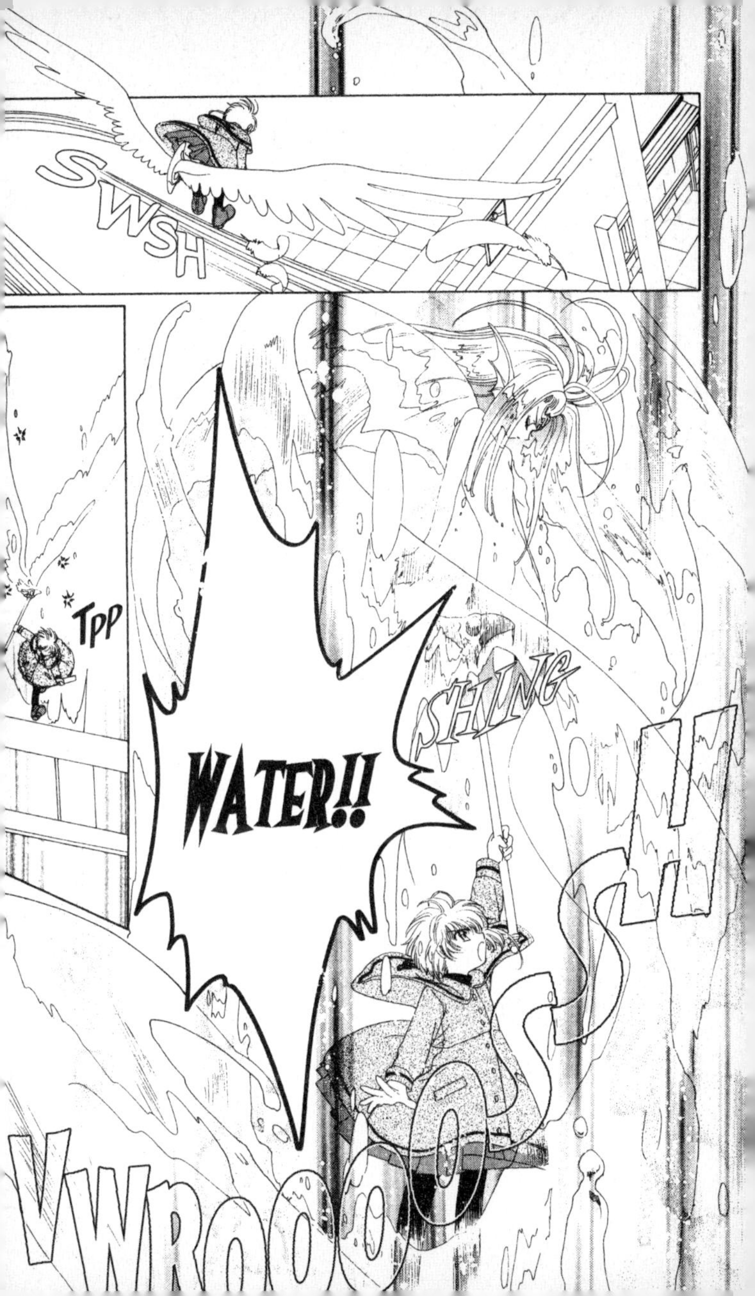
SWSH
TPP
SHING
WATER!!
SH!
VWROOOOO

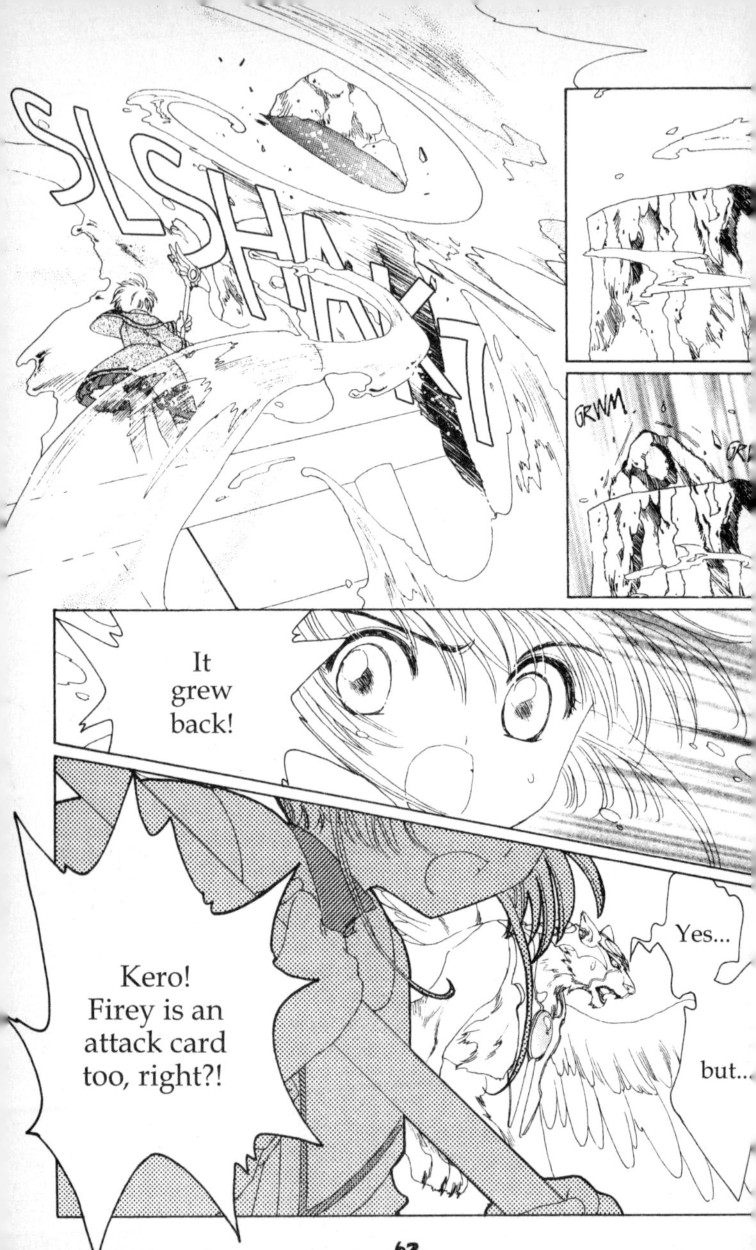
GRWM
SLSHAK
It grew back!
Yes...
but...
Kero! Firey is an attack card too, right?!

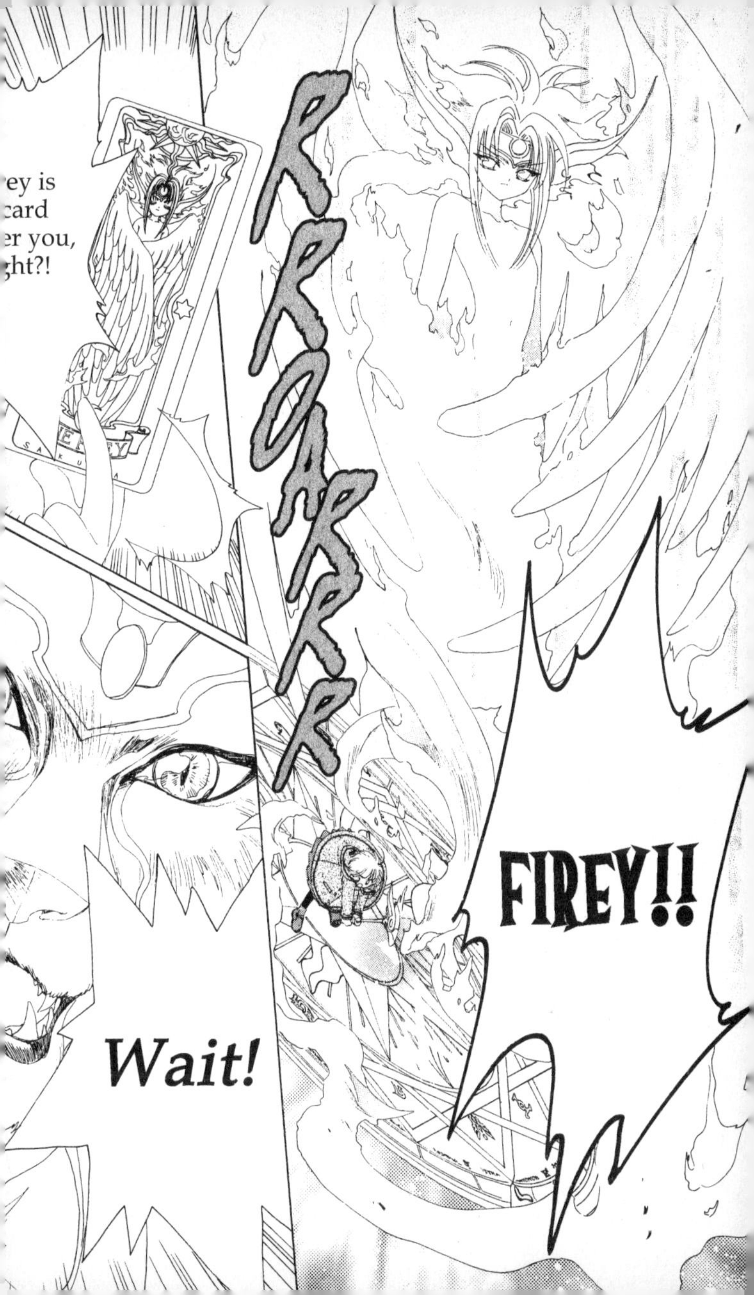
RROARRR
FIREY!!
ey is
card
er you,
ght?!
FIREY
Wait!

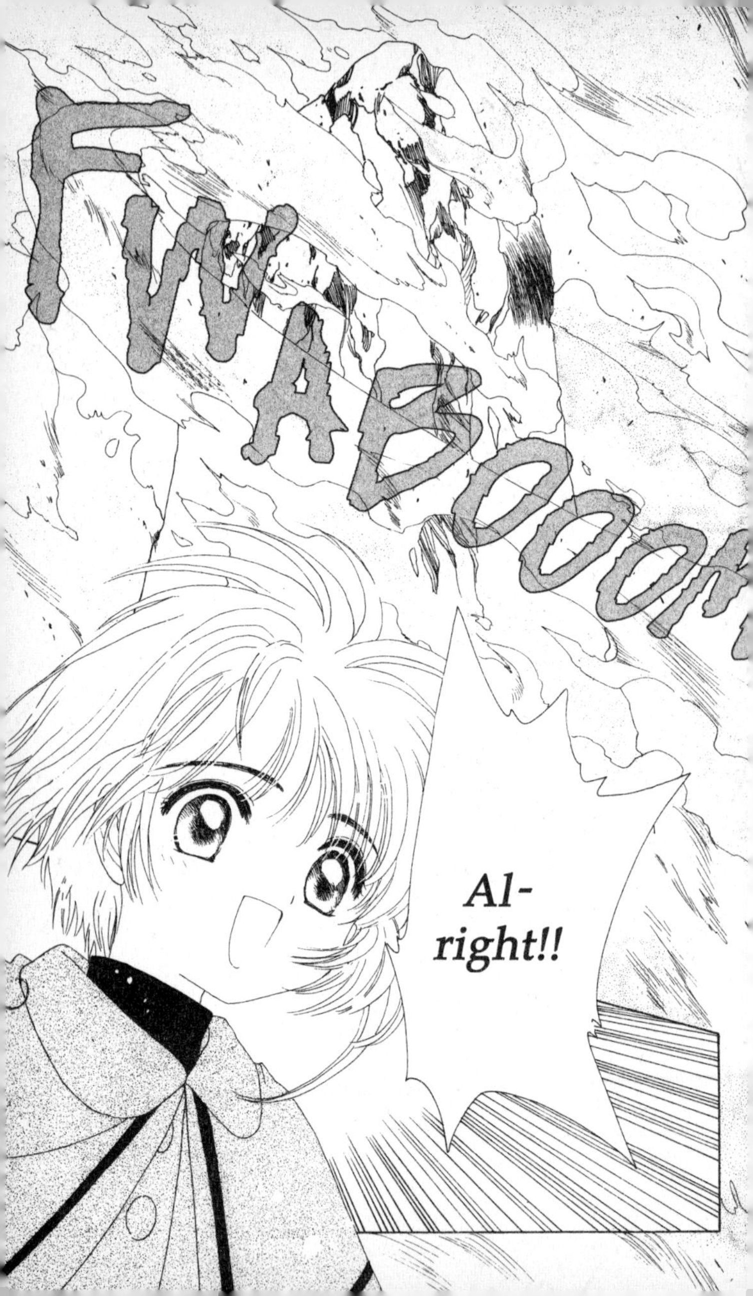
FWABOOOM
Al-
right!!

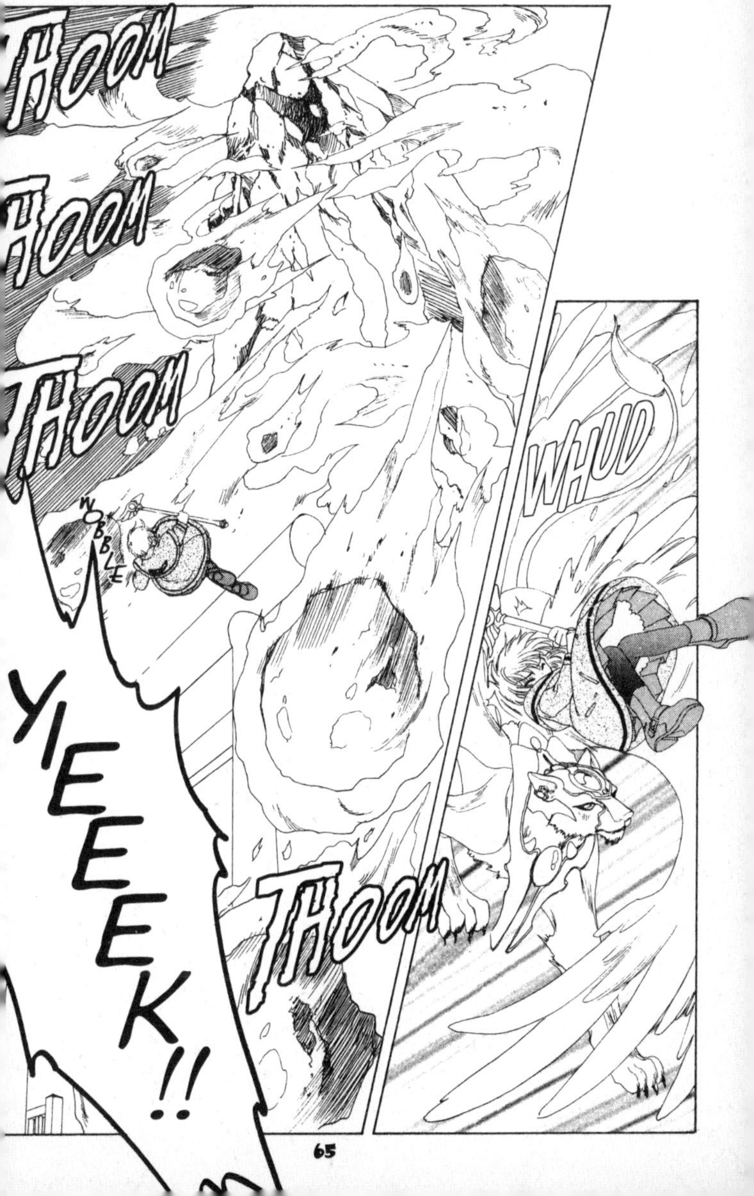

WHUD
THOOM
THOOM
THOOM
WOBBLE
YIEEEEK!!
THOOM

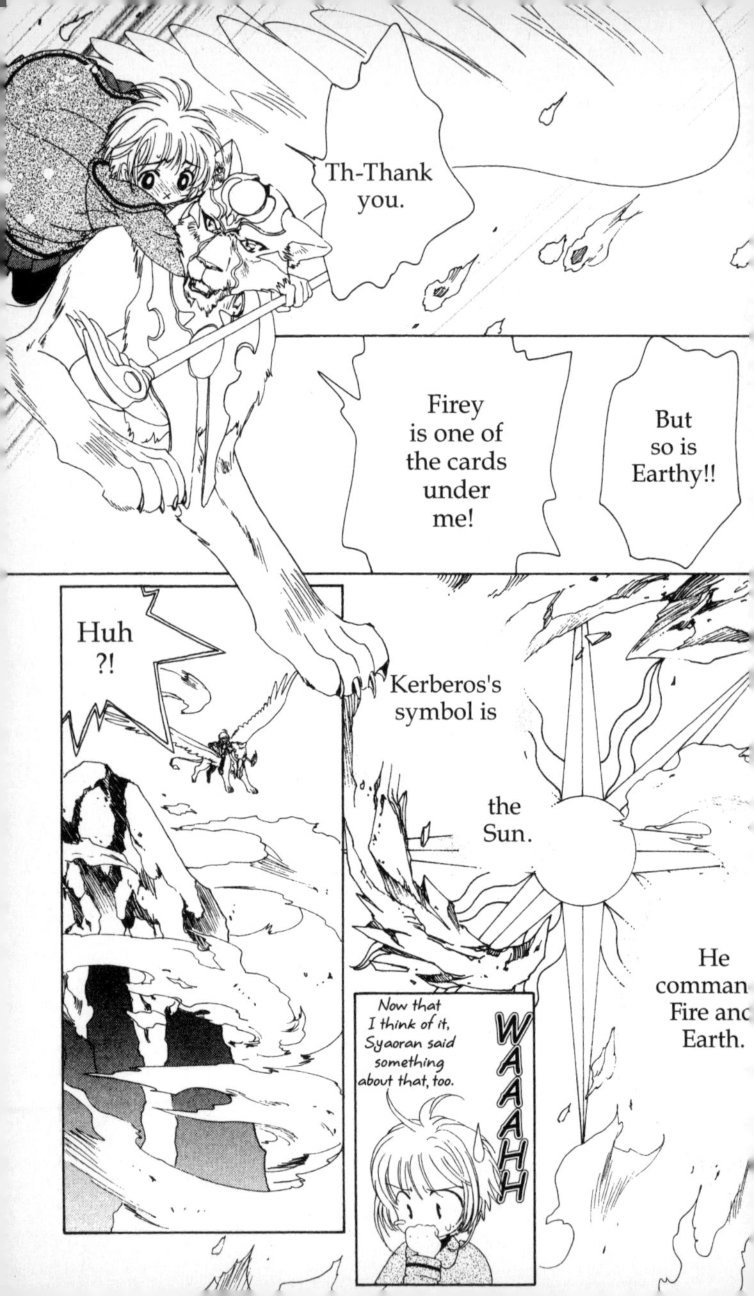
Th-Thank you.
Firey is one of the cards under me!
But so is Earthy!!
Huh?!
Kerberos's symbol is the Sun.
He comman Fire anc Earth.
Now that I think of it, Syaoran said something about that, too.
WAAAHH

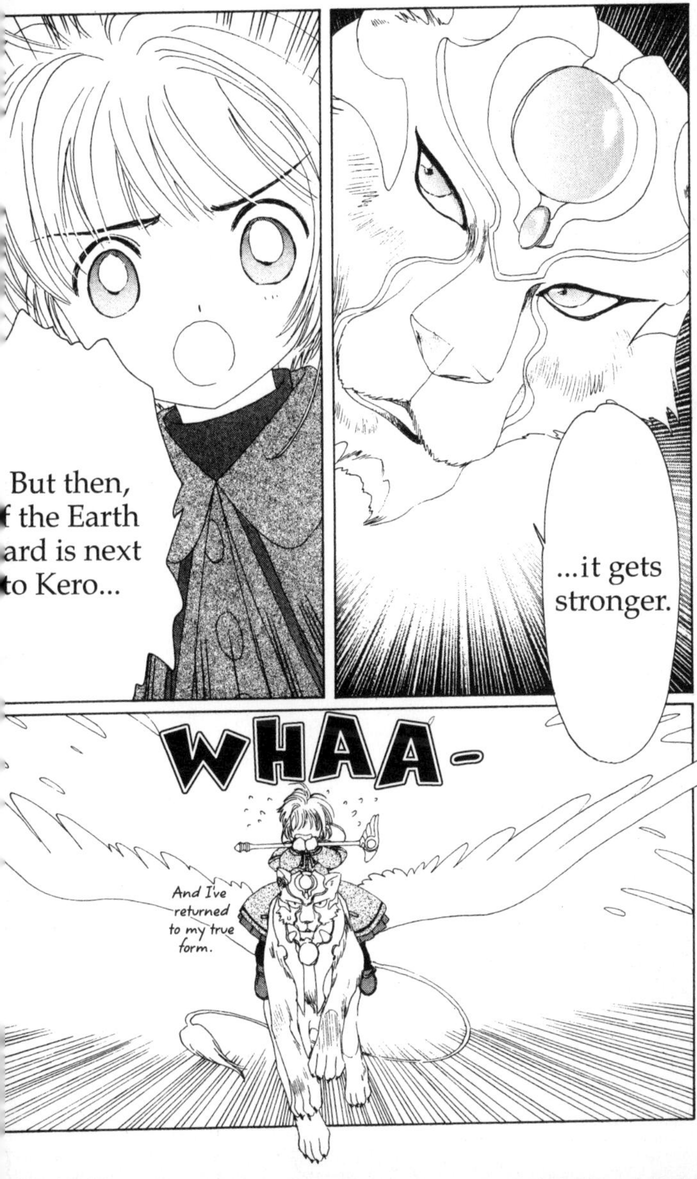
...it gets stronger.
But then,
f the Earth
ard is next
to Kero...
WHAA-
And I've returned to my true form.

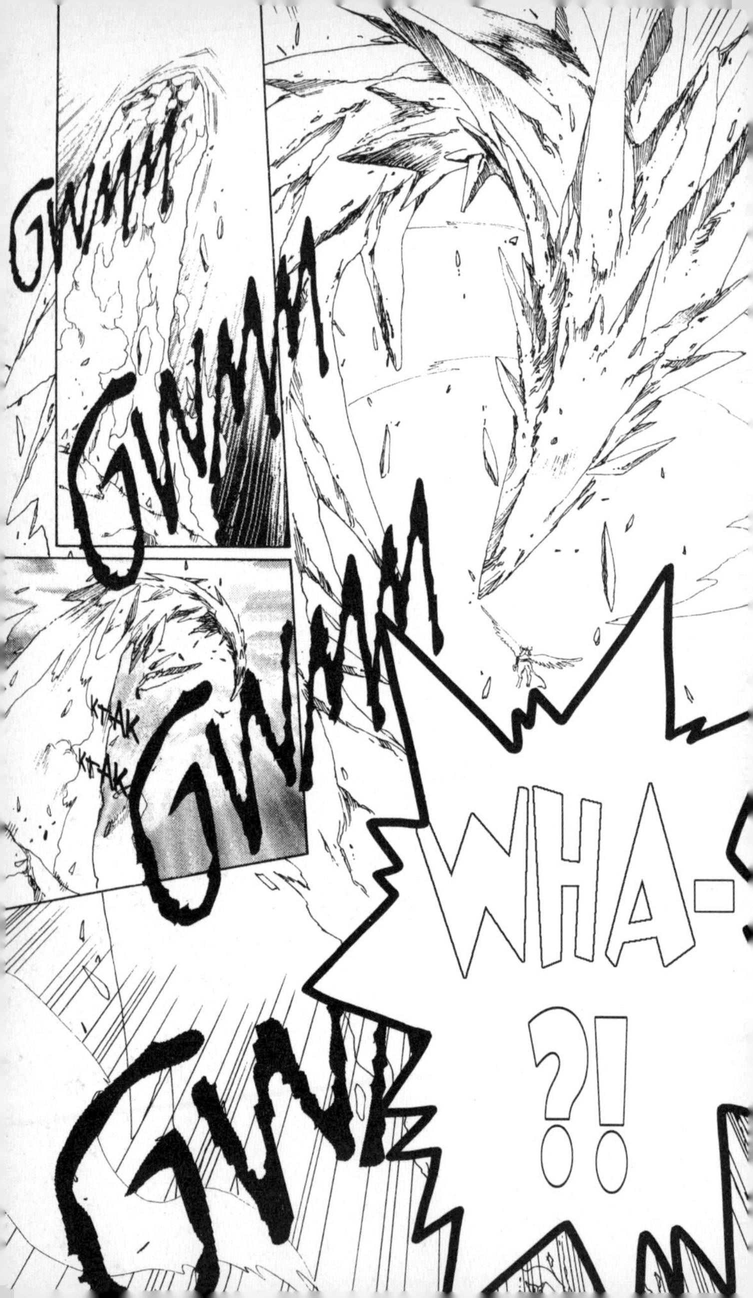
GWAM
GWAM
GWAM
KT-AK
KT-AK
WHA-?!
GWK

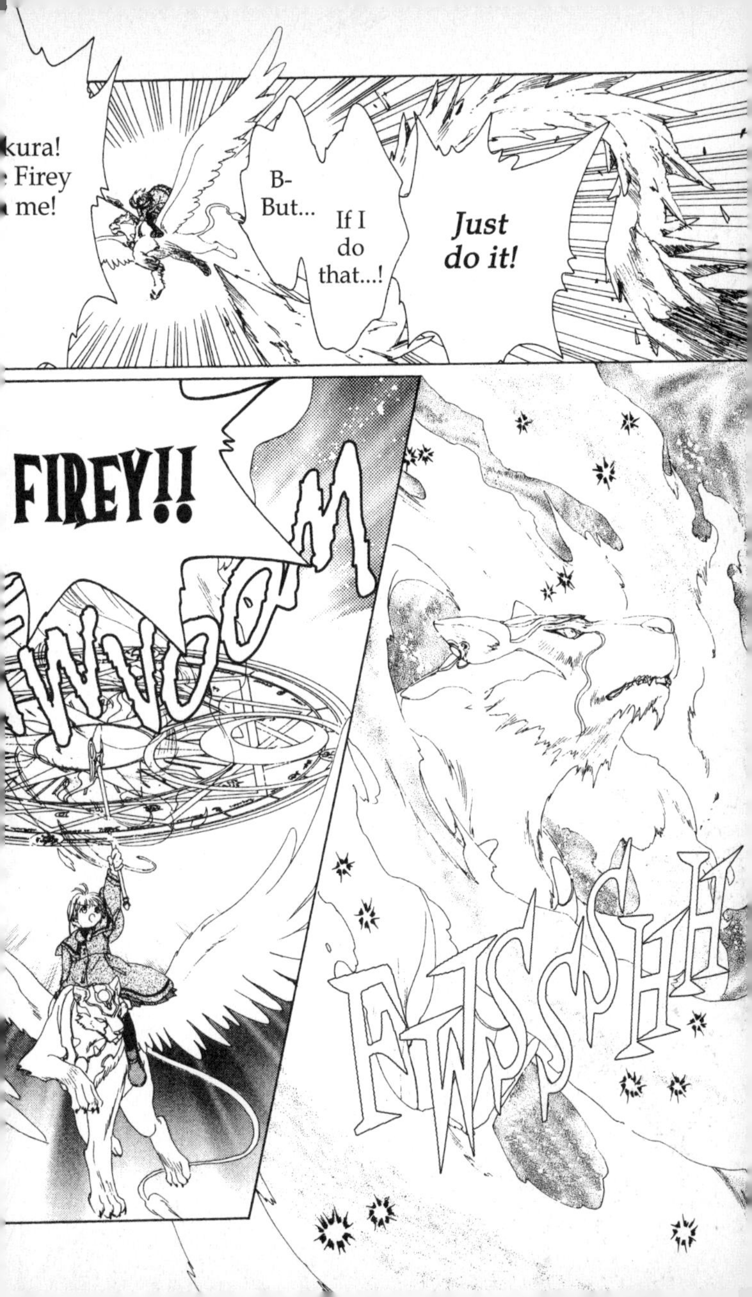
Just do it!
If I do that...!
B- But...
kura!
Firey
me!
FWSSHH
FIREY!!
WOOM

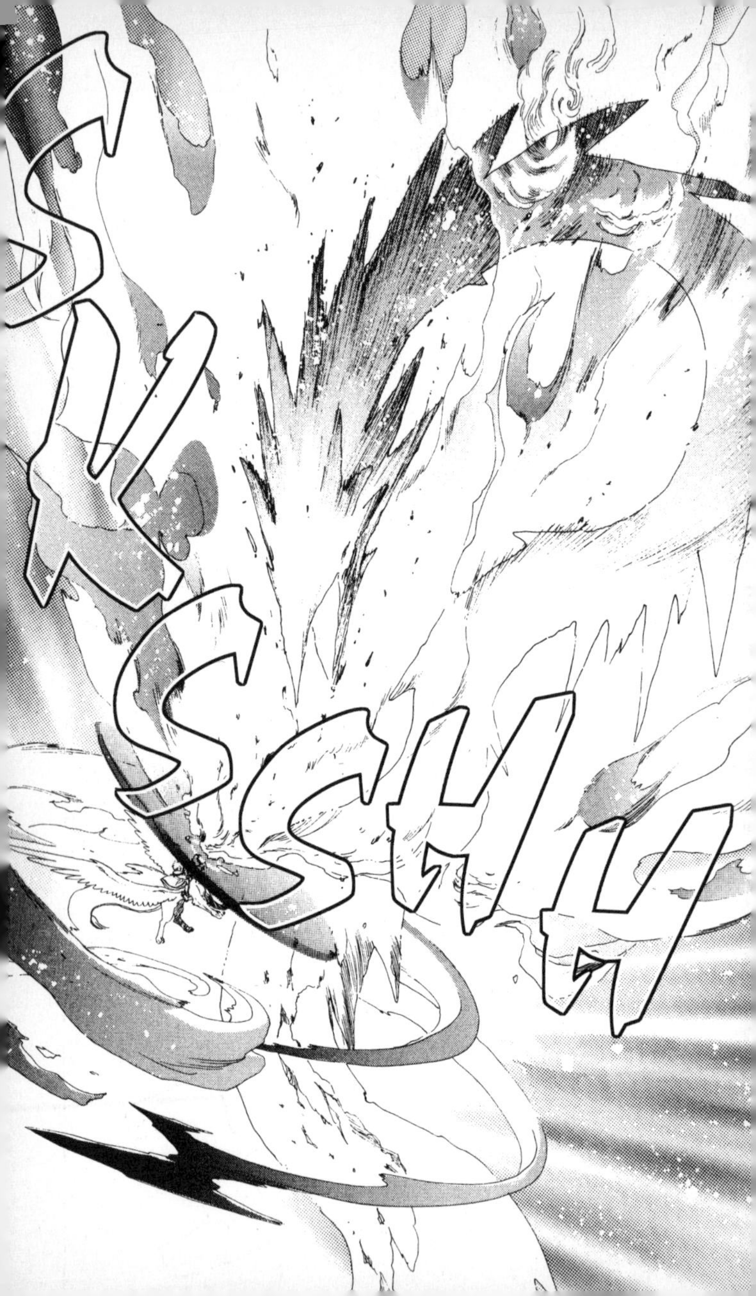
SSHH

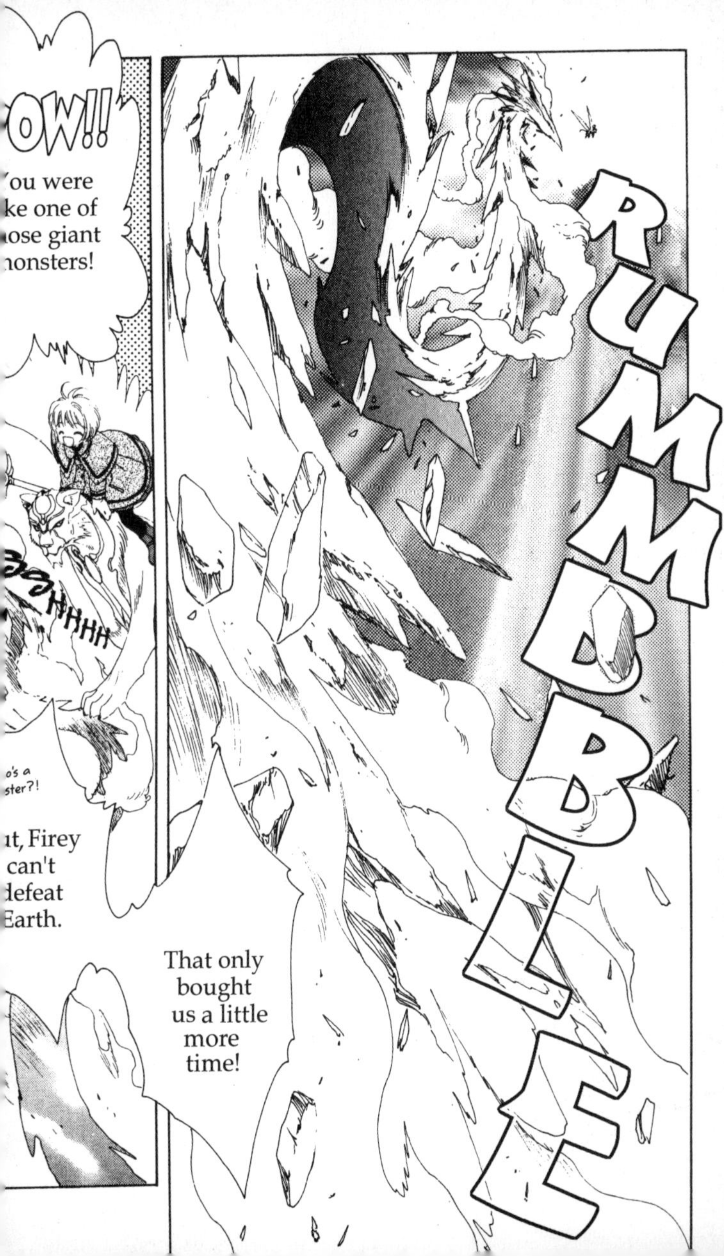
RUMMBBLE
That only bought us a little more time!
OW!!
ou were ke one of ose giant onsters!
o's a ster?!
it, Firey can't defeat Earth.

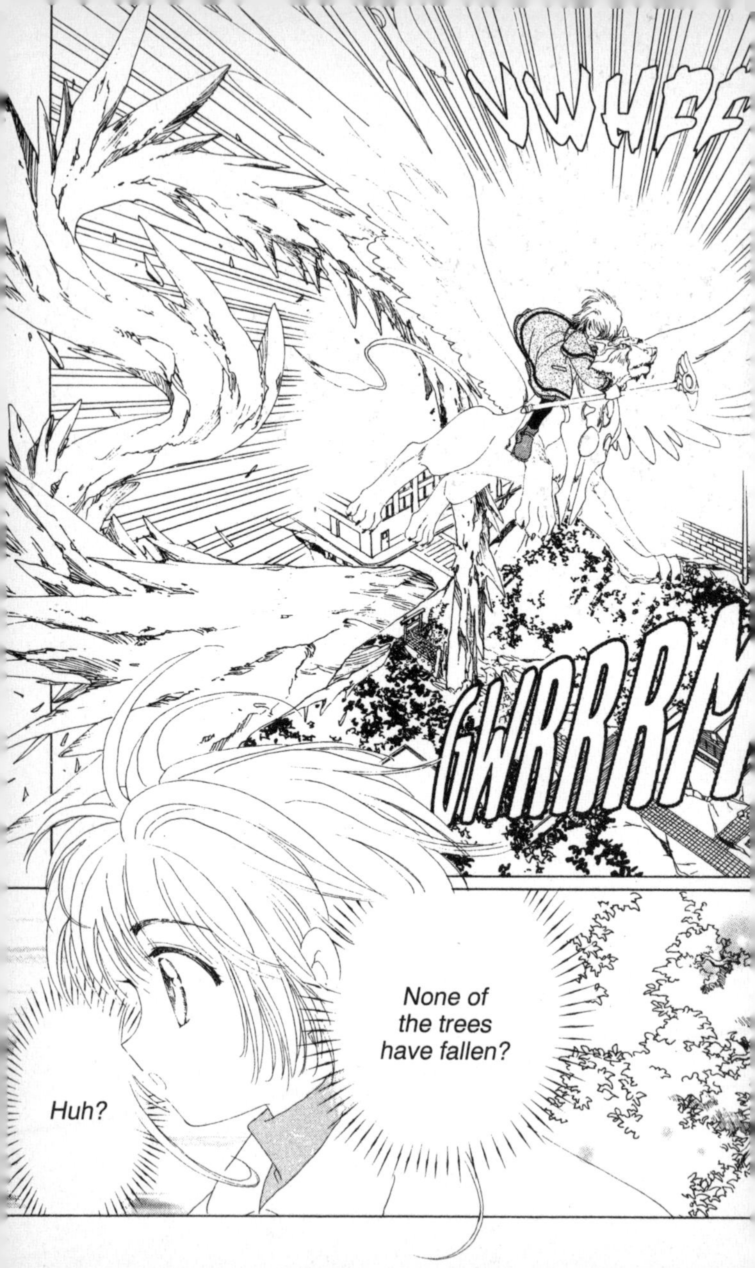
VWHEE
GWRRRM
None of the trees have fallen?
Huh?

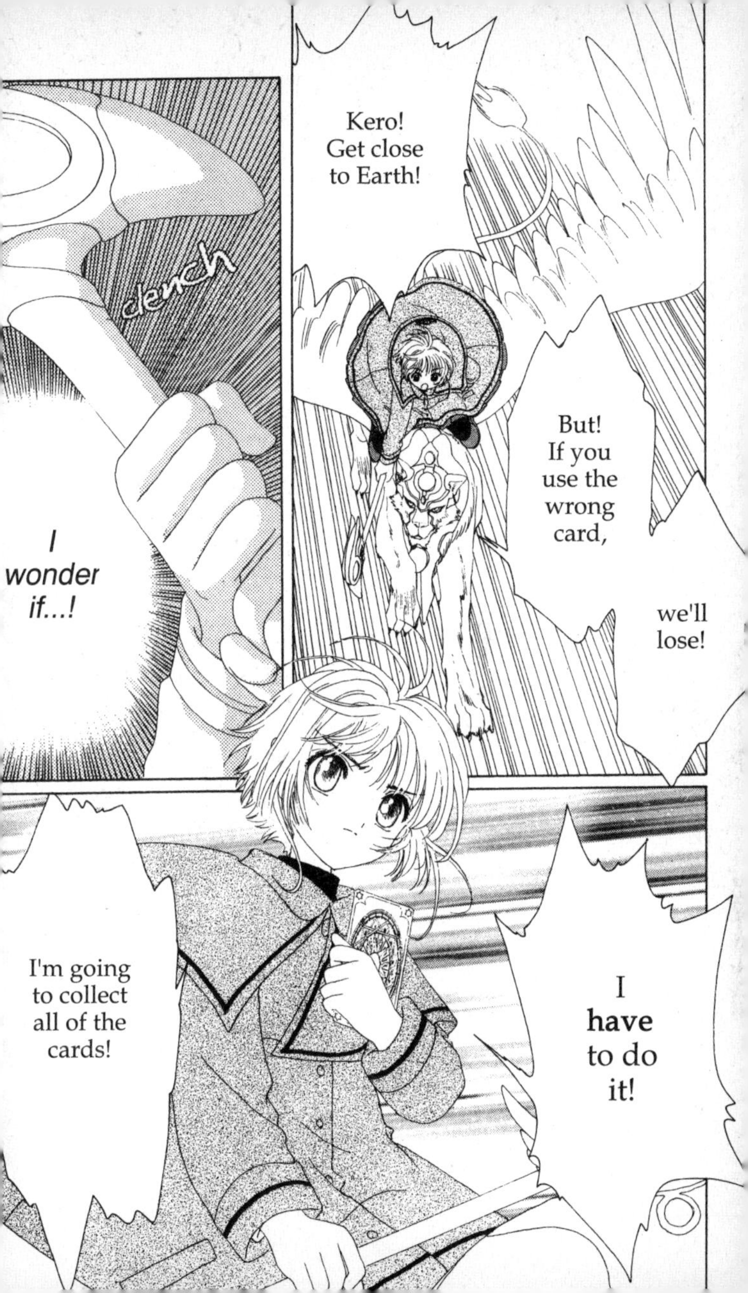
Kero! Get close to Earth!
But! If you use the wrong card,
we'll lose!
clench
I wonder if...!
I have to do it!
I'm going to collect all of the cards!

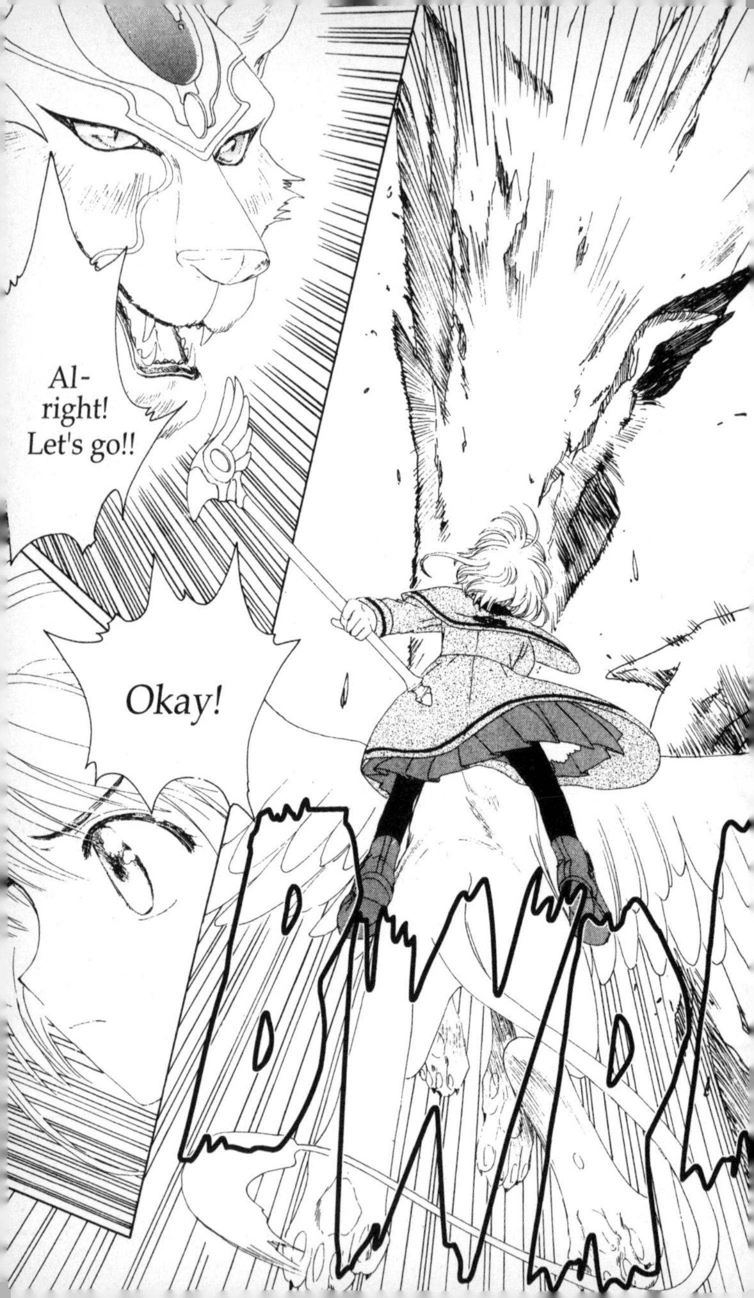
Al- right! Let's go!!
Okay!

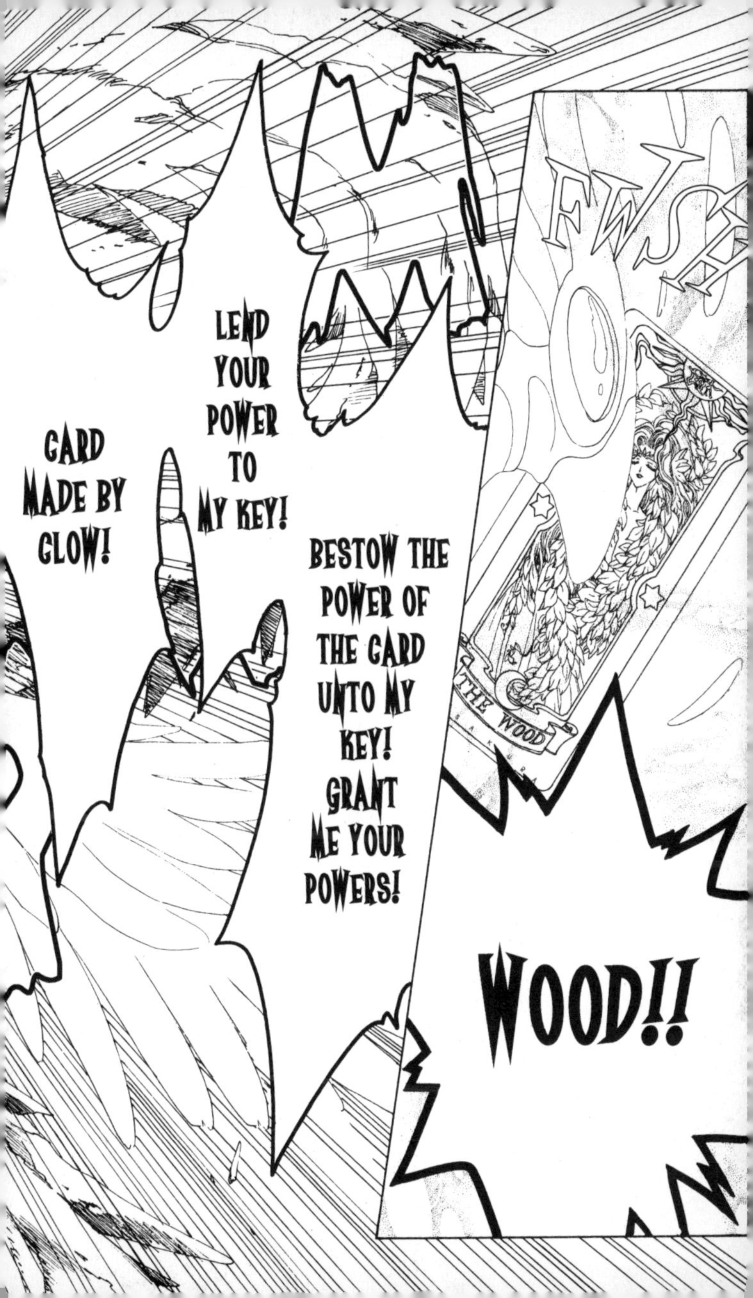
CARD MADE BY CLOW!
LEND YOUR POWER TO MY KEY!
BESTOW THE POWER OF THE CARD UNTO MY KEY! GRANT ME YOUR POWERS!
FWSH
THE WOOD
SAKURA
WOOD!!

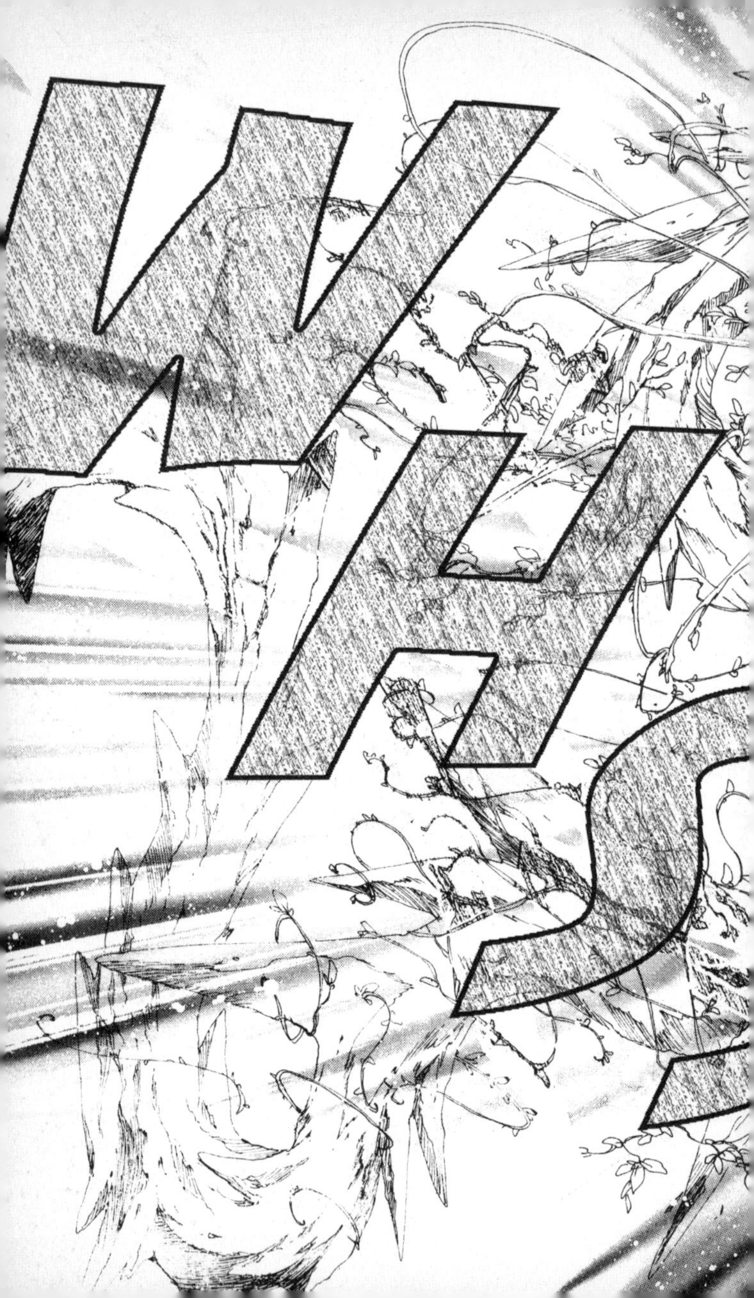
WHS

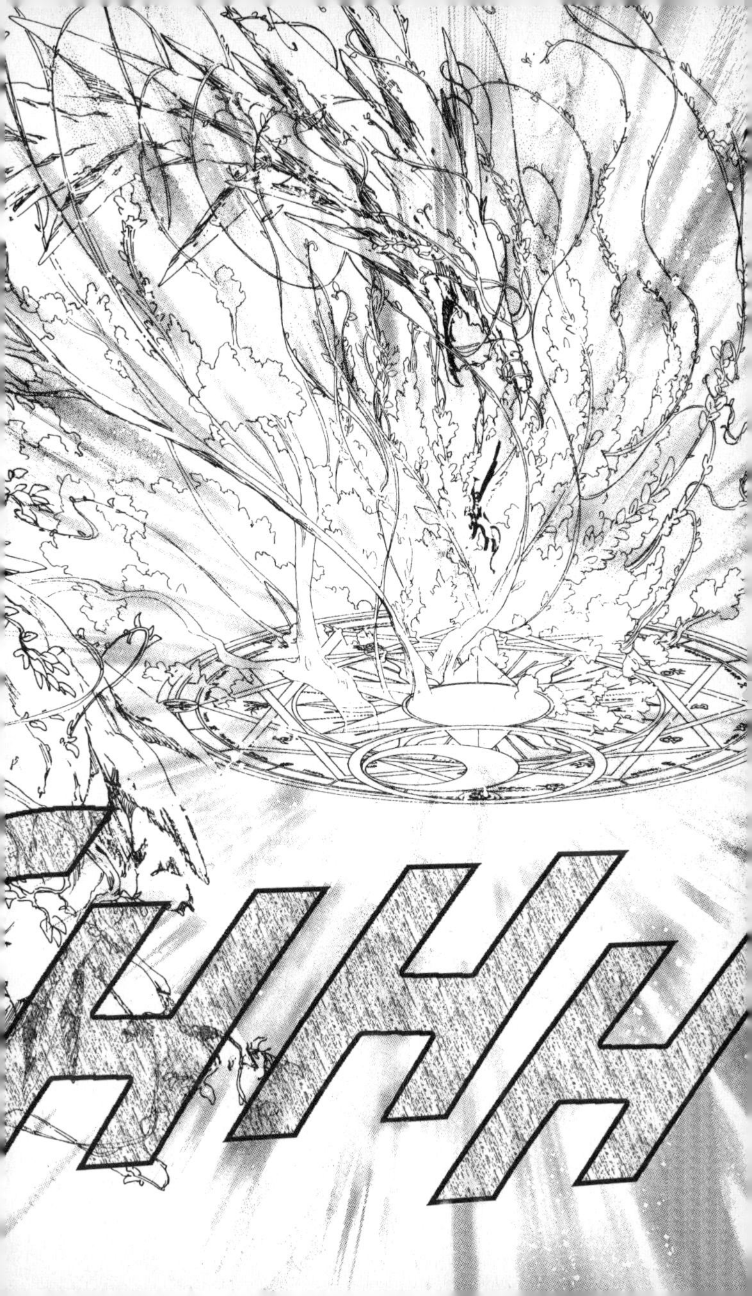

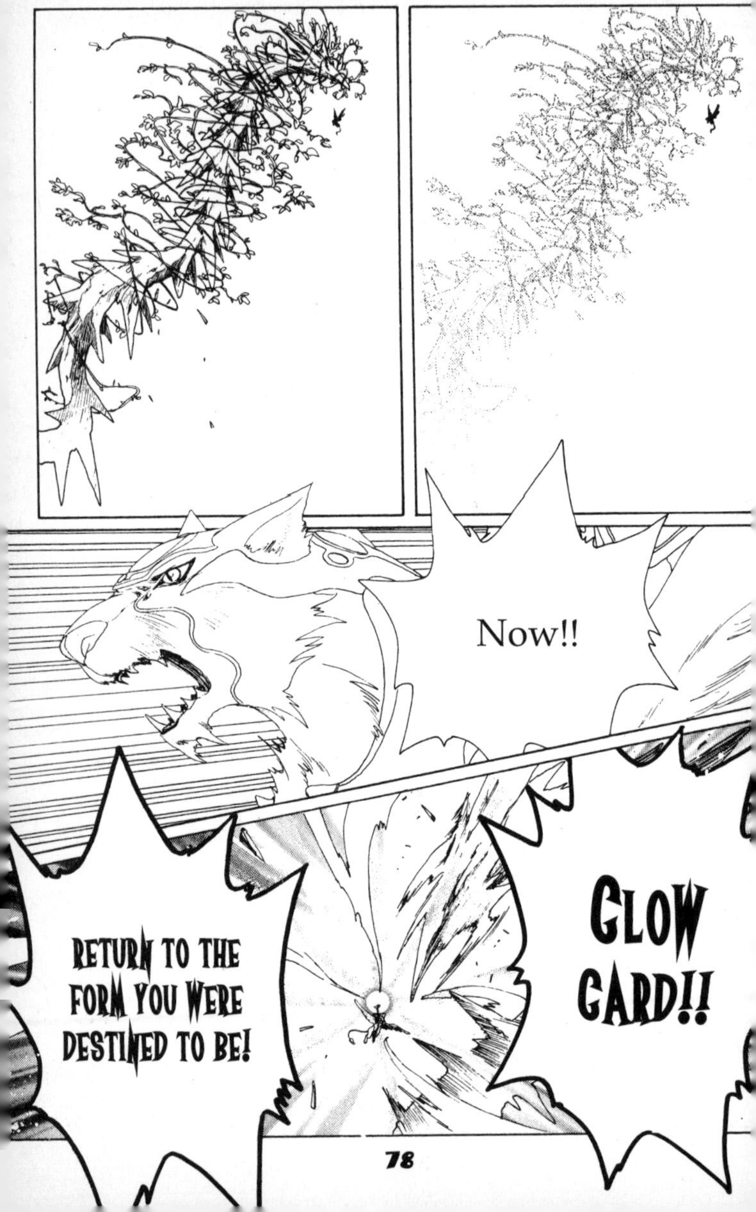
Now!!
GLOW CARD!!
RETURN TO THE FORM YOU WERE DESTINED TO BE!

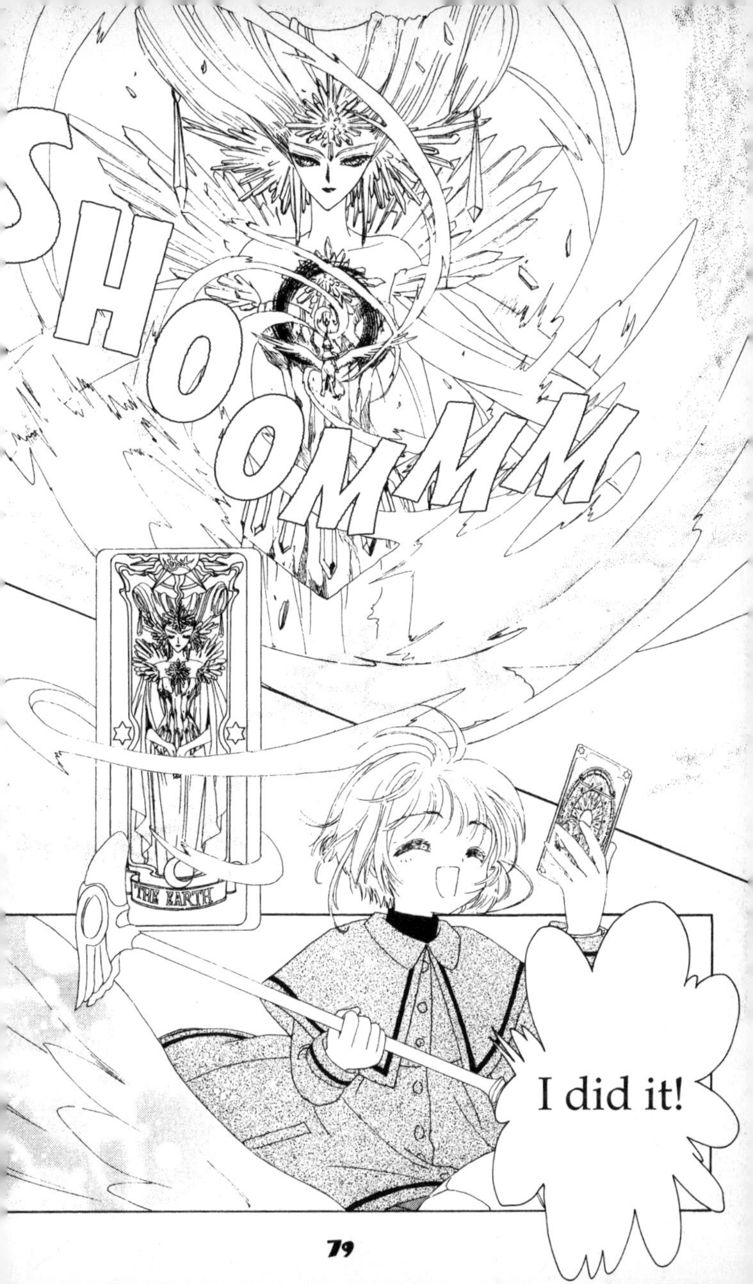
SHOOMMM
THE EARTH
I did it!

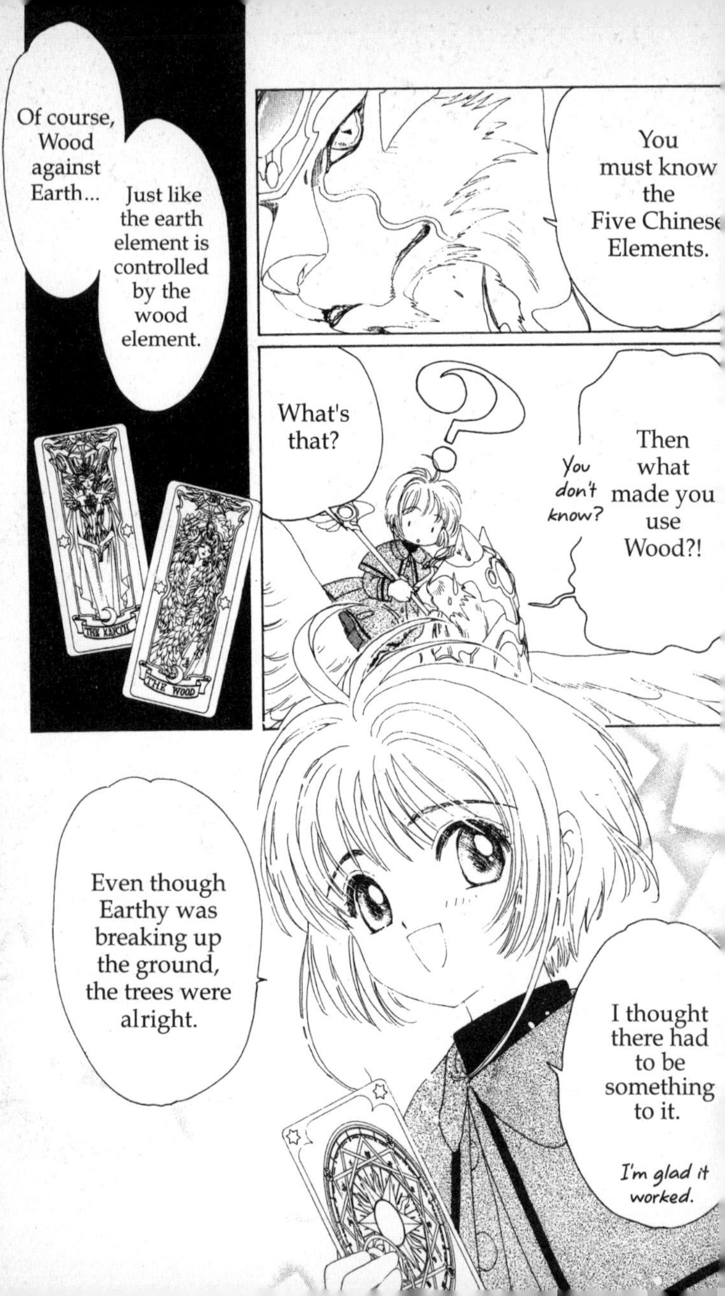
Of course, Wood against Earth...
Just like the earth element is controlled by the wood element.
You must know the Five Chinese Elements.
What's that?
You don't know?
Then what made you use Wood?!
Even though Earthy was breaking up the ground, the trees were alright.
I thought there had to be something to it.
I'm glad it worked.

The Five Elements...

In ancient China, it was believed that the universe was made of five elements.

Wood - Fire - Earth - Metal - Water. Each of the elements reacts in a certain way with the others.

Wood exists at the expense of Earth.

Trees grow from Earth, after all.

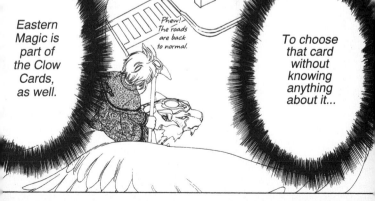

Eastern Magic is part of the Clow Cards, as well.

Phew! The roads are back to normal.

To choose that card without knowing anything about it...

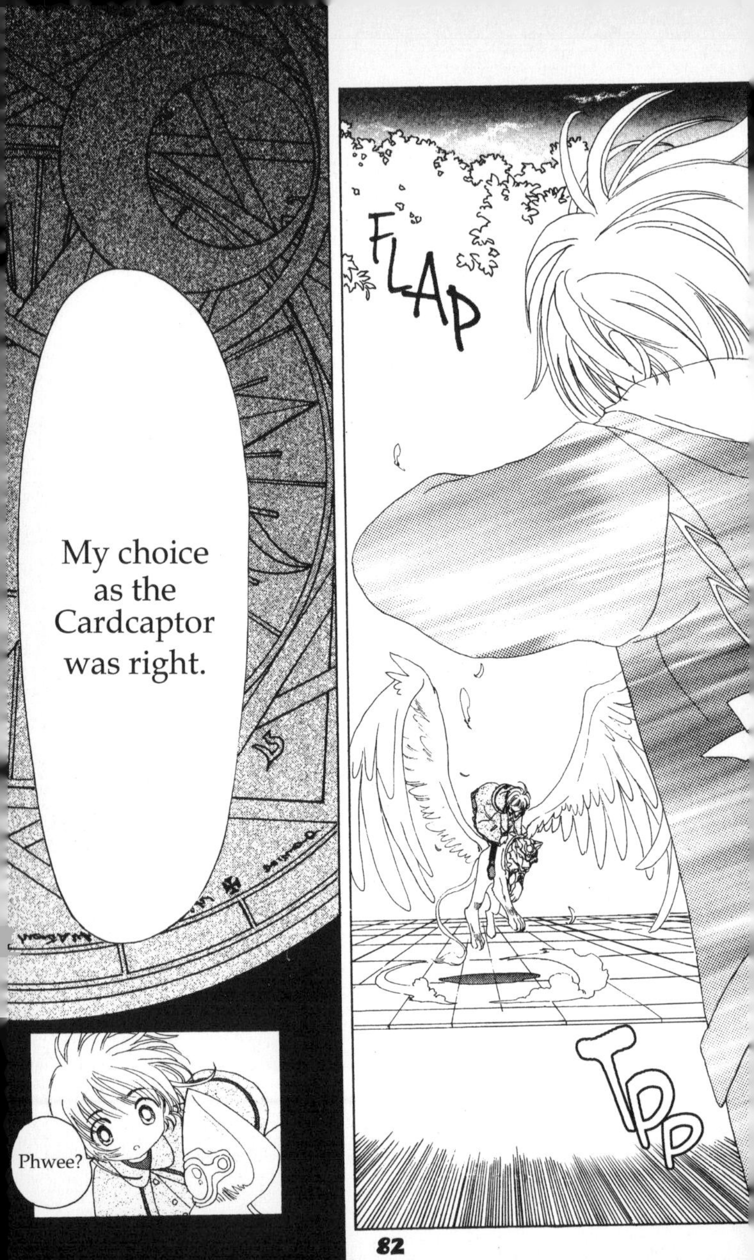
FLAP
TPP
My choice as the Cardcaptor was right.
Phwee?

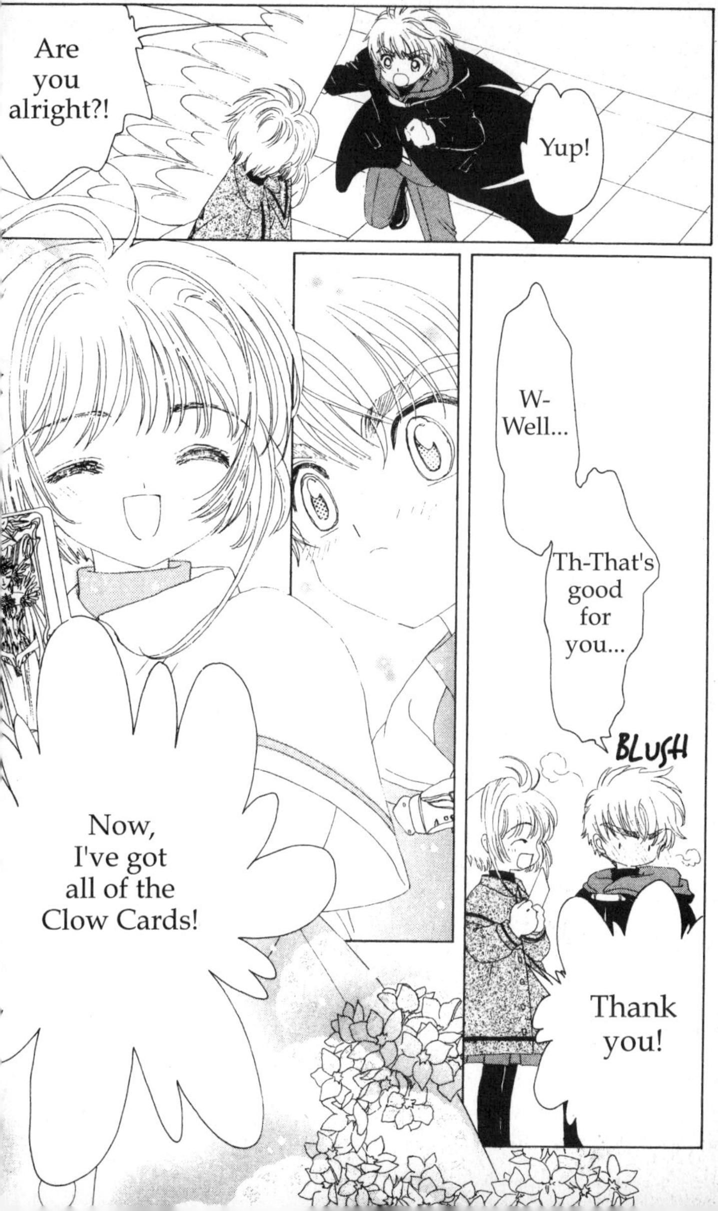
Are you alright?!
Yup!
Now, I've got all of the Clow Cards!
W-Well...
Th-That's good for you...
BLUSH
Thank you!

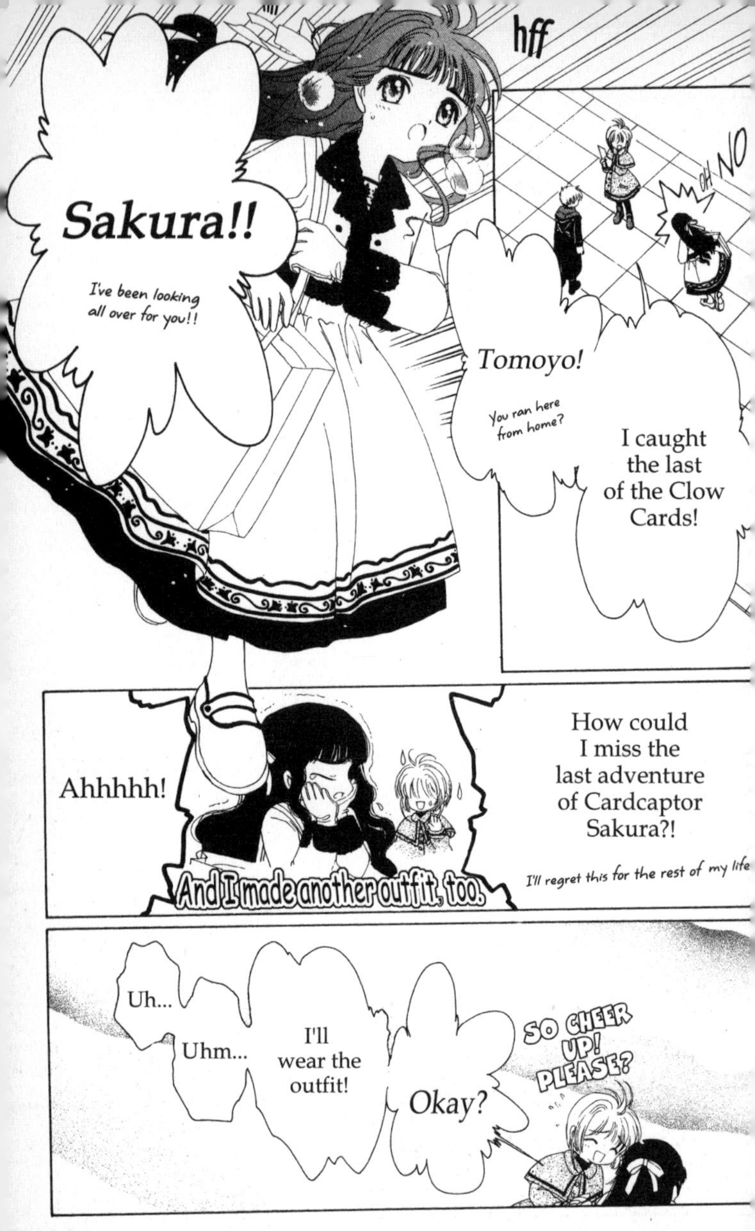
hff
Sakura!!
I've been looking all over for you!!
Tomoyo!
You ran here from home?
I caught the last of the Clow Cards!
OH NO
Ahhhhh!
How could I miss the last adventure of Cardcaptor Sakura?!
I'll regret this for the rest of my life
And I made another outfit, too.
Uh...
Uhm...
I'll wear the outfit!
Okay?
SO CHEER UP! PLEASE?

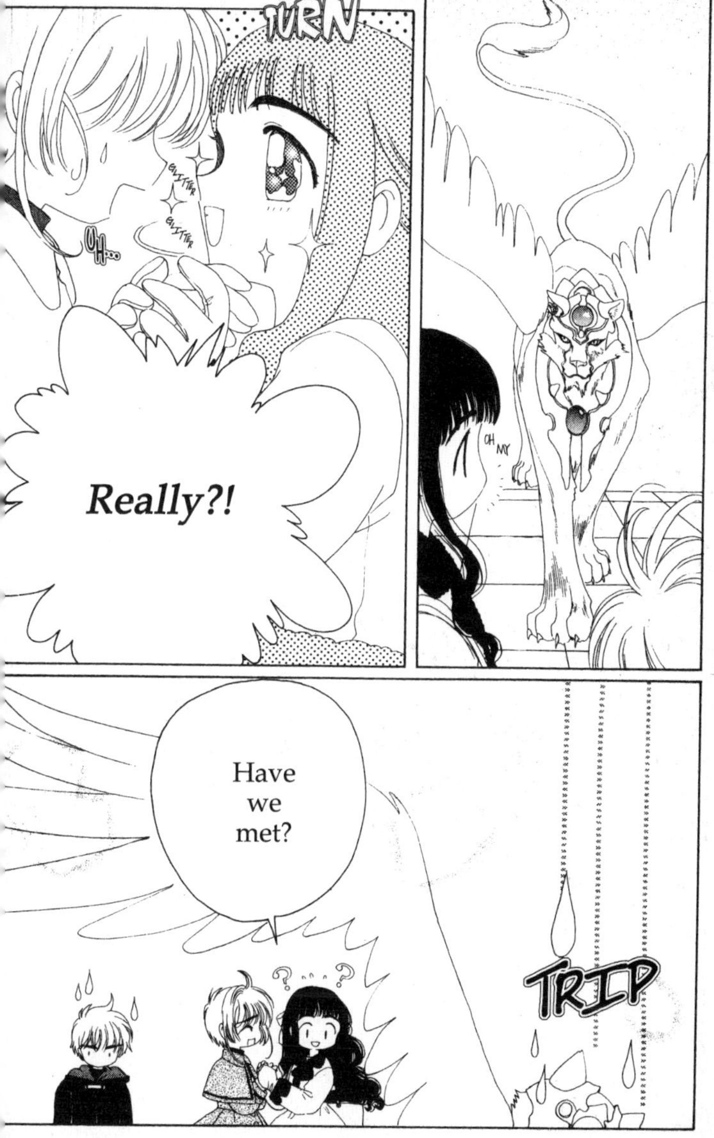
OH MY
TURN
GLITTER
GLITTER
UH...
Really?!
Have we met?
TRIP

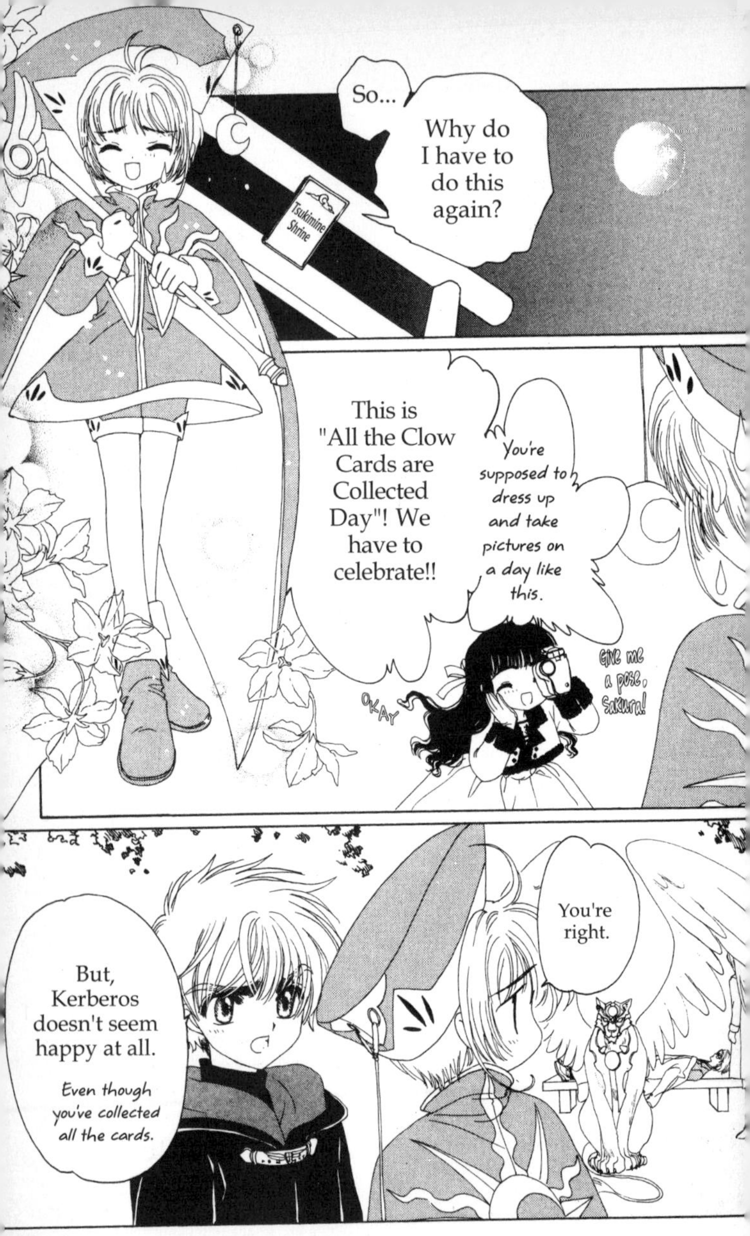
So...
Why do I have to do this again?
Tsukimine Shrine
This is "All the Clow Cards are Collected Day"! We have to celebrate!!
You're supposed to dress up and take pictures on a day like this.
Give me a pose, Sakura!
OKAY
But, Kerberos doesn't seem happy at all.
Even though you've collected all the cards.
You're right.

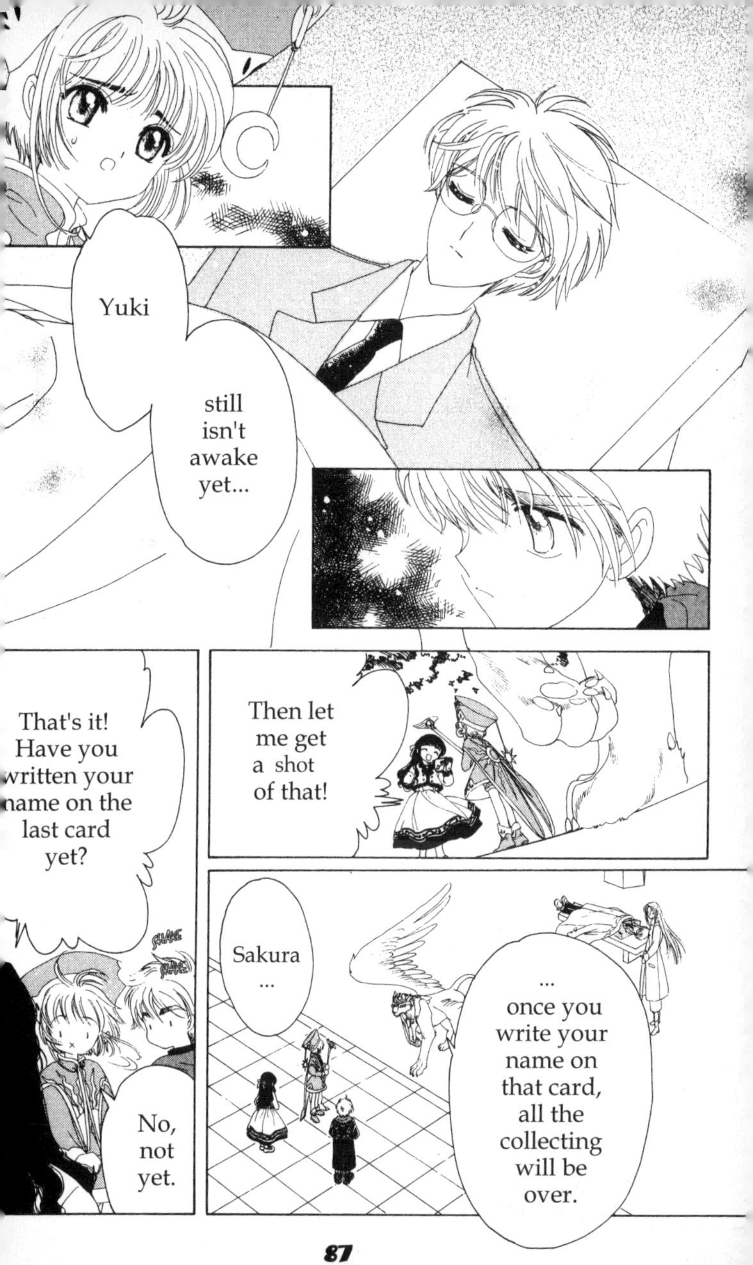
Yuki
still isn't awake yet...
Then let me get a shot of that!
That's it! Have you written your name on the last card yet?
SHAKE
SHAKE
No, not yet.
Sakura ...
... once you write your name on that card, all the collecting will be over.

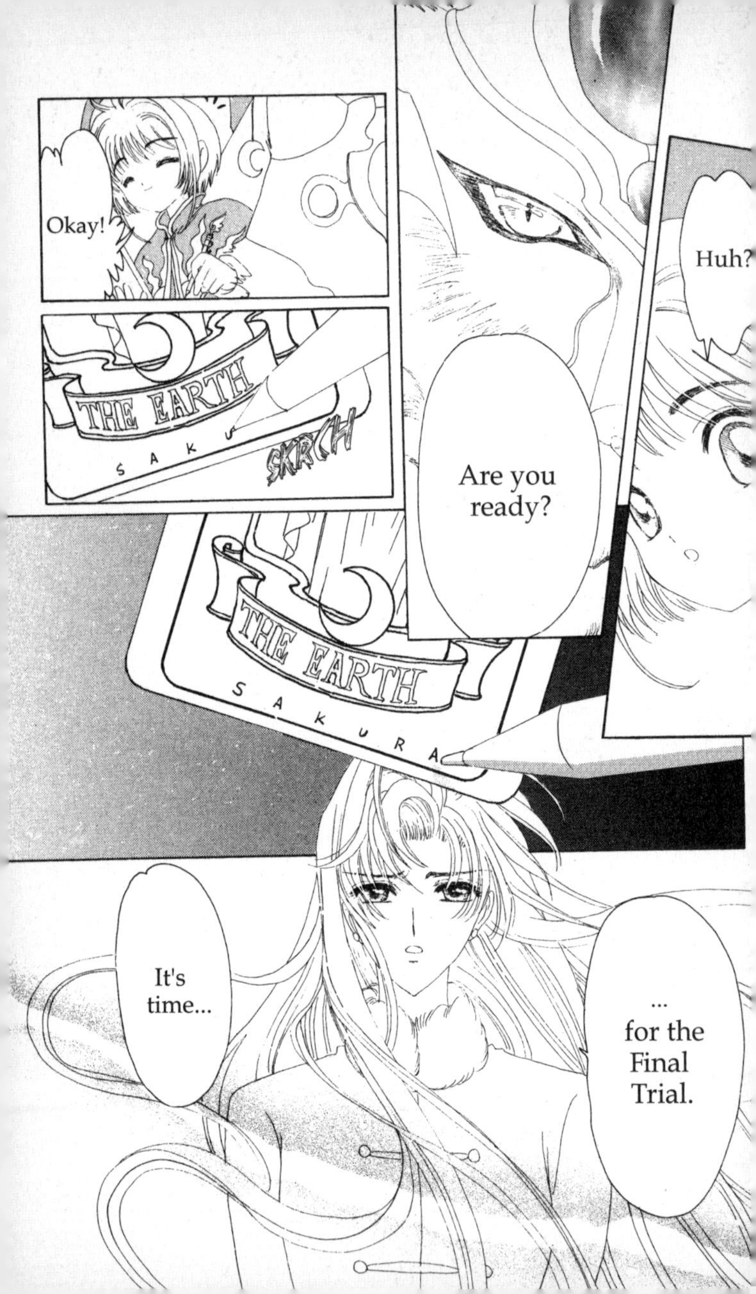
Okay!
THE EARTH
S A K U
SKRCH
Are you ready?
Huh?
THE EARTH
S A K U R A
It's time...
... for the Final Trial.

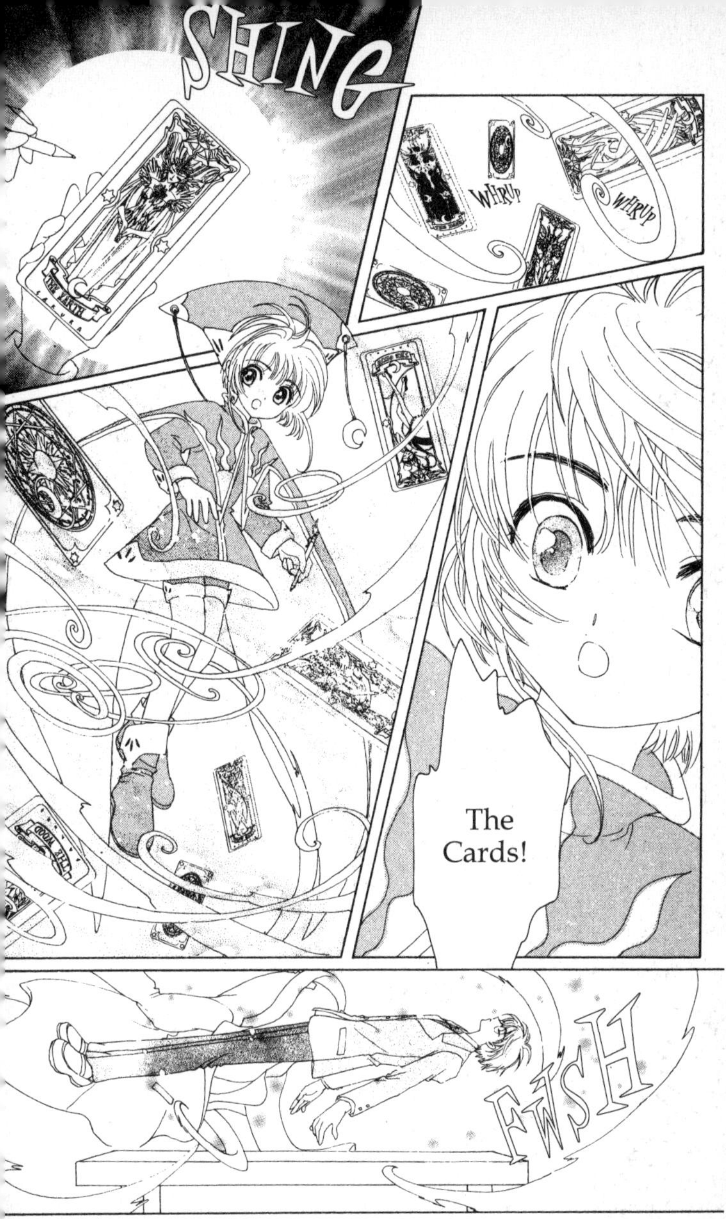
SHING
WHRUP
WHRUP
The Cards!
FWSH

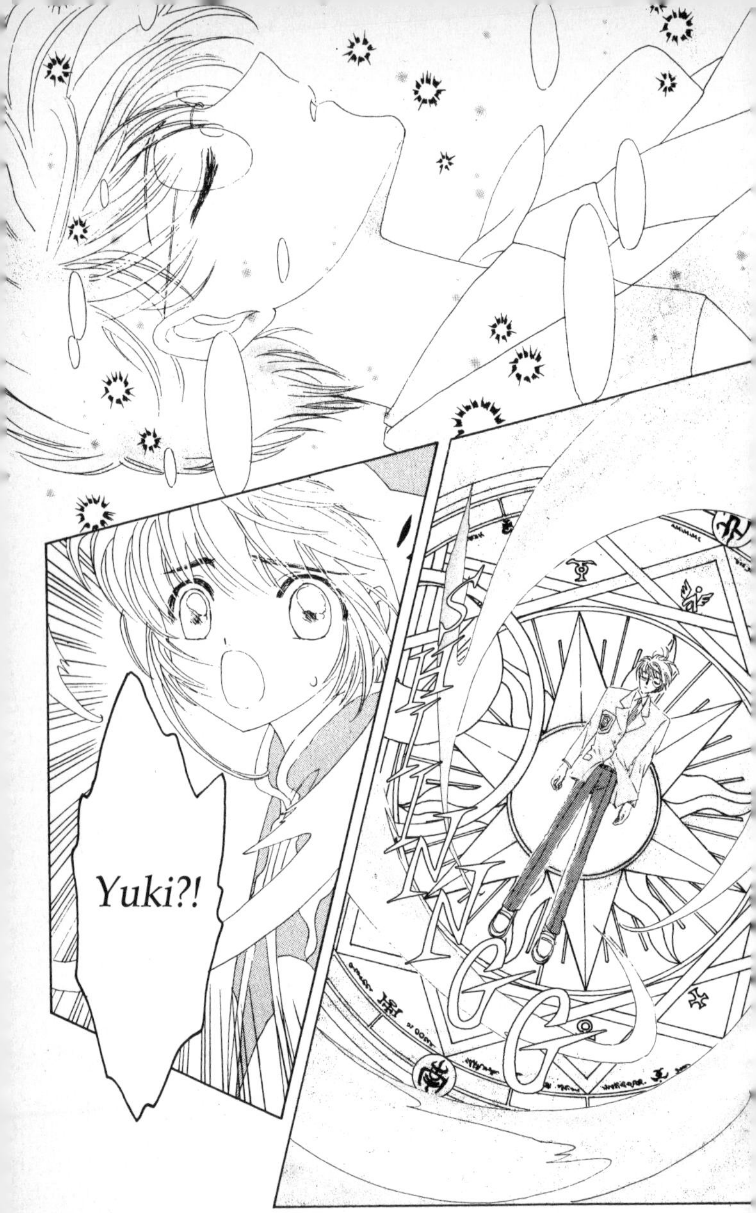
SHINING
Yuki?!

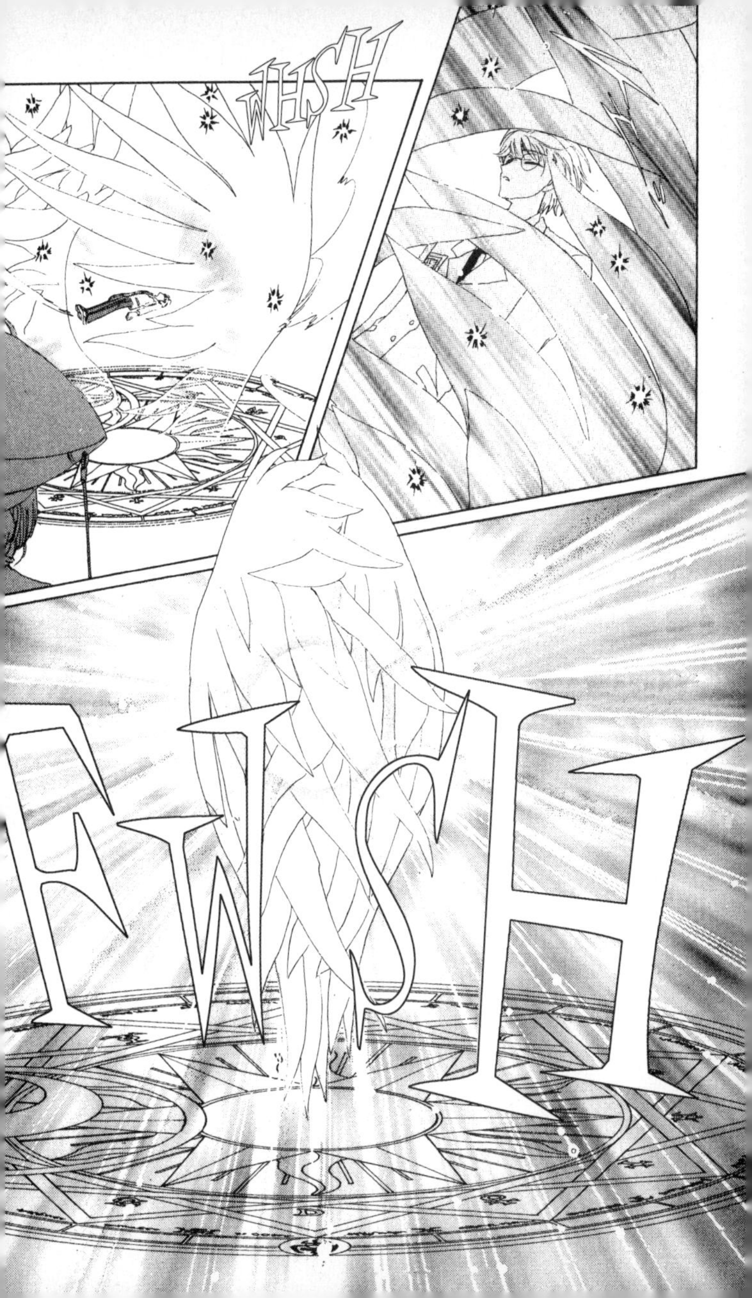
WHSH
FWSH

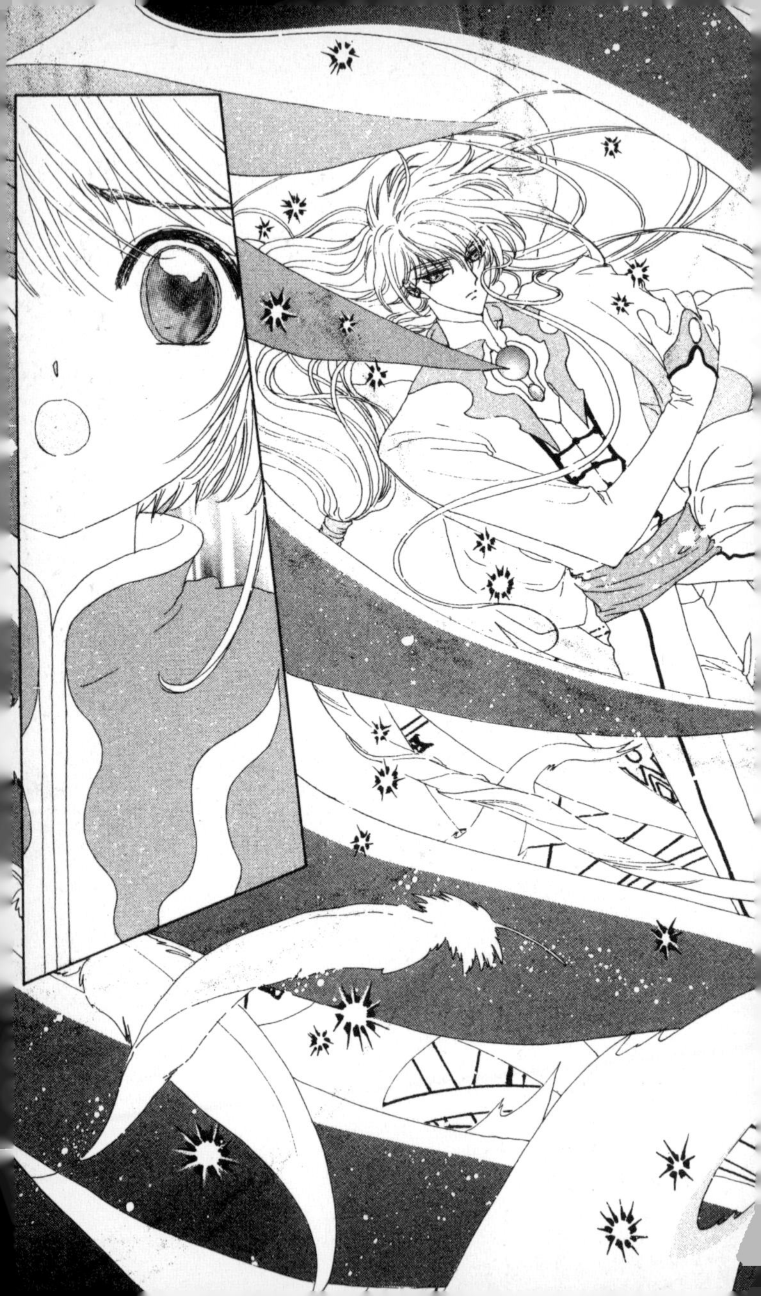

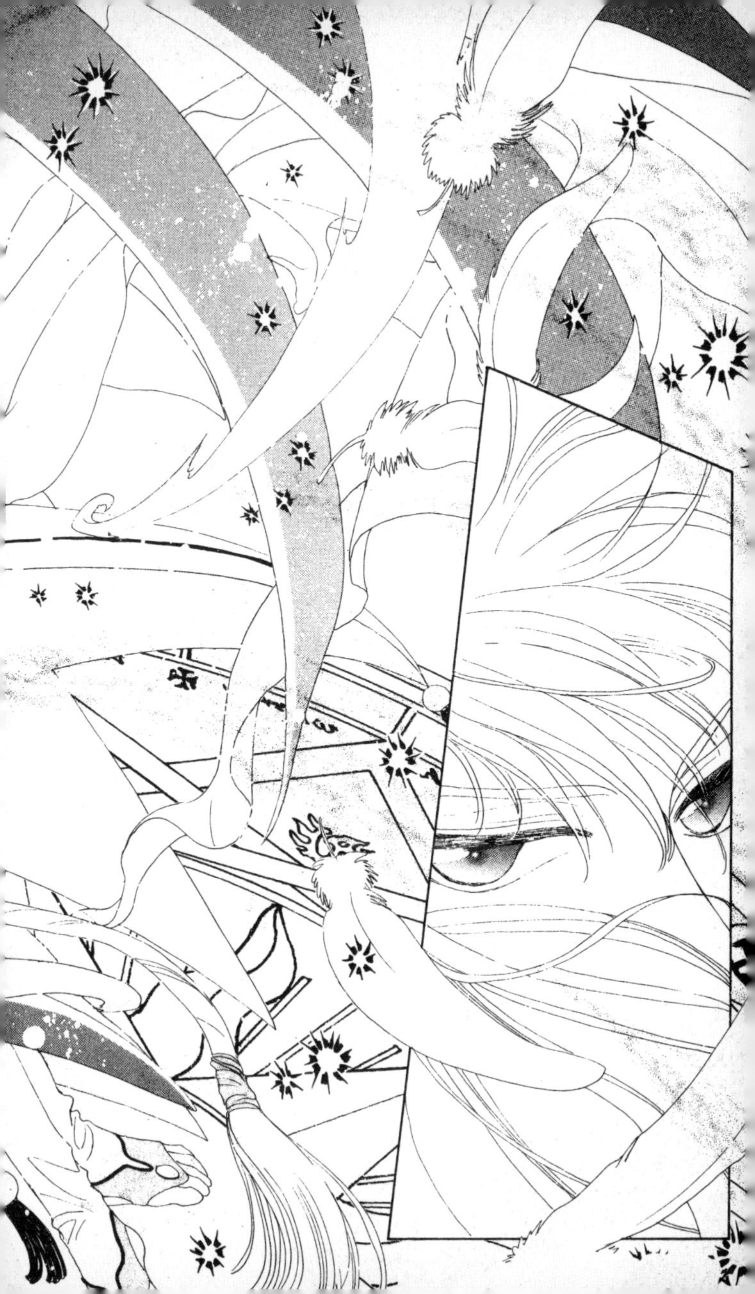

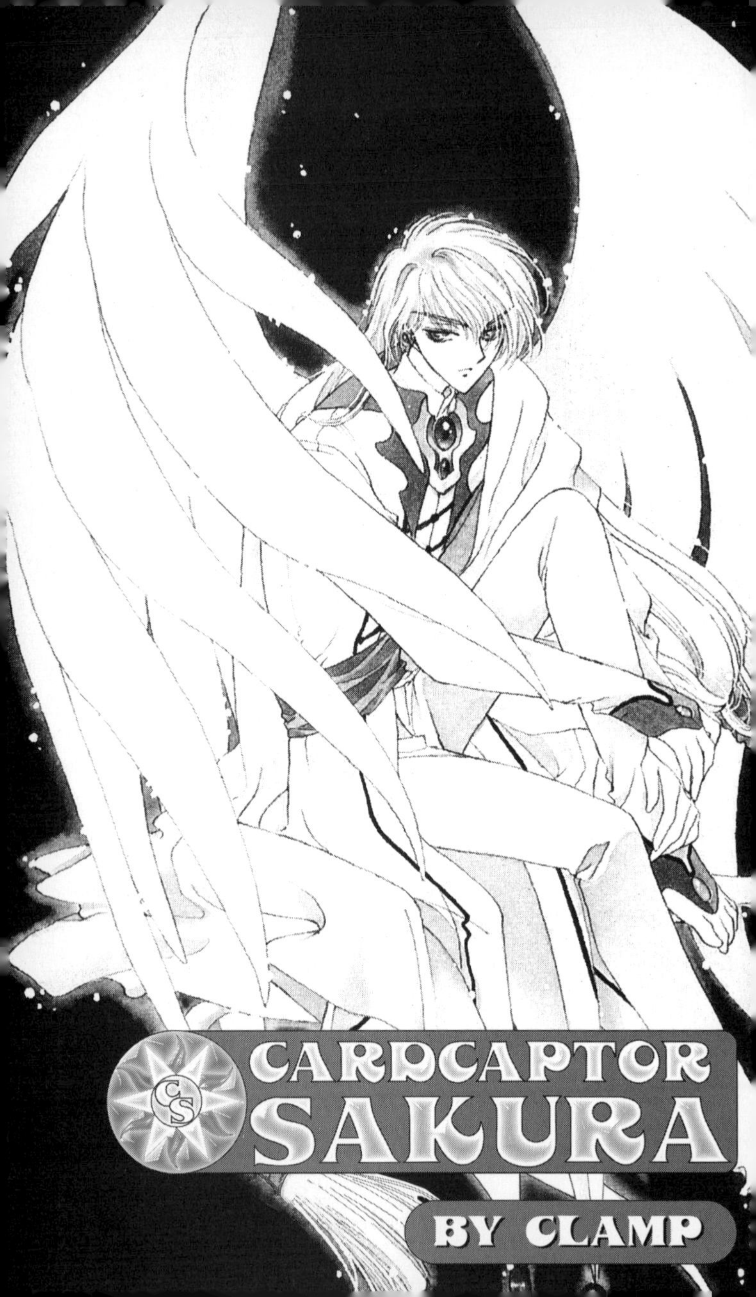
CARDCAPTOR
SAKURA
BY CLAMP

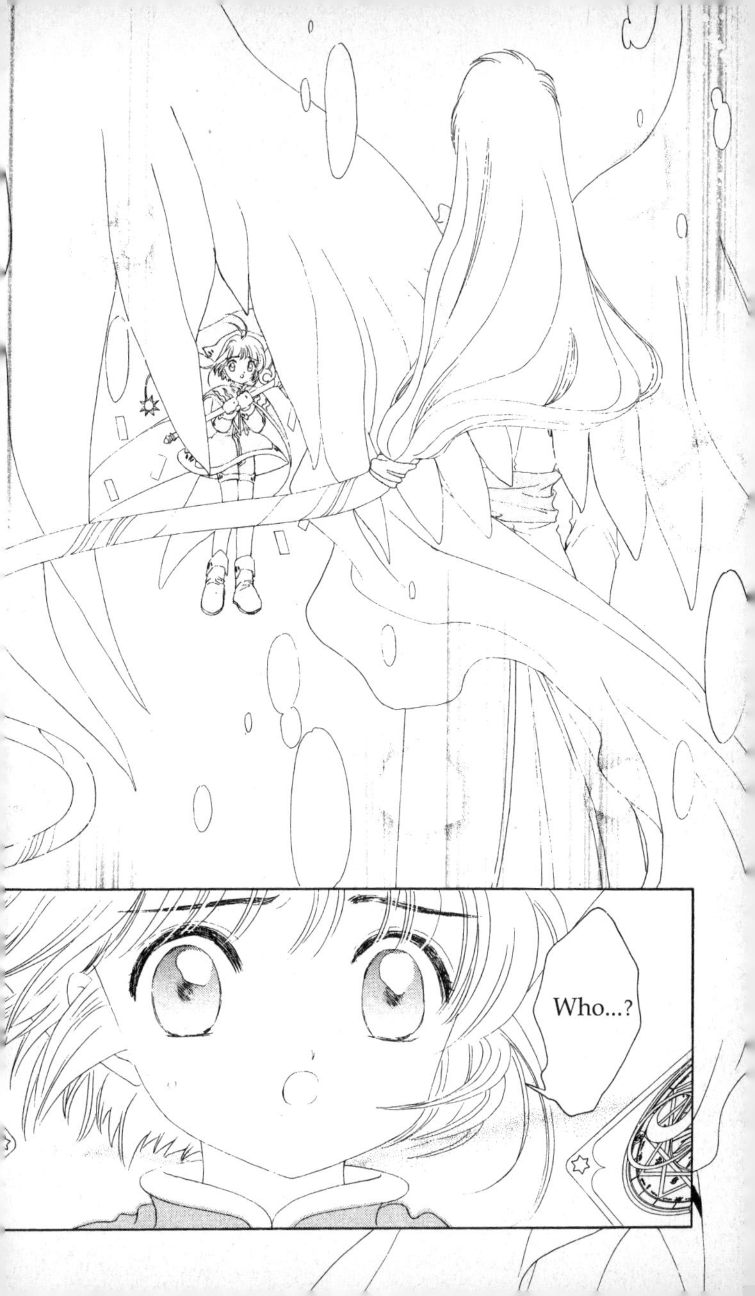
Who...?

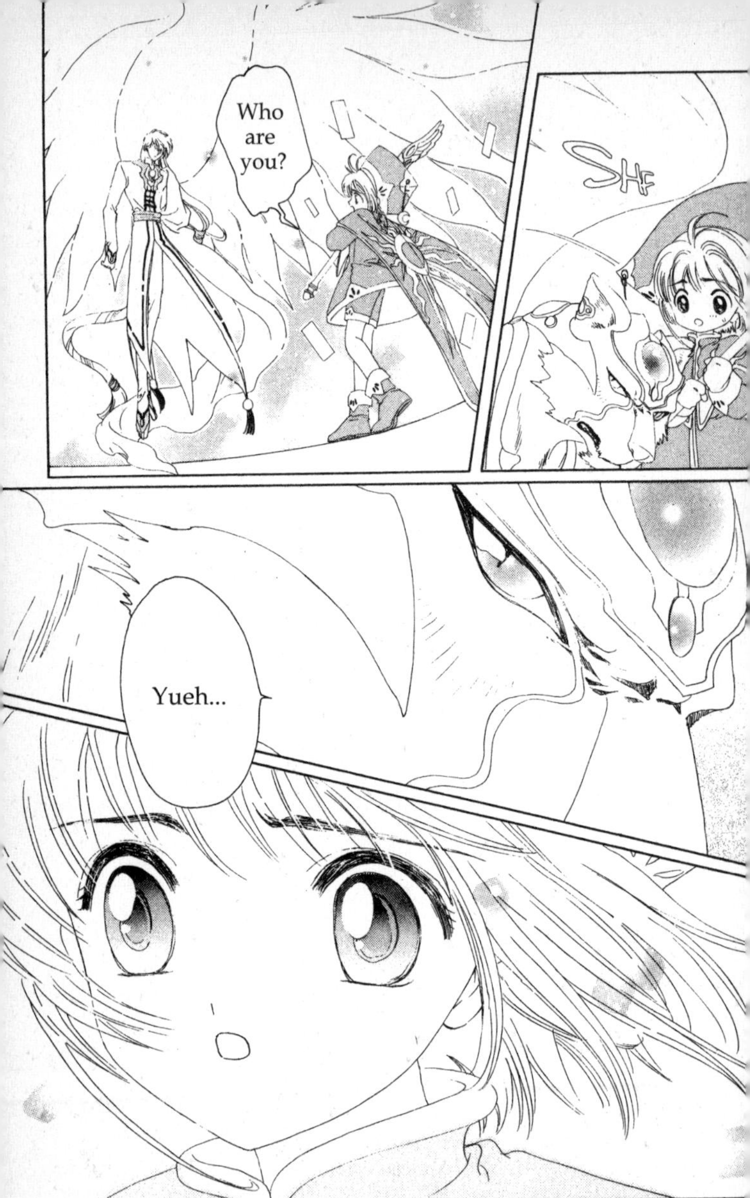
SHF
Who are you?
Yueh...

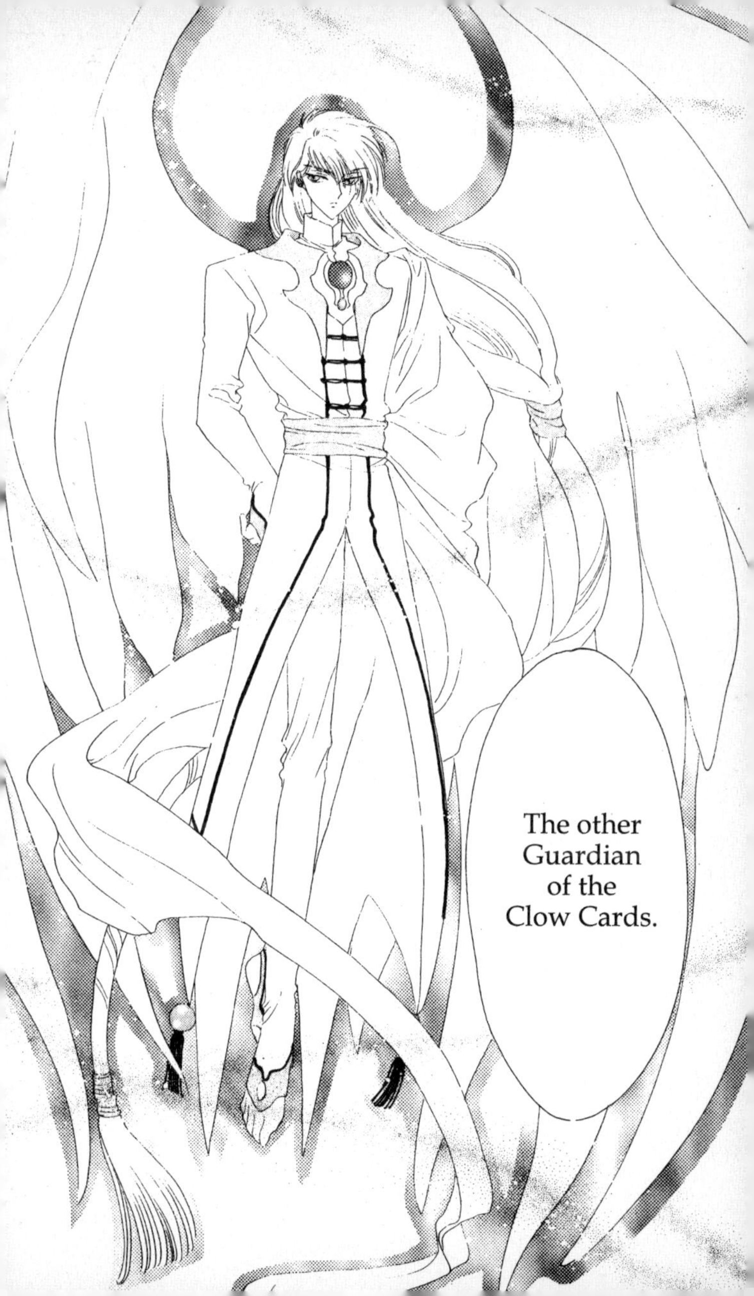
The other Guardian of the Clow Cards.

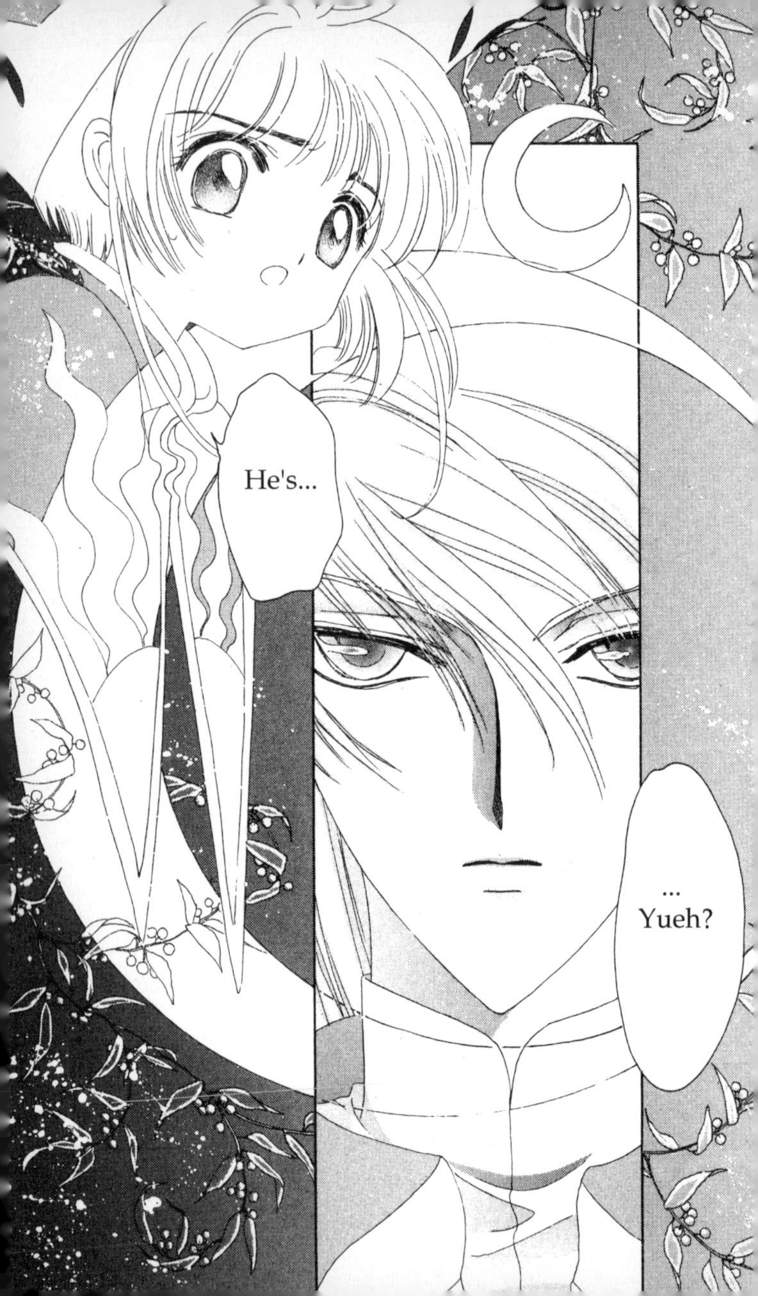
He's...
... Yueh?

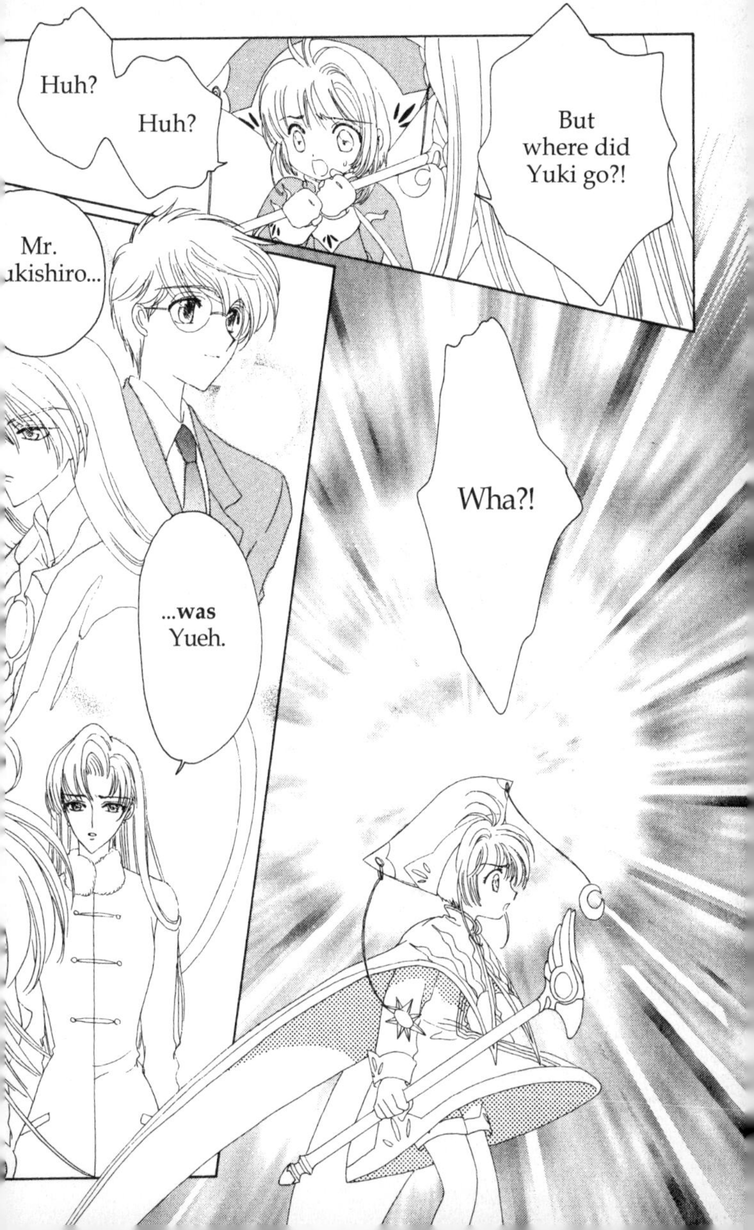
But where did Yuki go?!
Huh?
Huh?
Mr. ukishiro...
...was Yueh.
Wha?!

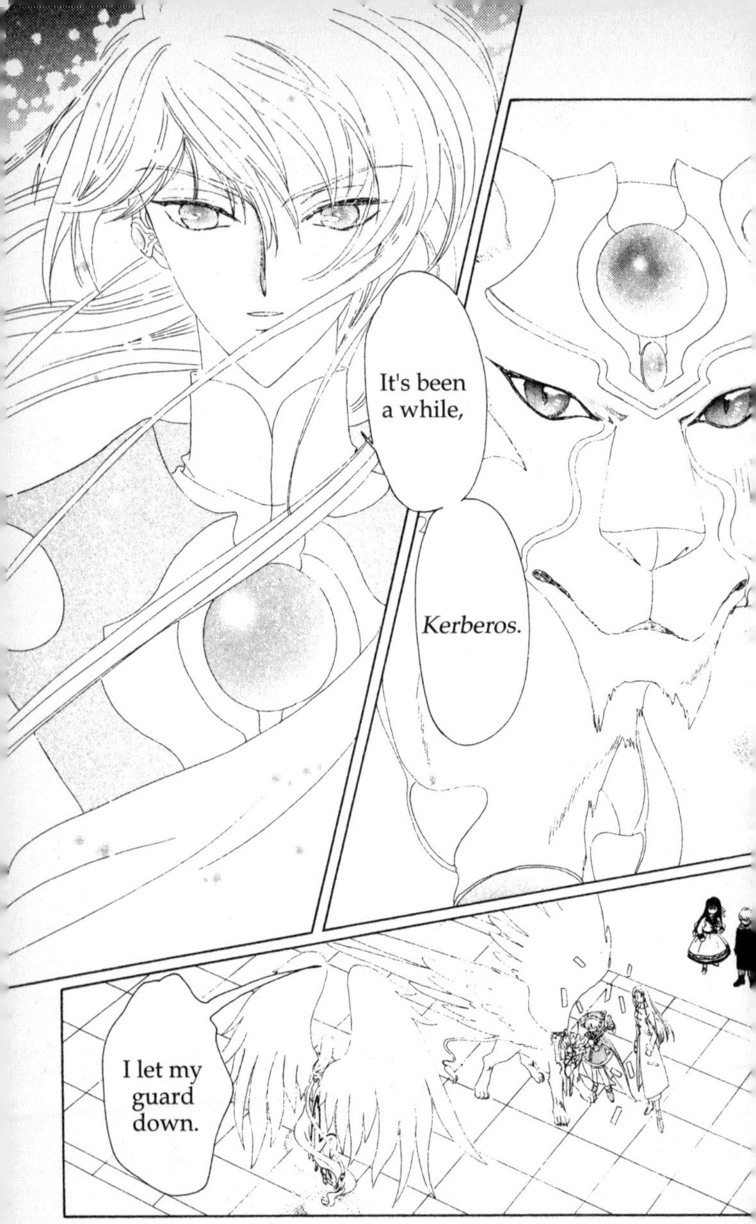
It's been a while,
Kerberos.
I let my guard down.

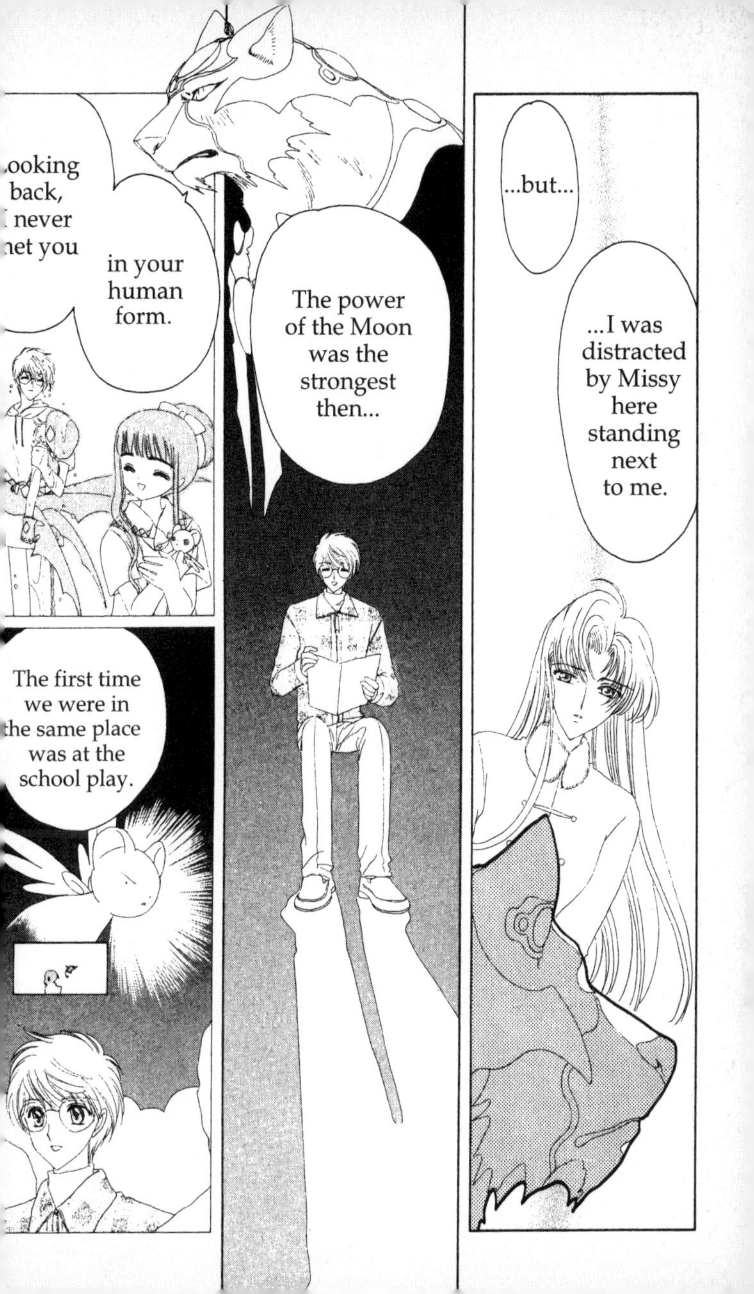
...but...
...I was distracted by Missy here standing next to me.
The power of the Moon was the strongest then...
ooking back, never net you
in your human form.
The first time we were in the same place was at the school play.

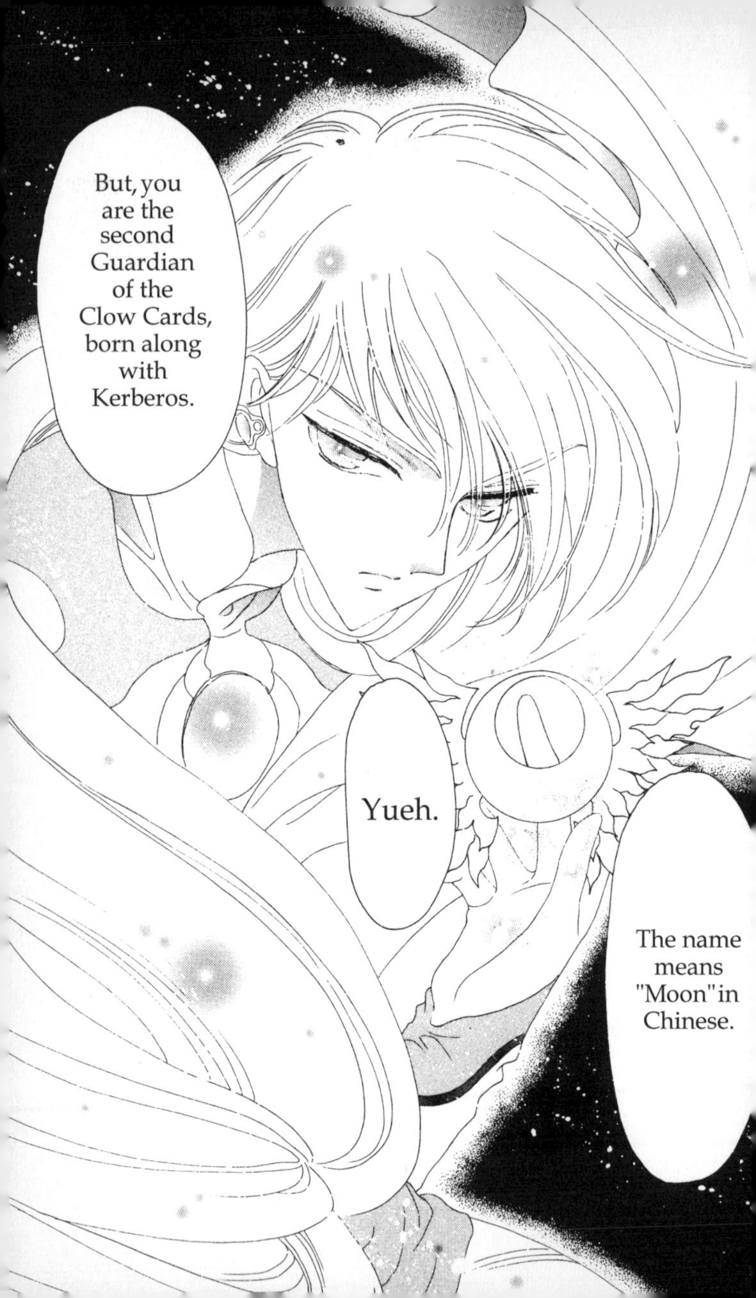
But, you are the second Guardian of the Clow Cards, born along with Kerberos.
Yueh.
The name means "Moon" in Chinese.

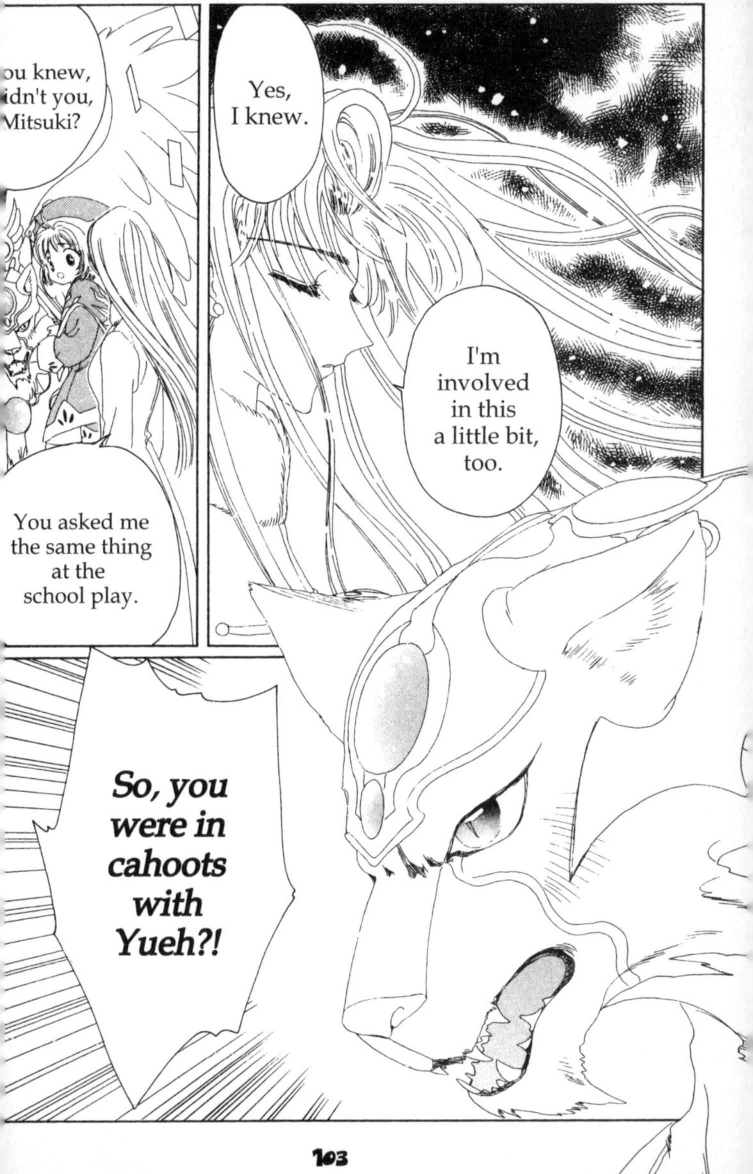
ou knew, idn't you, Mitsuki?
You asked me the same thing at the school play.
Yes, I knew.
I'm involved in this a little bit, too.
So, you were in cahoots with Yueh?!

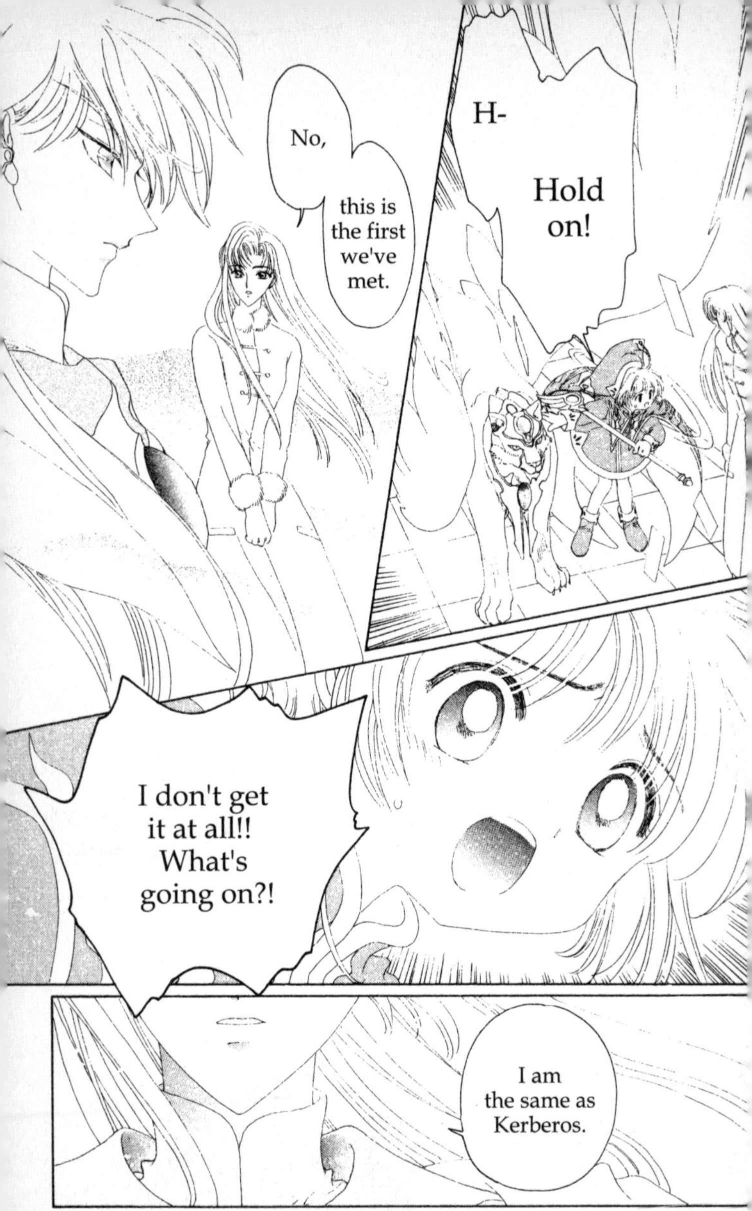
No, this is the first we've met.
H- Hold on!
I don't get it at all!! What's going on?!
I am the same as Kerberos.

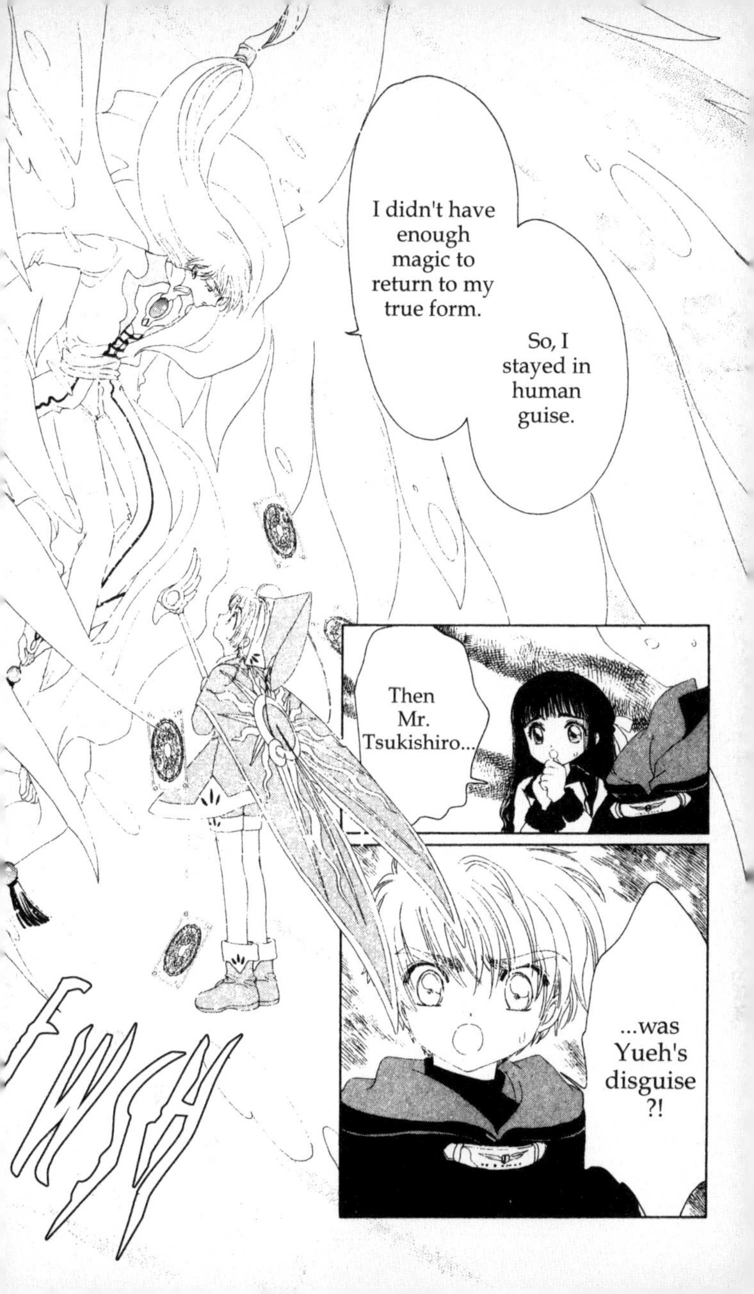
I didn't have enough magic to return to my true form.
So, I stayed in human guise.
FWSH
Then Mr. Tsukishiro...
...was Yueh's disguise ?!

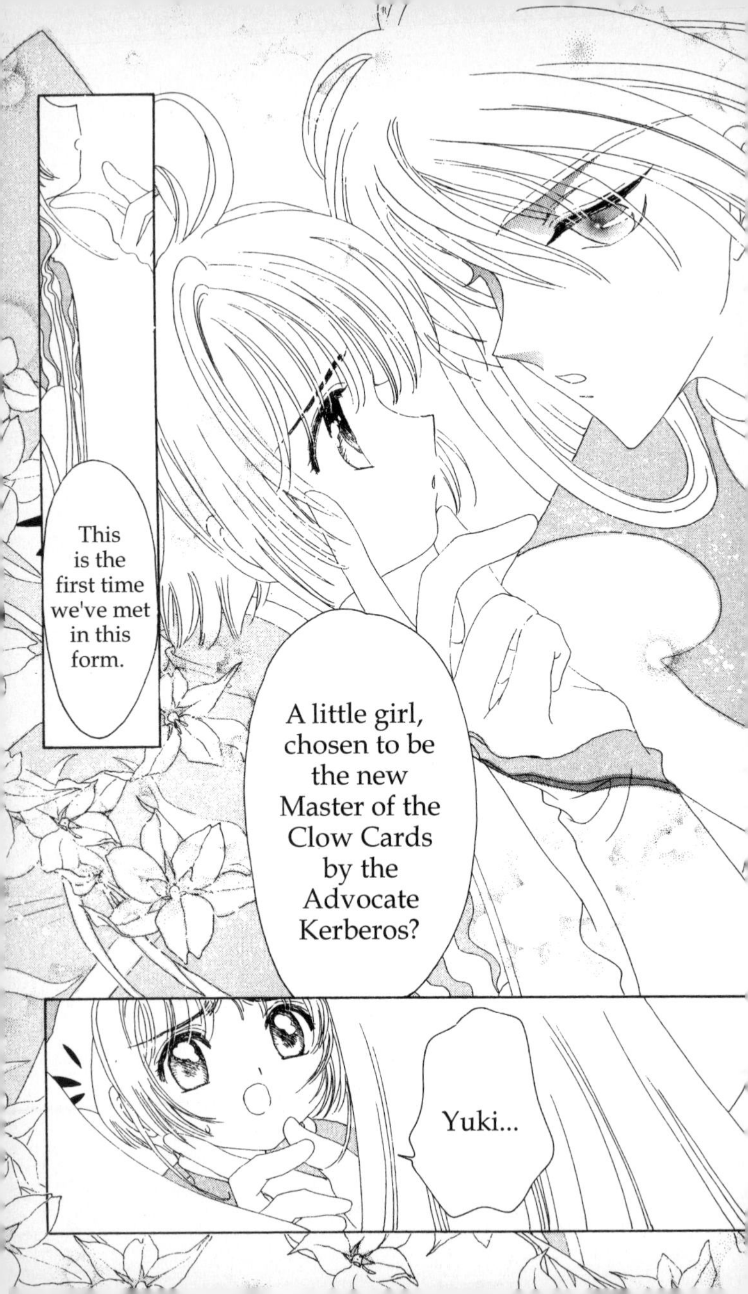
A little girl, chosen to be the new Master of the Clow Cards by the Advocate Kerberos?
This is the first time we've met in this form.
Yuki...

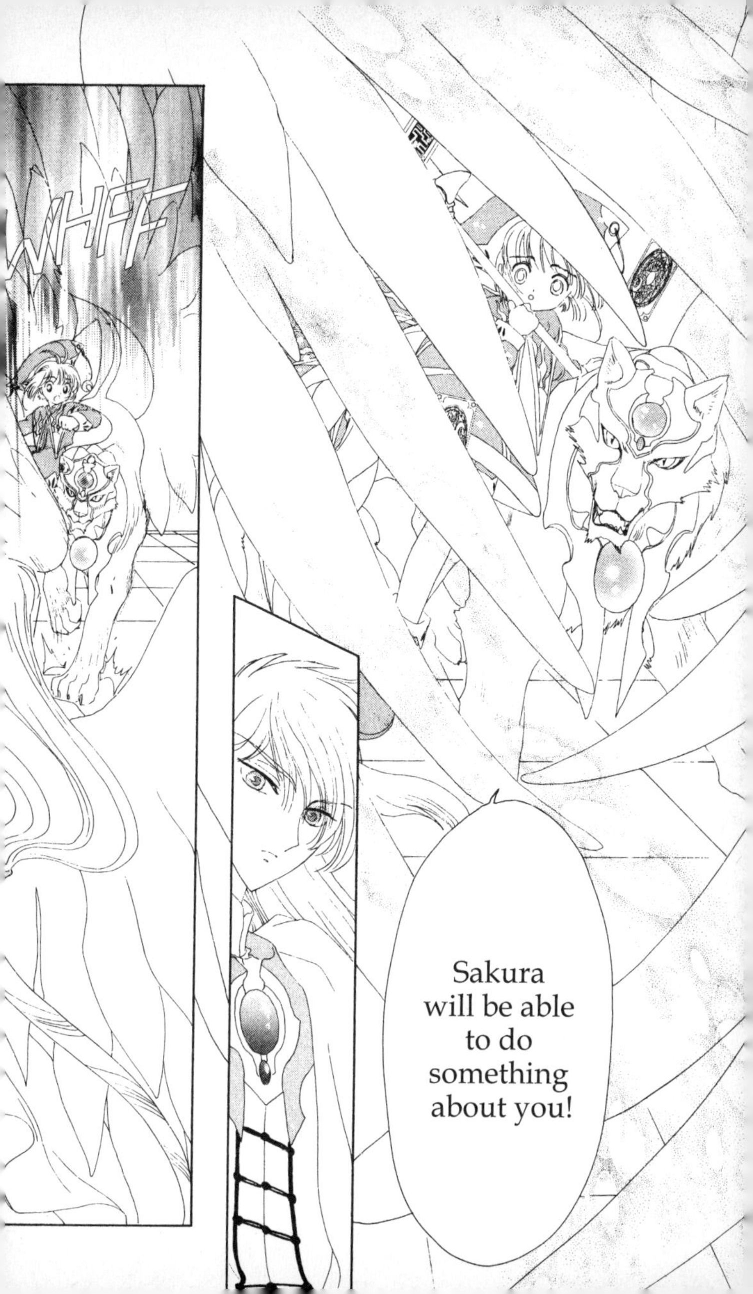
WHFF
Sakura will be able to do something about you!

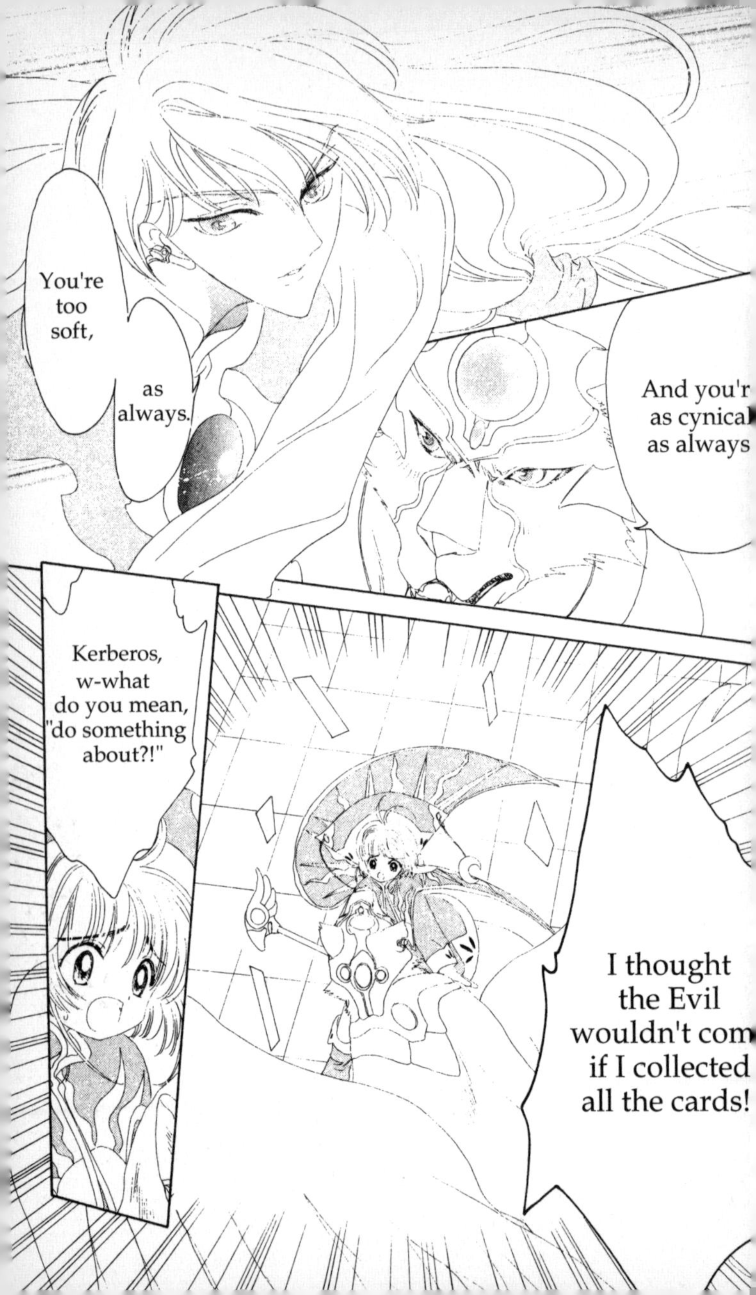
You're too soft,
as always.
And you'r as cynical as always
I thought the Evil wouldn't com if I collected all the cards!
Kerberos, w-what do you mean, "do something about?!"

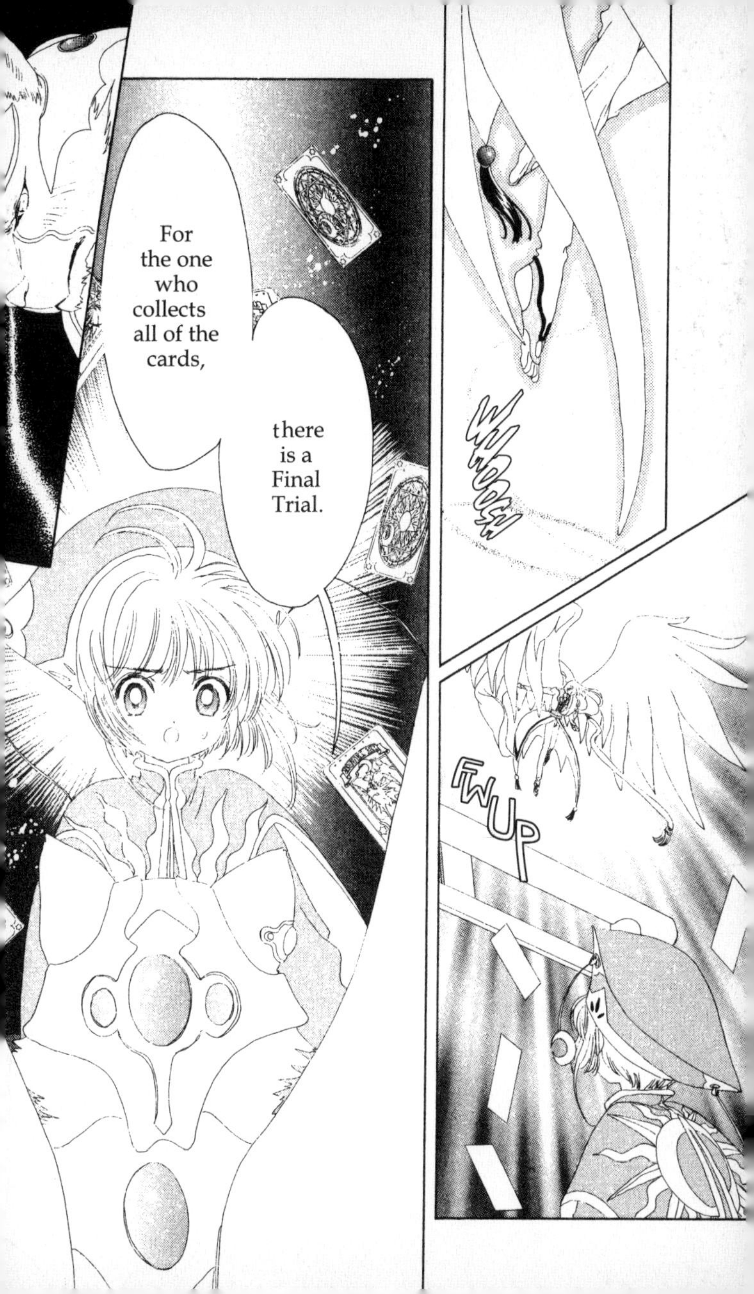
WHOOSH
FWUP
For the one who collects all of the cards,
there is a Final Trial.

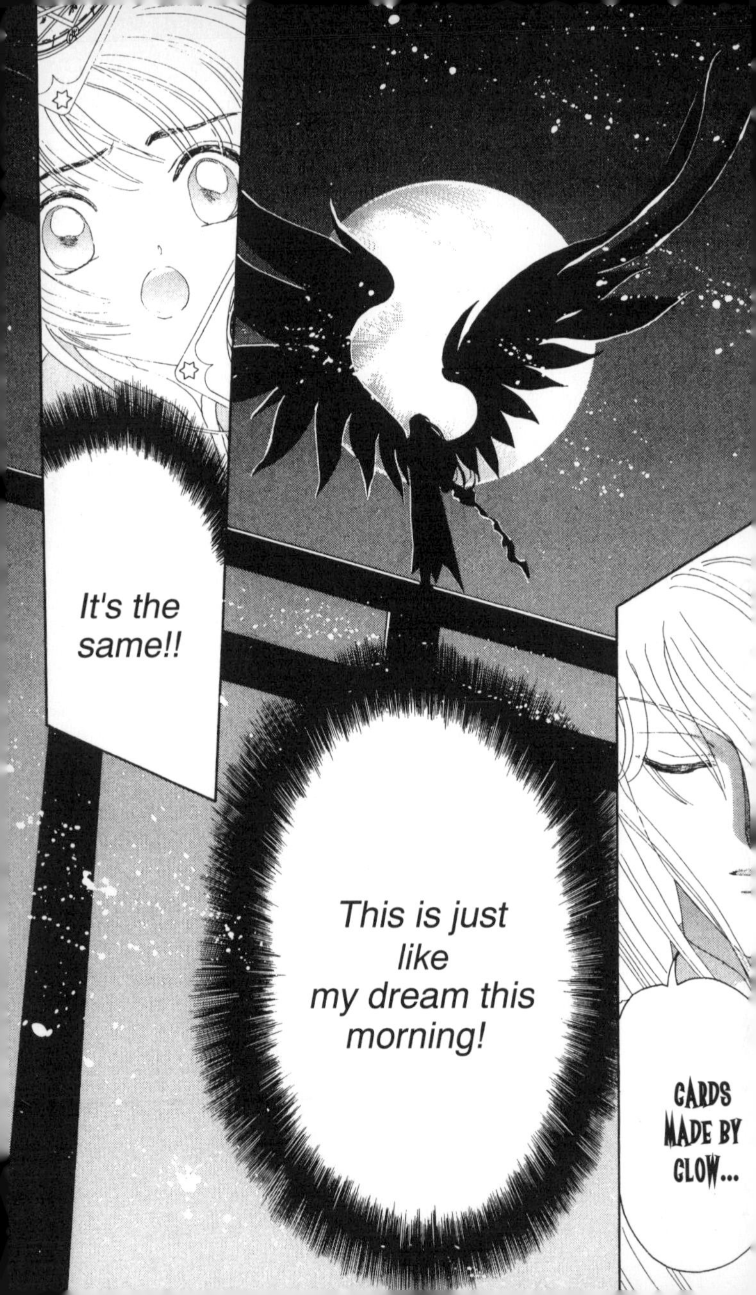
It's the same!!
This is just like my dream this morning!
CARDS MADE BY CLOW...

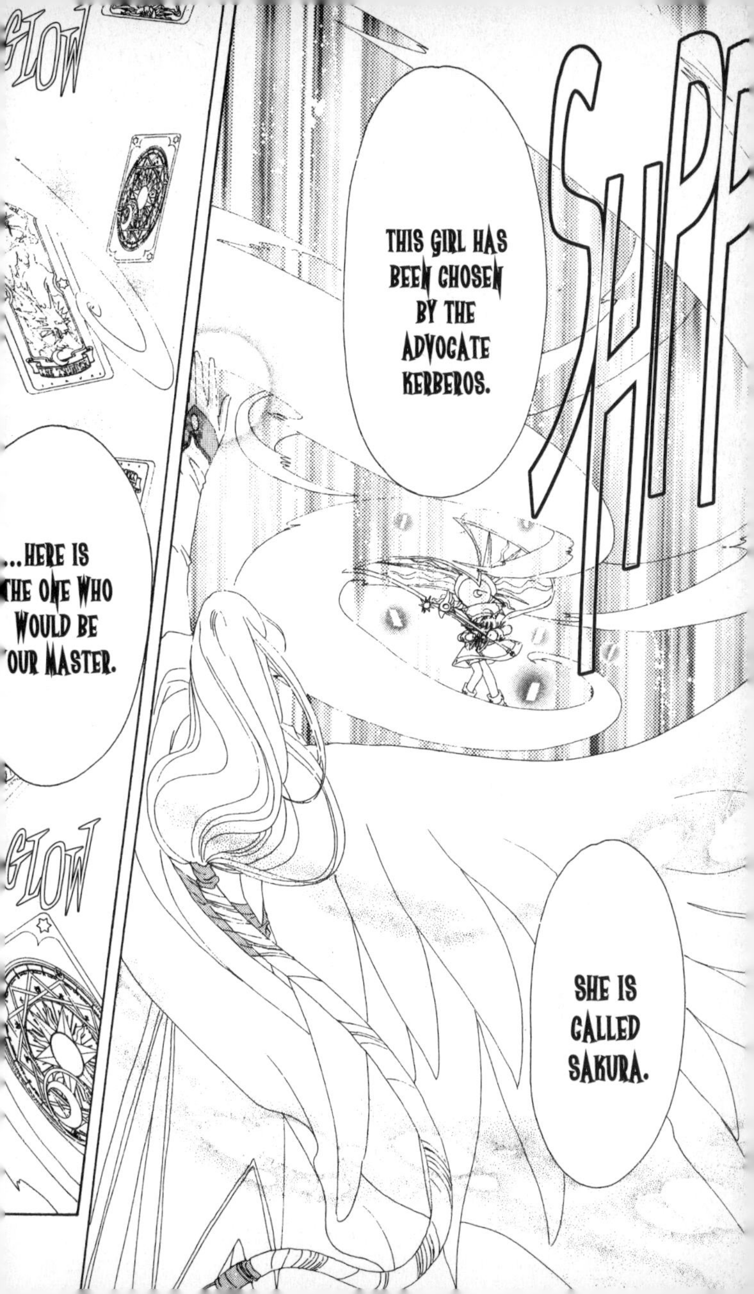
SHPP
THIS GIRL HAS BEEN CHOSEN BY THE ADVOCATE KERBEROS.
SHE IS CALLED SAKURA.
GLOW
...HERE IS THE ONE WHO WOULD BE OUR MASTER.
GLOW

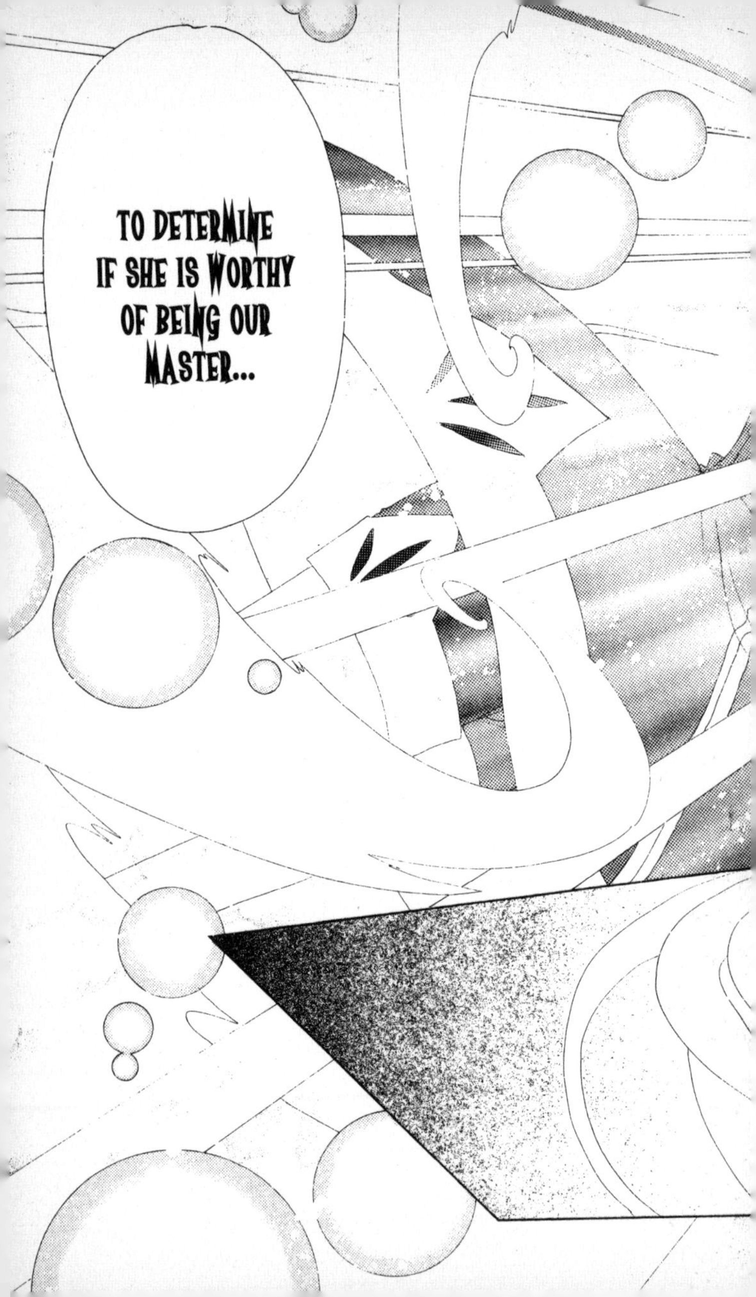
TO DETERMINE IF SHE IS WORTHY OF BEING OUR MASTER...

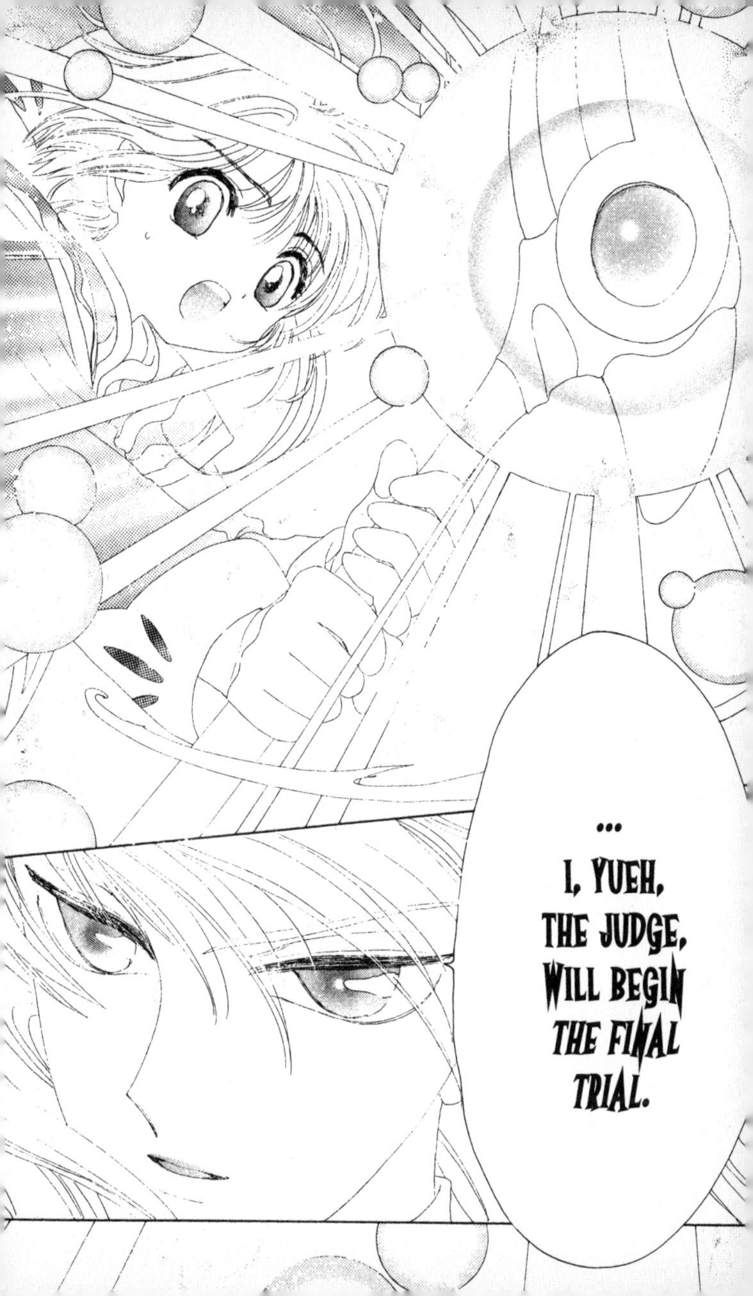
... I, YUEH, THE JUDGE, WILL BEGIN THE FINAL TRIAL.

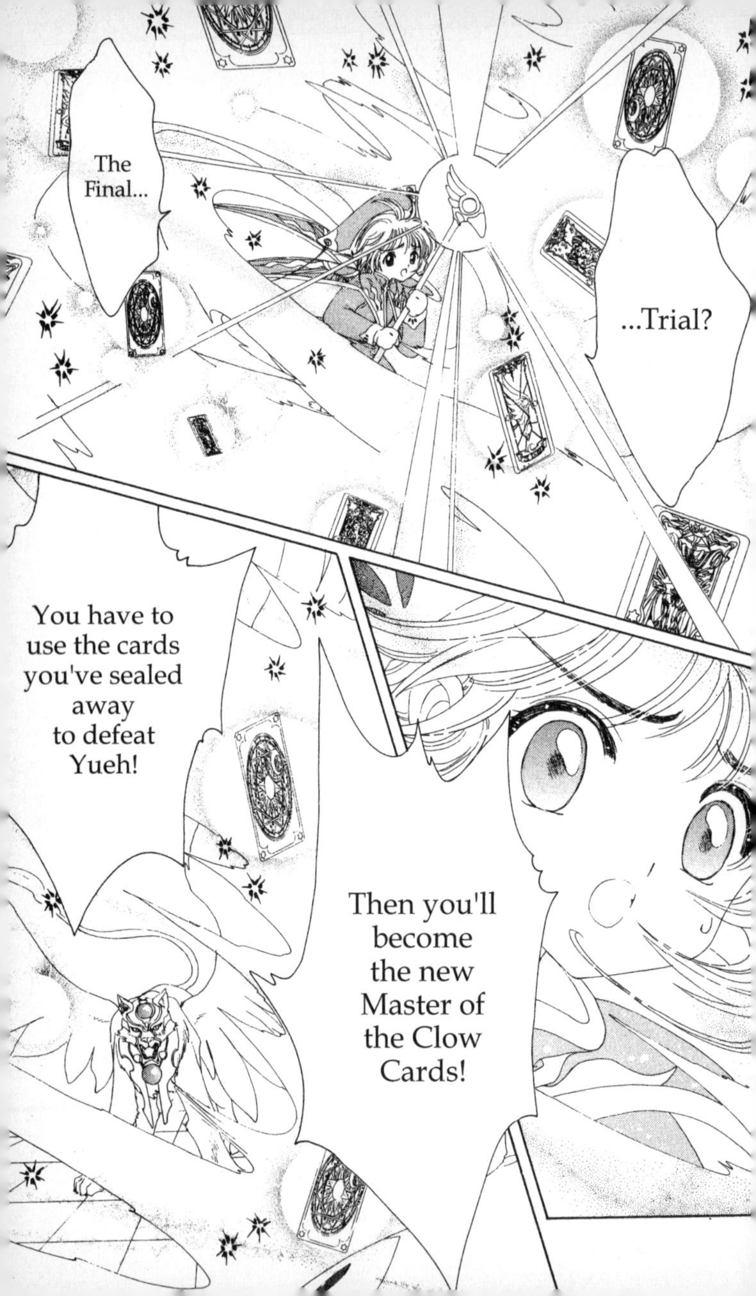
The Final...
...Trial?
You have to use the cards you've sealed away to defeat Yueh!
Then you'll become the new Master of the Clow Cards!

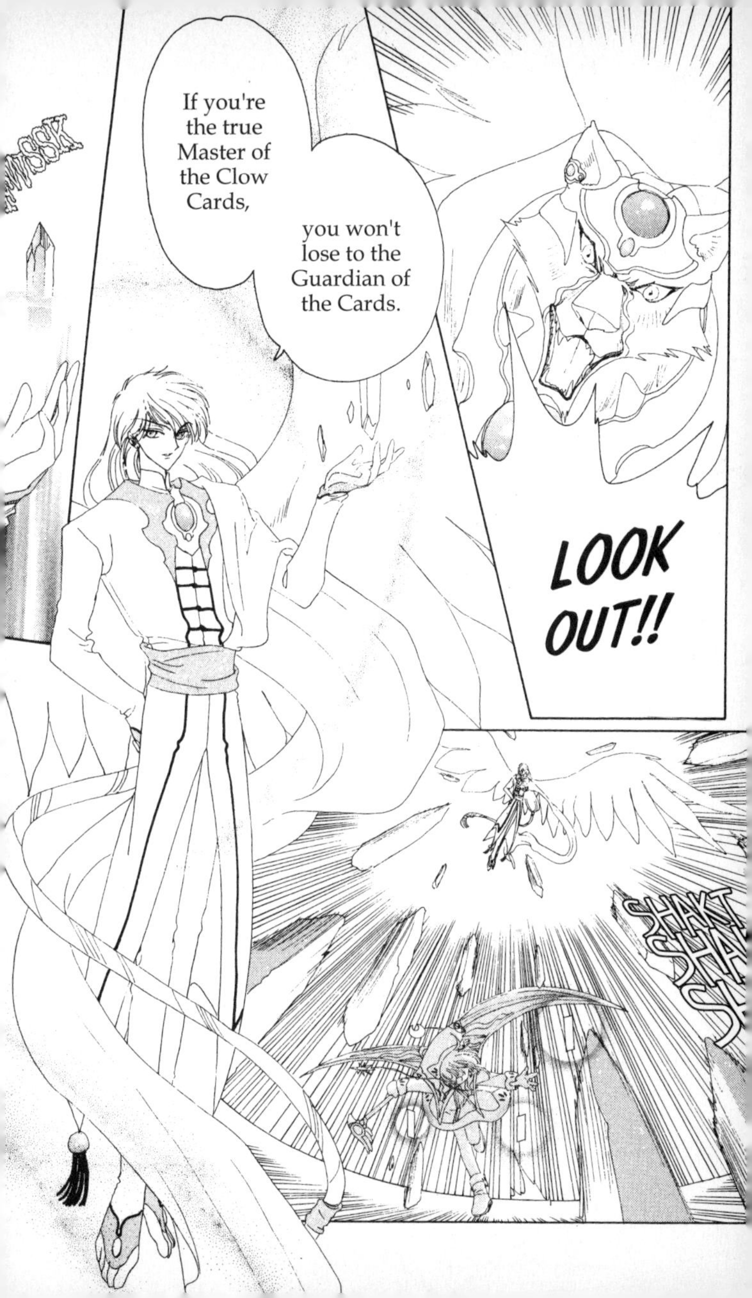
If you're the true Master of the Clow Cards,
you won't lose to the Guardian of the Cards.
LOOK OUT!!
FWSSK
SHAK SHA SH

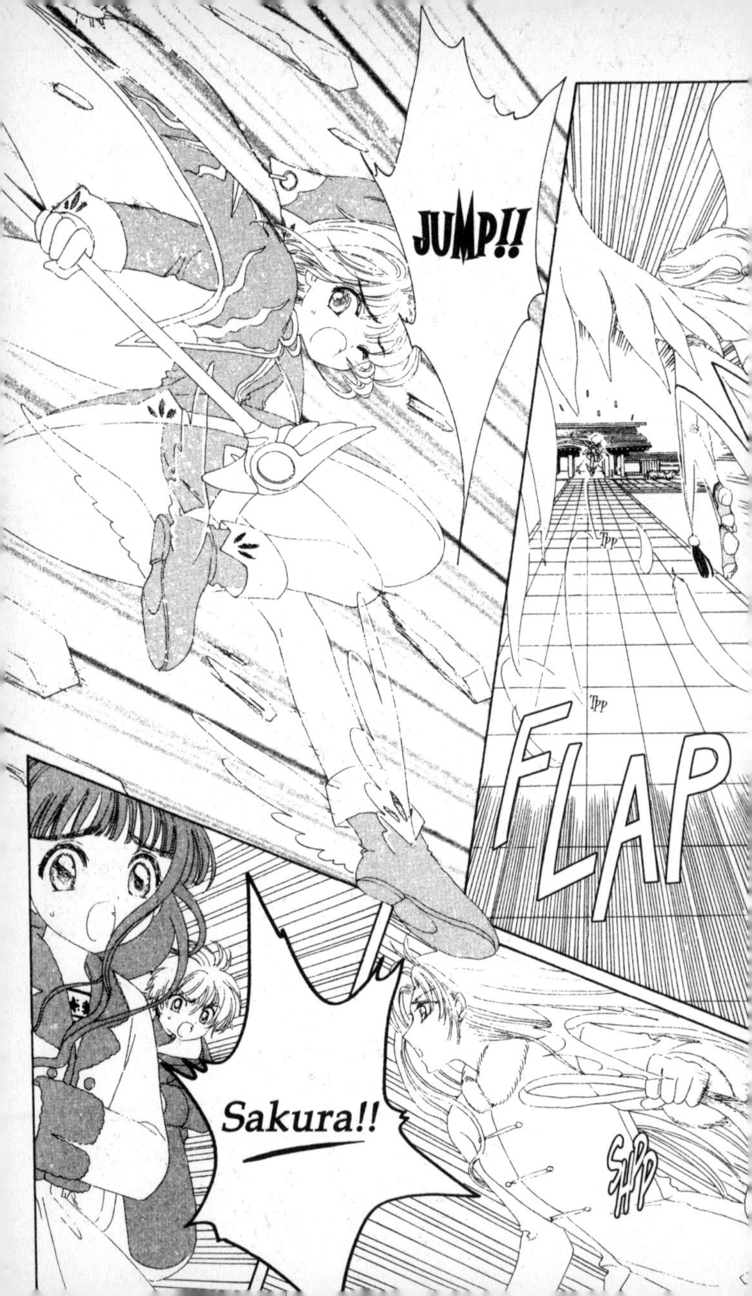
Tpp
Tpp
FLAP
JUMP!!
Sakura!!

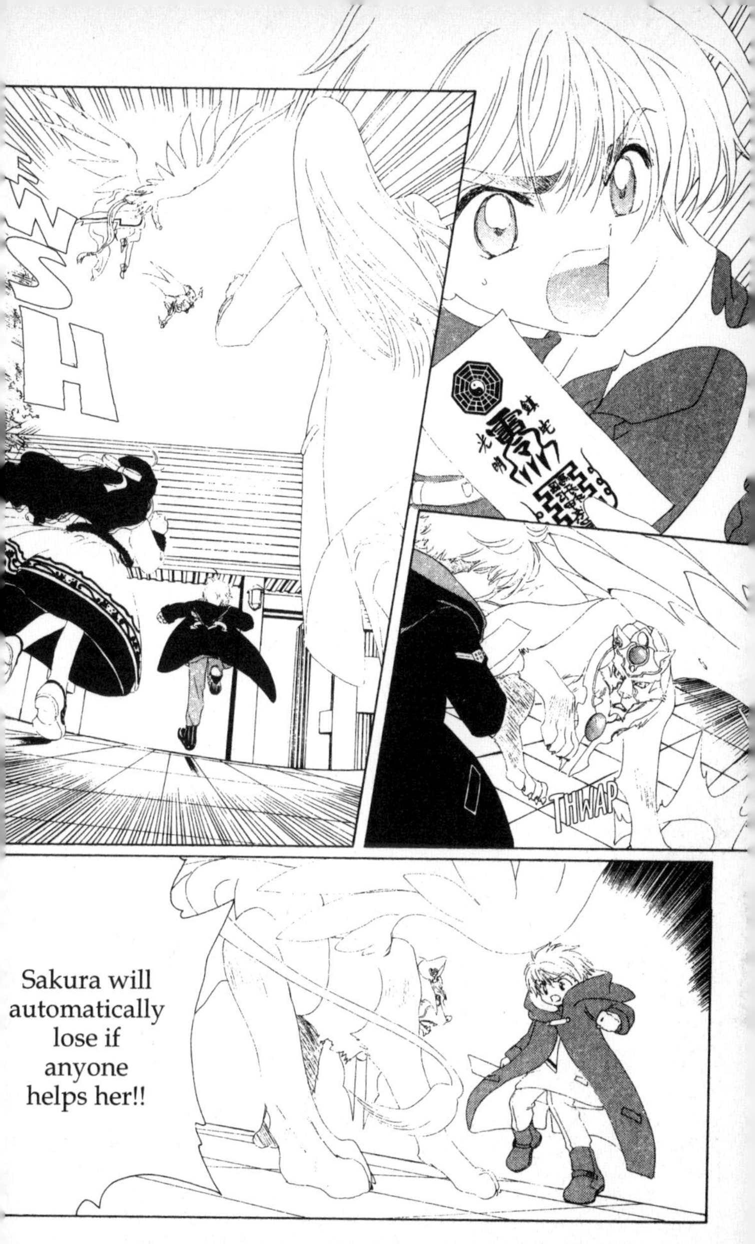
SWISH
THWAP
Sakura will automatically lose if anyone helps her!!

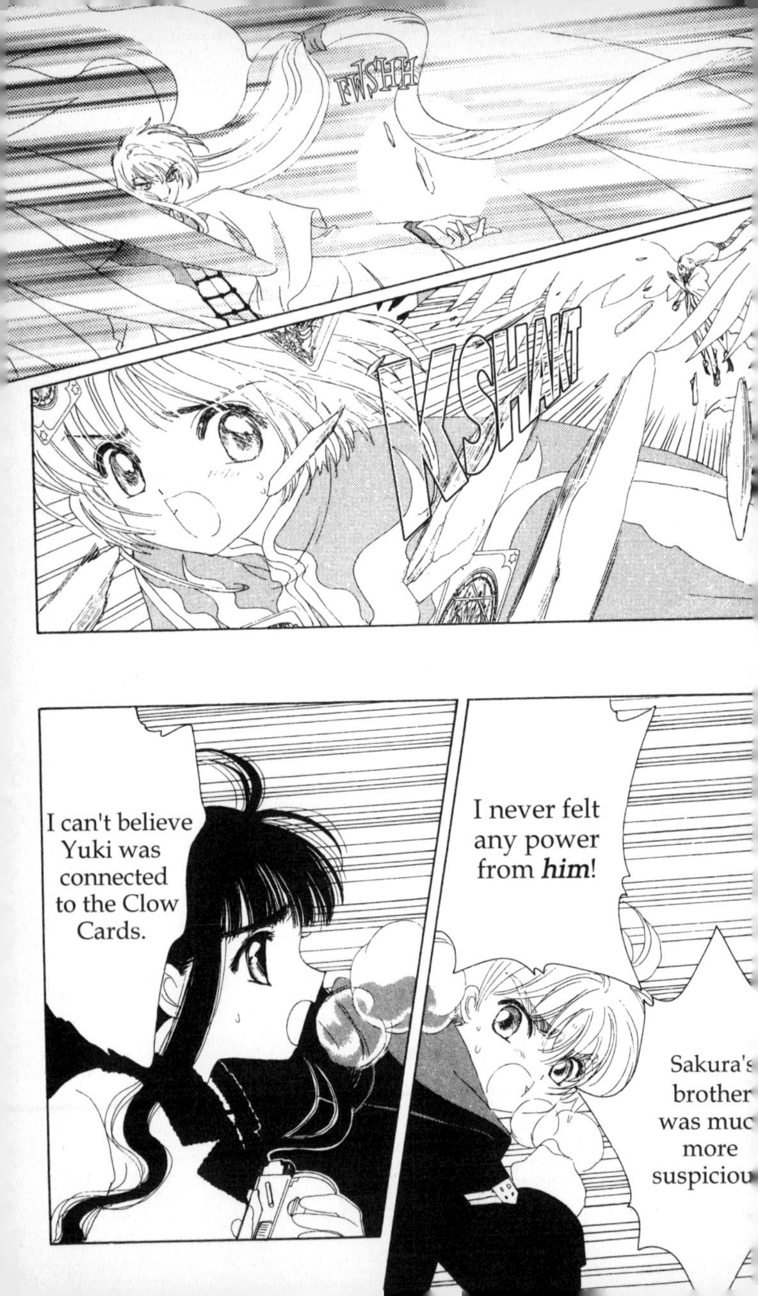
FWSHHH
KSHAKT
I never felt any power from *him*!
Sakura's brother was muc more suspiciou
I can't believe Yuki was connected to the Clow Cards.

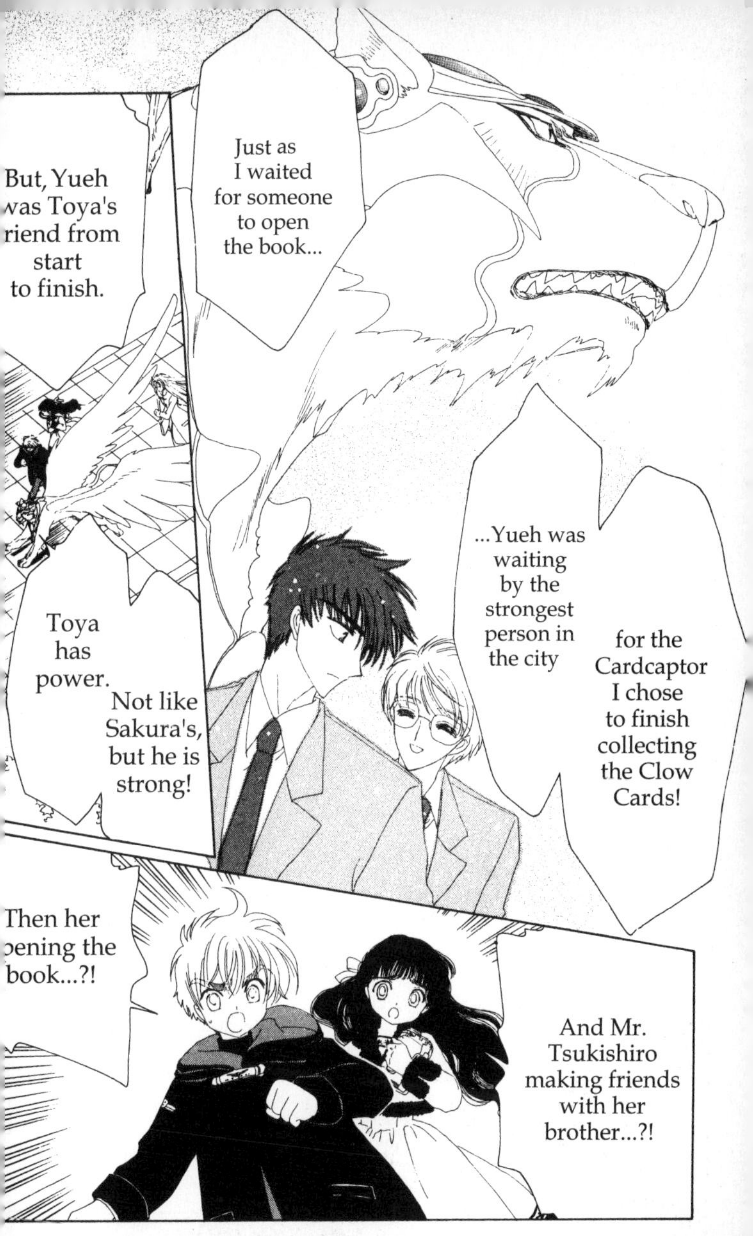
Just as I waited for someone to open the book...
...Yueh was waiting by the strongest person in the city
for the Cardcaptor I chose to finish collecting the Clow Cards!
But, Yueh vas Toya's riend from start to finish.
Toya has power.
Not like Sakura's, but he is strong!
And Mr. Tsukishiro making friends with her brother...?!
Then her pening the book...?!

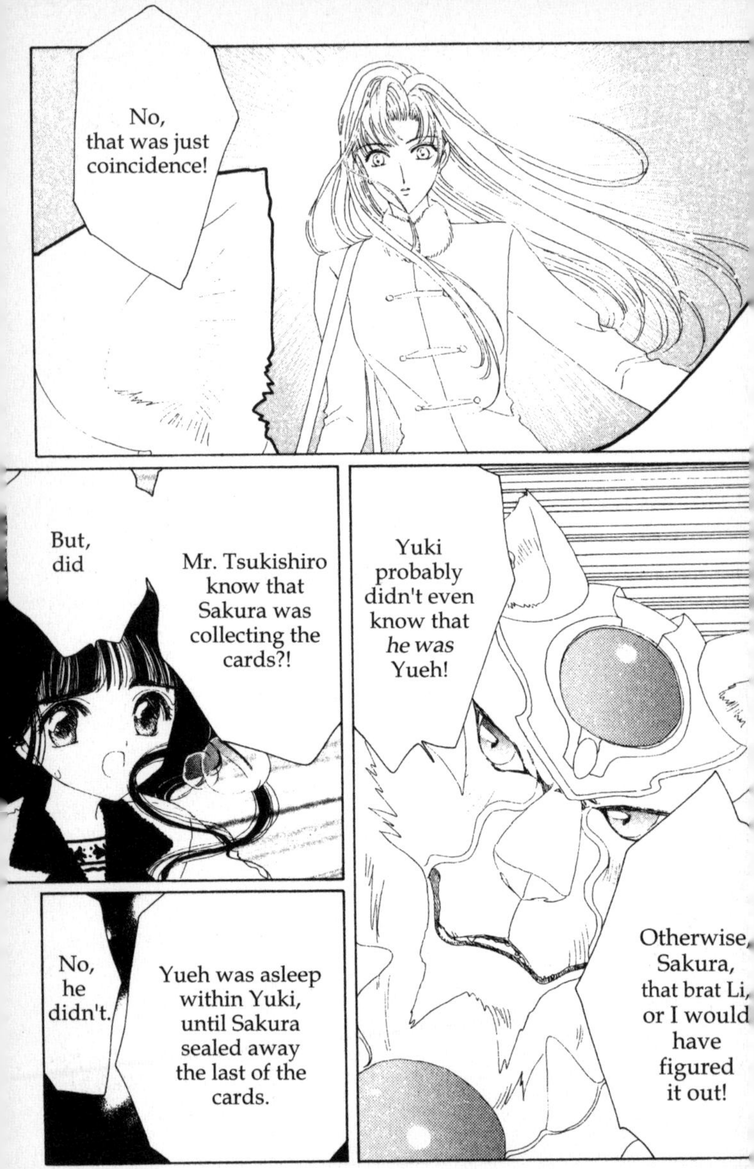
No, that was just coincidence!
But, did
Mr. Tsukishiro know that Sakura was collecting the cards?!
No, he didn't.
Yueh was asleep within Yuki, until Sakura sealed away the last of the cards.
Yuki probably didn't even know that *he was* Yueh!
Otherwise, Sakura, that brat Li, or I would have figured it out!

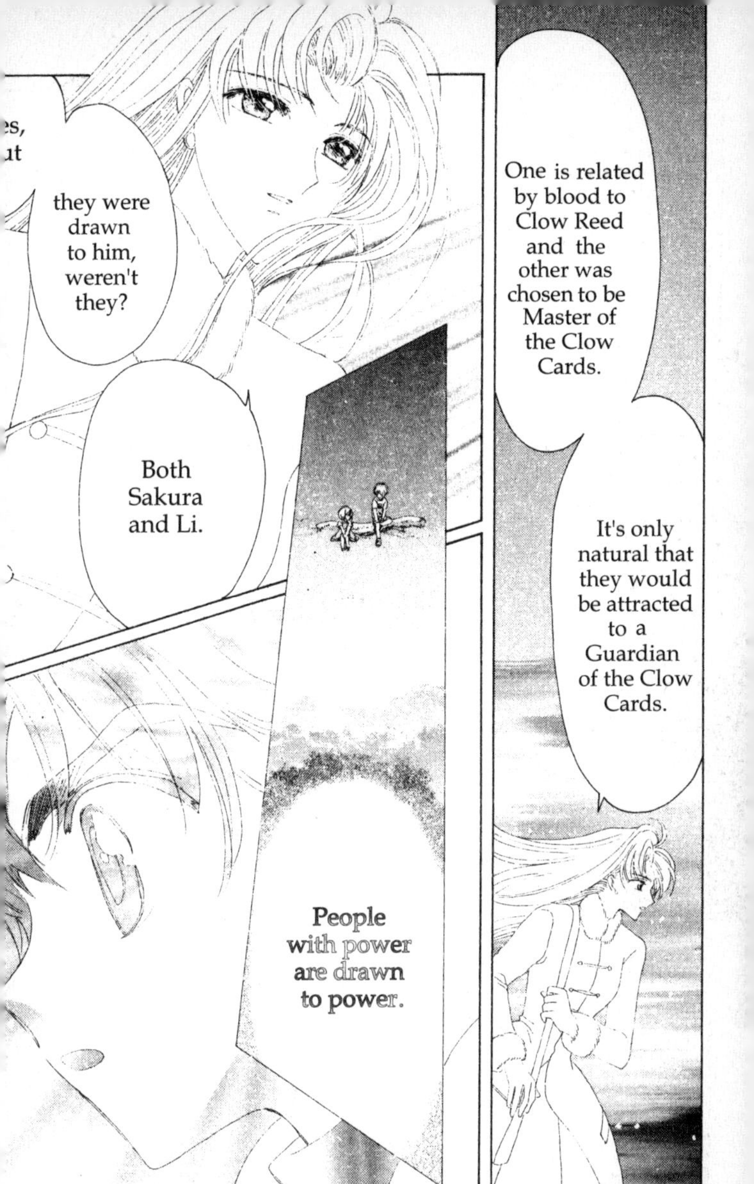
they were drawn to him, weren't they?
Both Sakura and Li.
People with power are drawn to power.
One is related by blood to Clow Reed and the other was chosen to be Master of the Clow Cards.
It's only natural that they would be attracted to a Guardian of the Clow Cards.

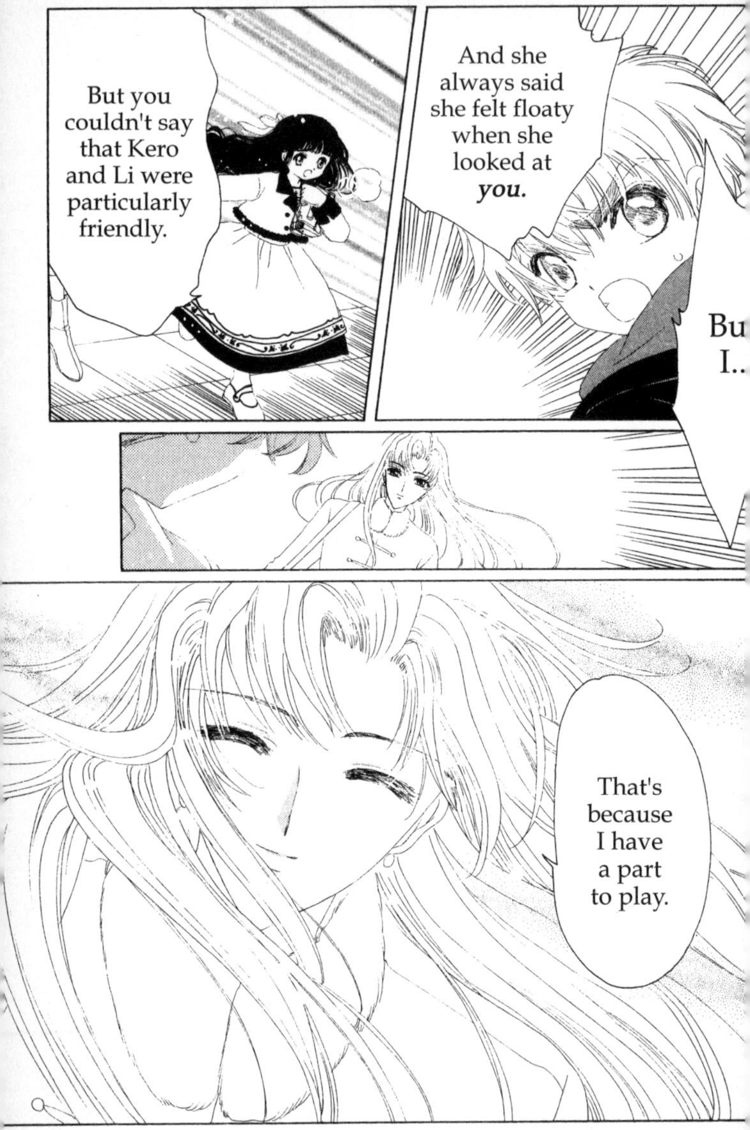
But you couldn't say that Kero and Li were particularly friendly.
And she always said she felt floaty when she looked at *you.*
Bu I..
That's because I have a part to play.

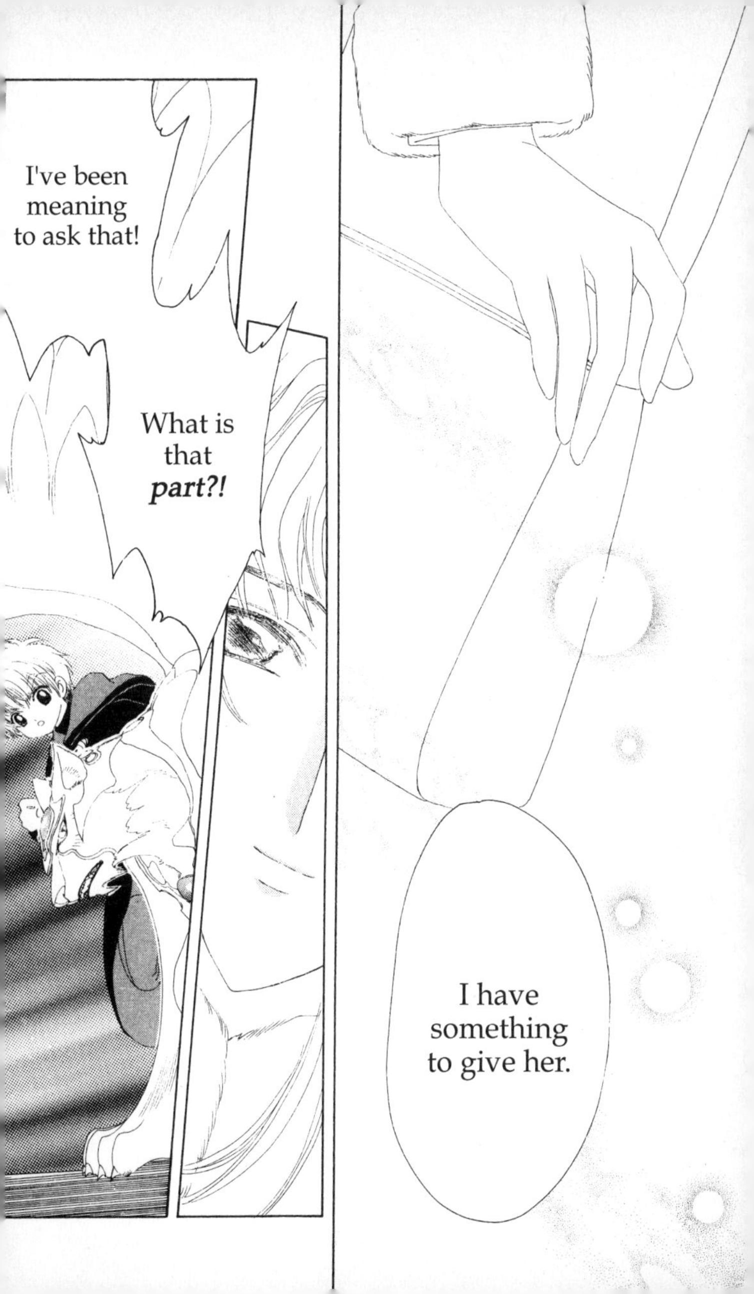
I have something to give her.
I've been meaning to ask that!
What is that *part?!*

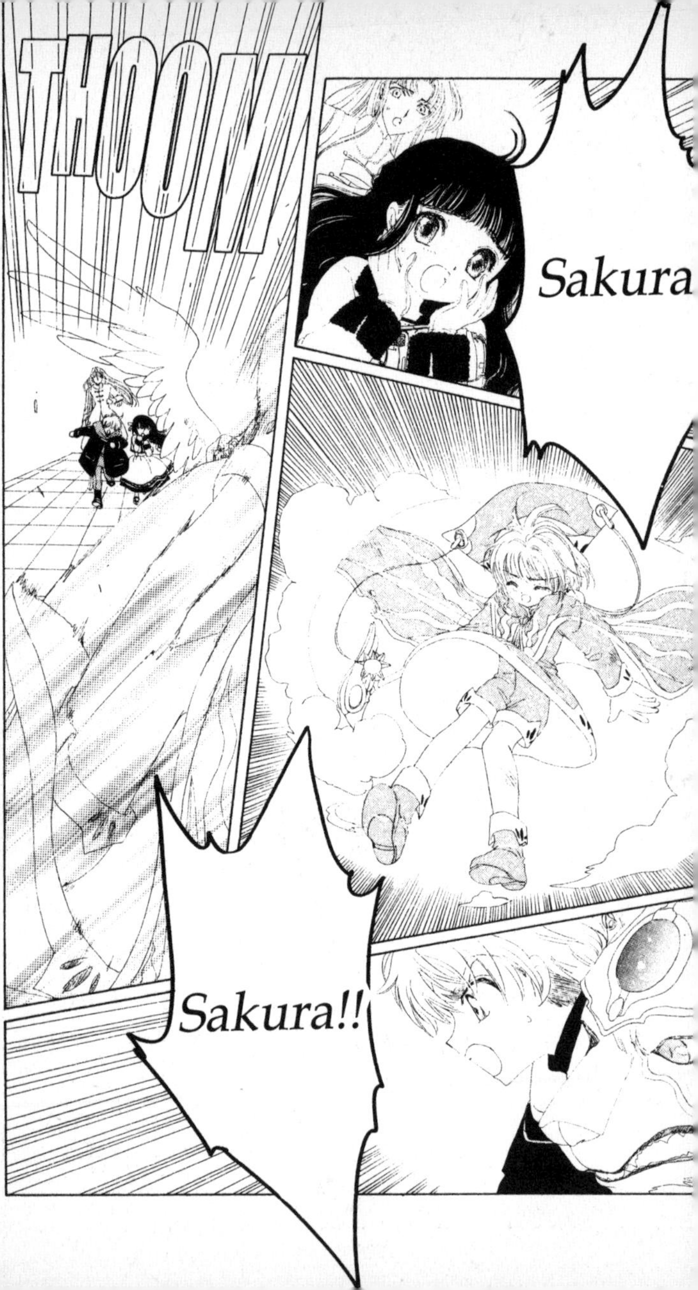
Sakura
THOOM
Sakura!!

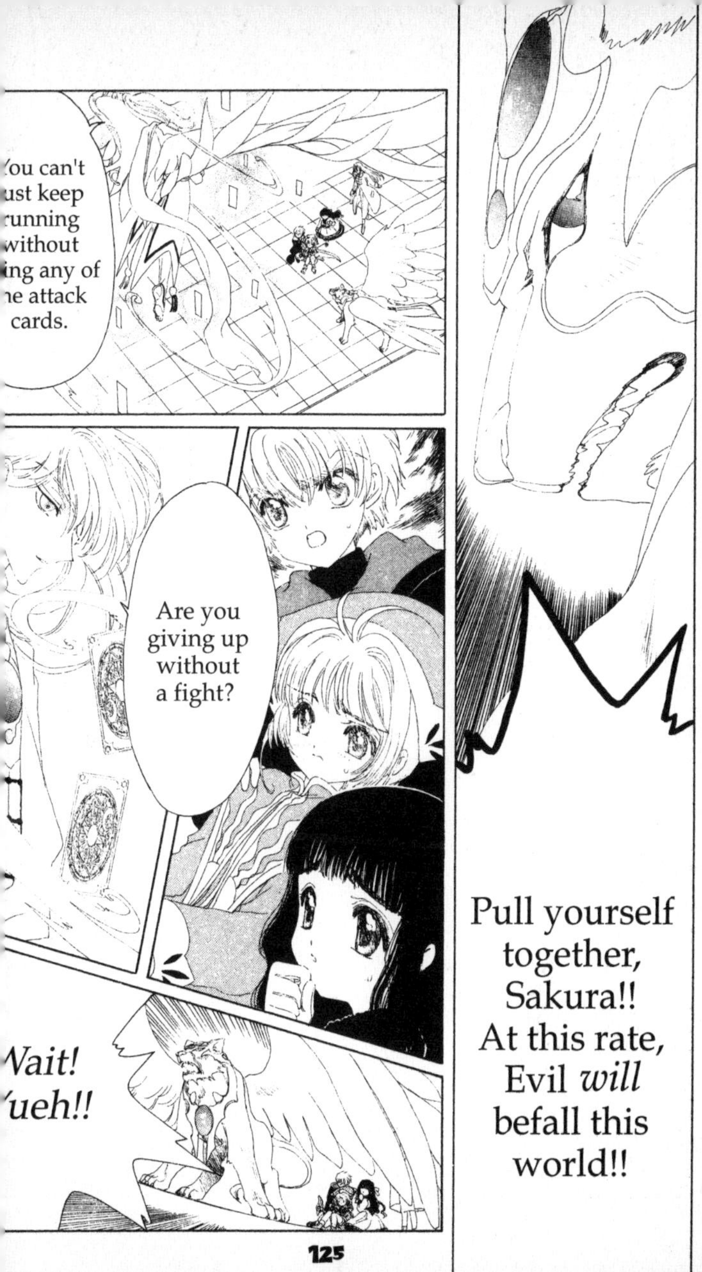
Pull yourself together, Sakura!! At this rate, Evil *will* befall this world!!
ou can't ust keep unning without ing any of e attack cards.
Are you giving up without a fight?
Vait! ueh!!

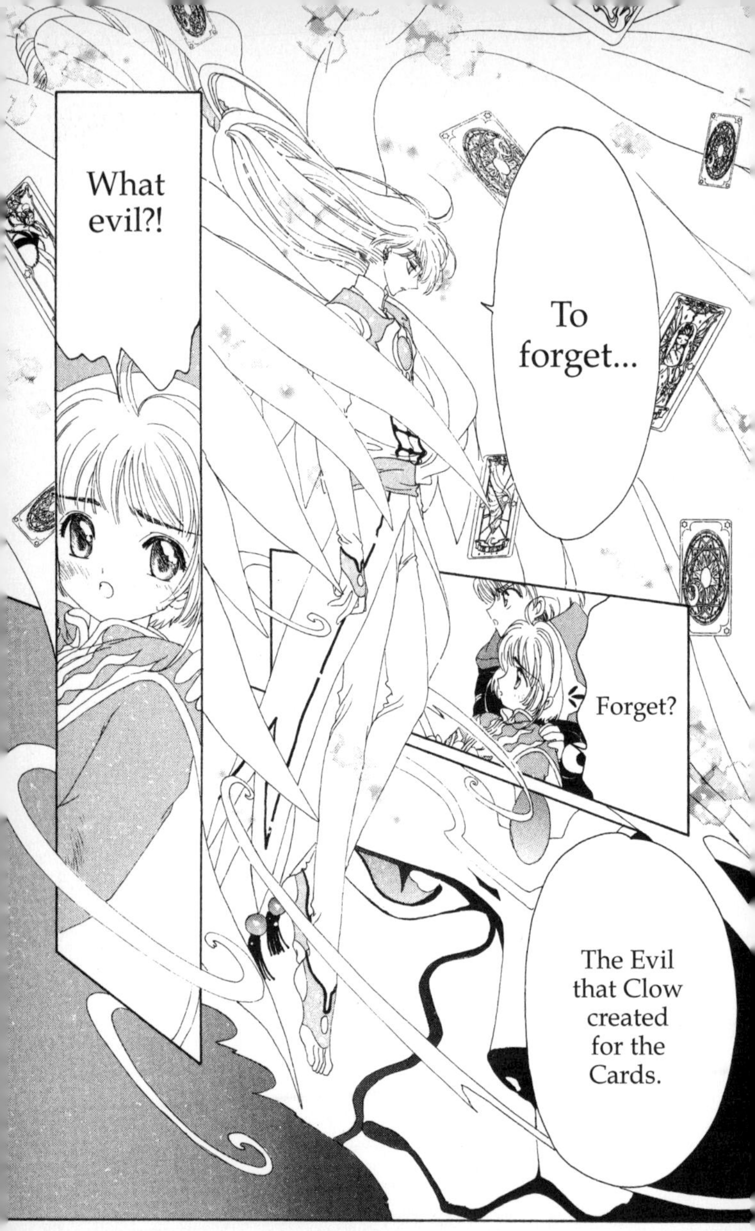
To forget...
Forget?
The Evil that Clow created for the Cards.
What evil?!

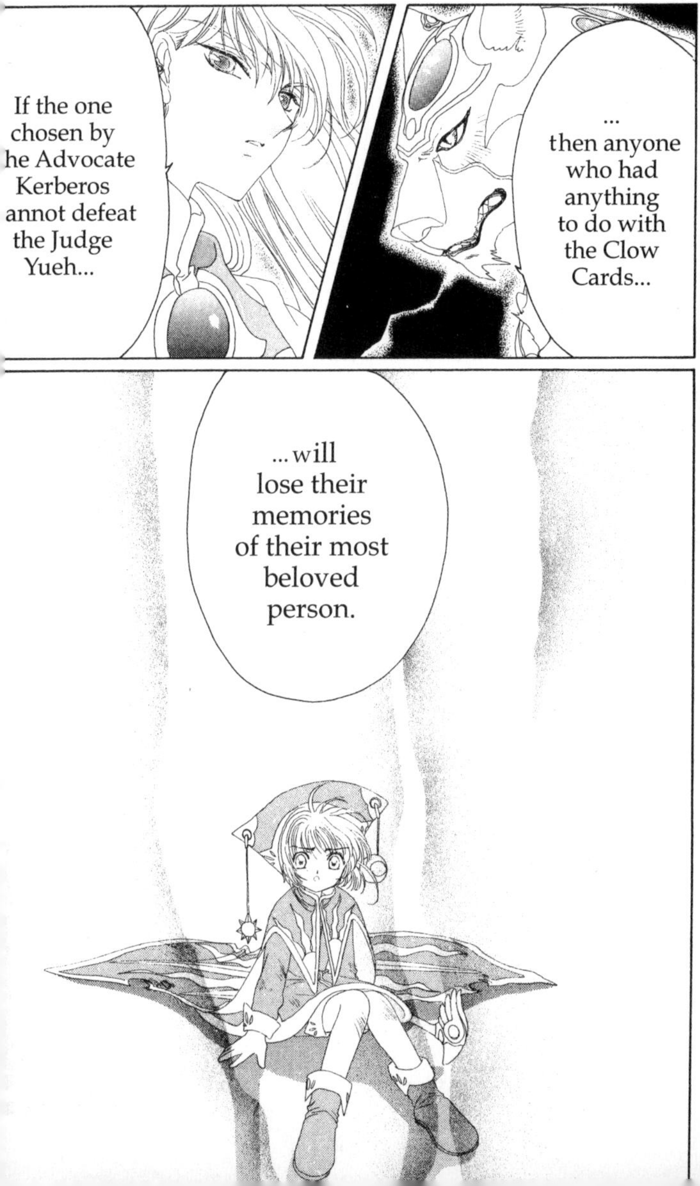
If the one chosen by he Advocate Kerberos annot defeat the Judge Yueh...
... then anyone who had anything to do with the Clow Cards...
...will lose their memories of their most beloved person.

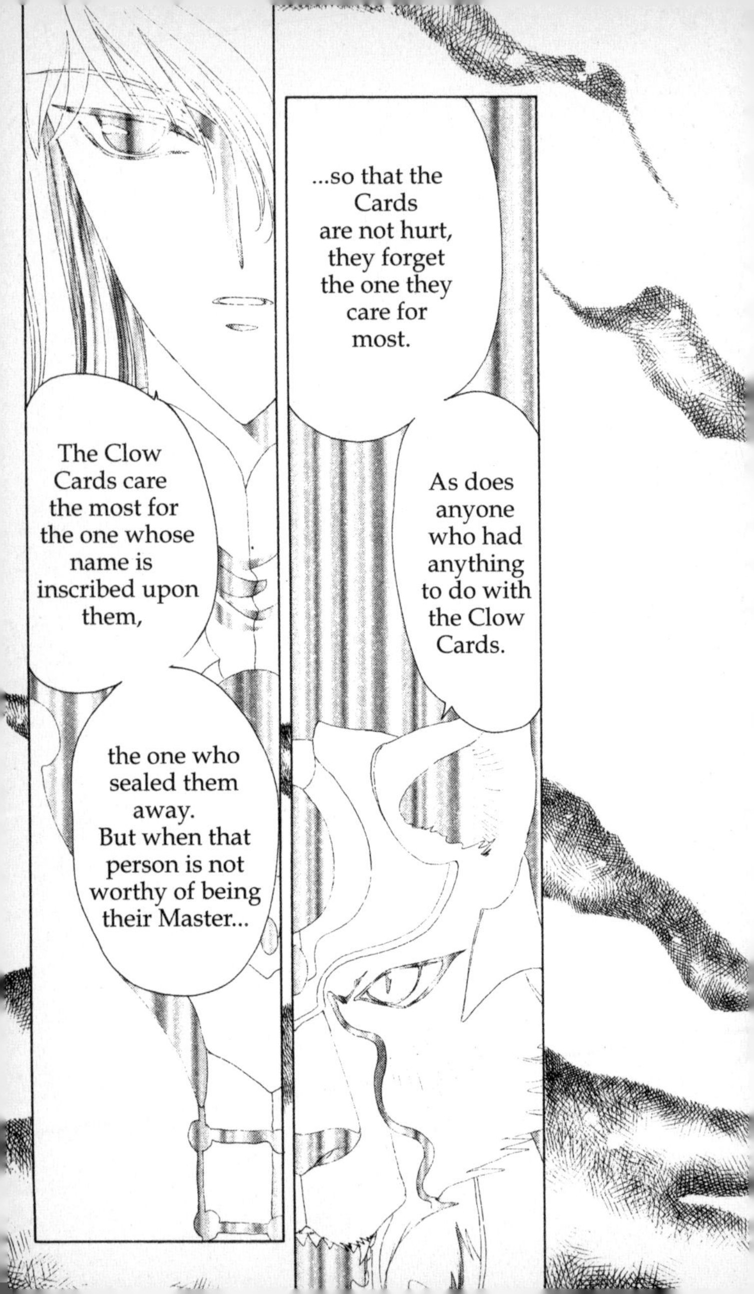
The Clow Cards care the most for the one whose name is inscribed upon them,
the one who sealed them away. But when that person is not worthy of being their Master...
...so that the Cards are not hurt, they forget the one they care for most.
As does anyone who had anything to do with the Clow Cards.

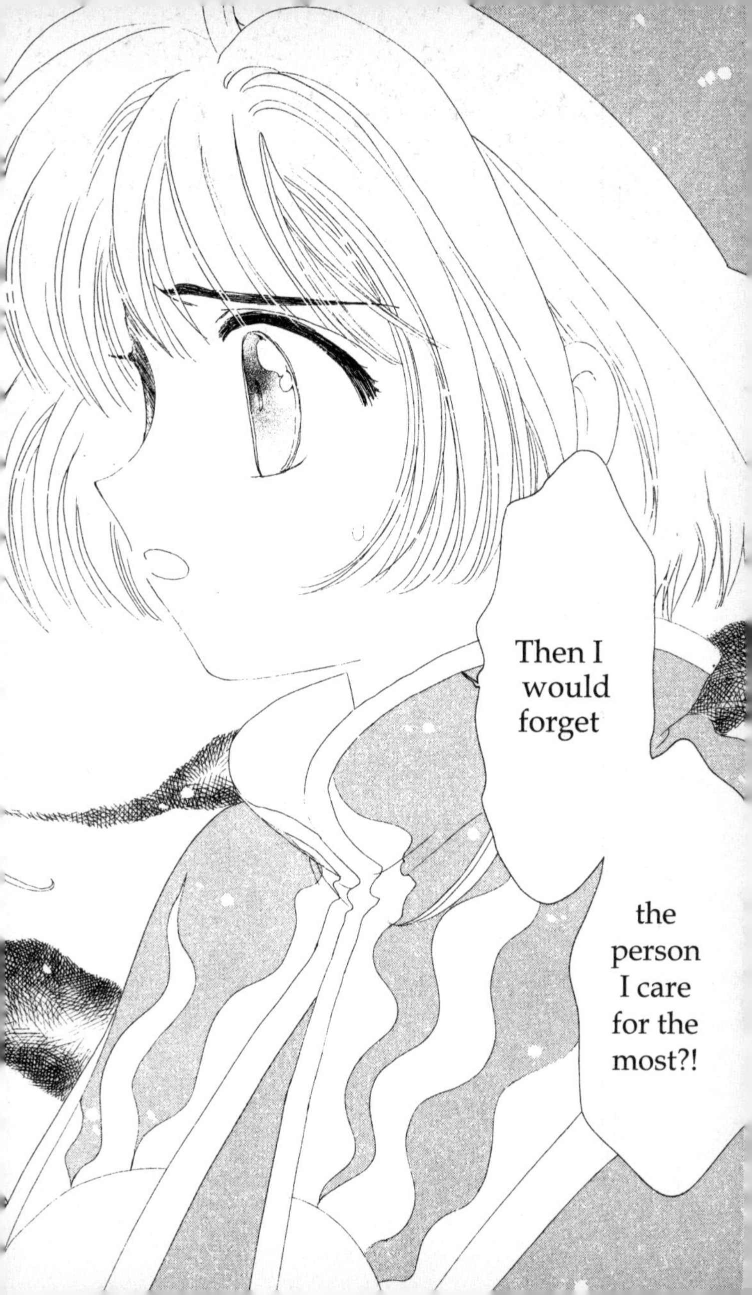
Then I would forget
the person I care for the most?!

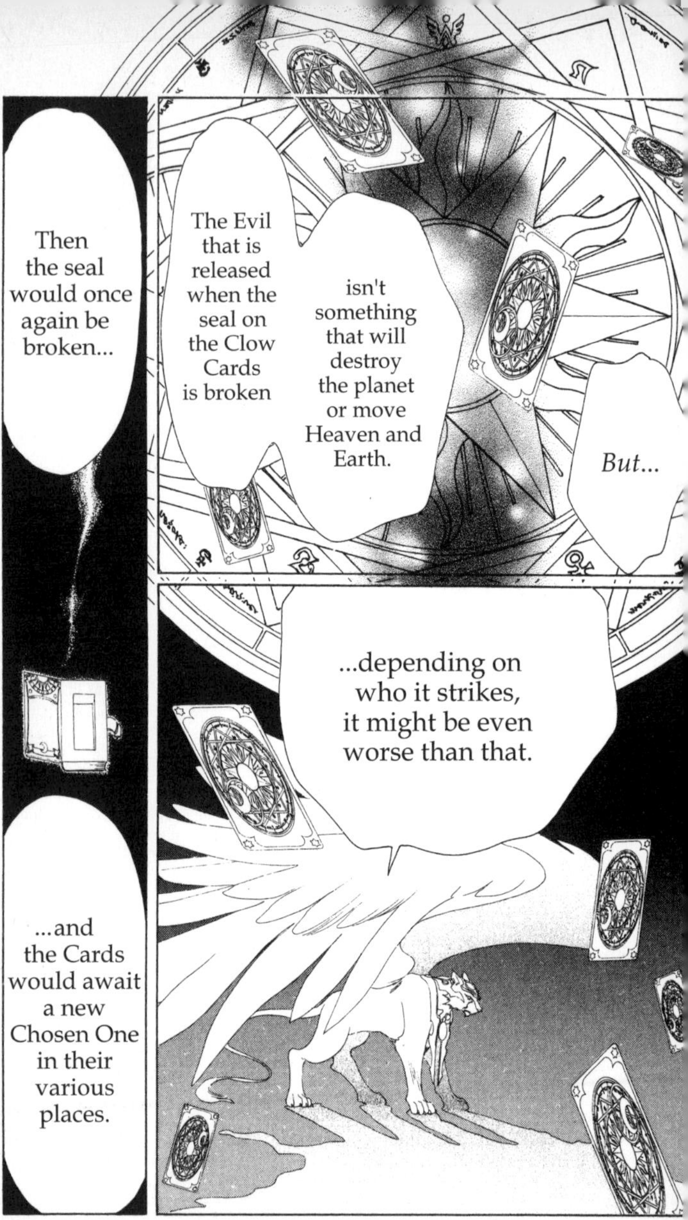
Then the seal would once again be broken...
...and the Cards would await a new Chosen One in their various places.
The Evil that is released when the seal on the Clow Cards is broken
isn't something that will destroy the planet or move Heaven and Earth.
But...
...depending on who it strikes, it might be even worse than that.

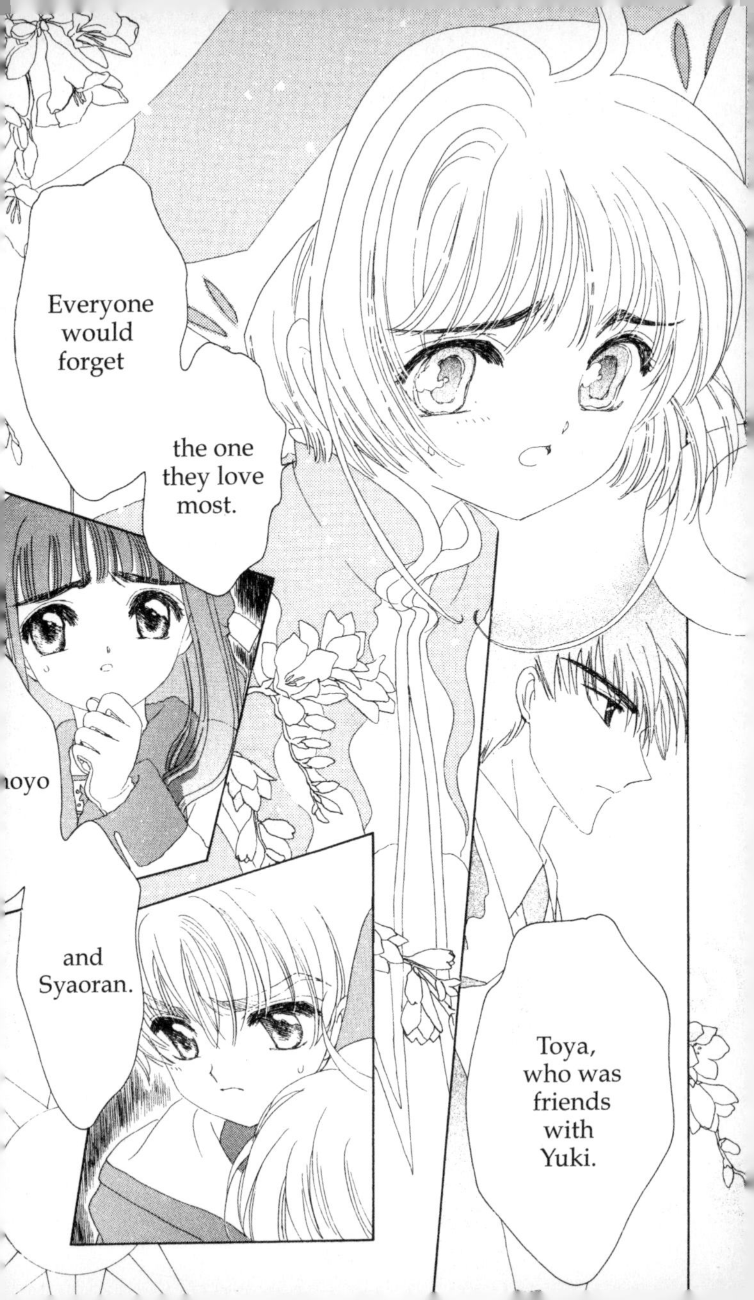
Everyone would forget
the one they love most.
Toya, who was friends with Yuki.
oyo
and Syaoran.

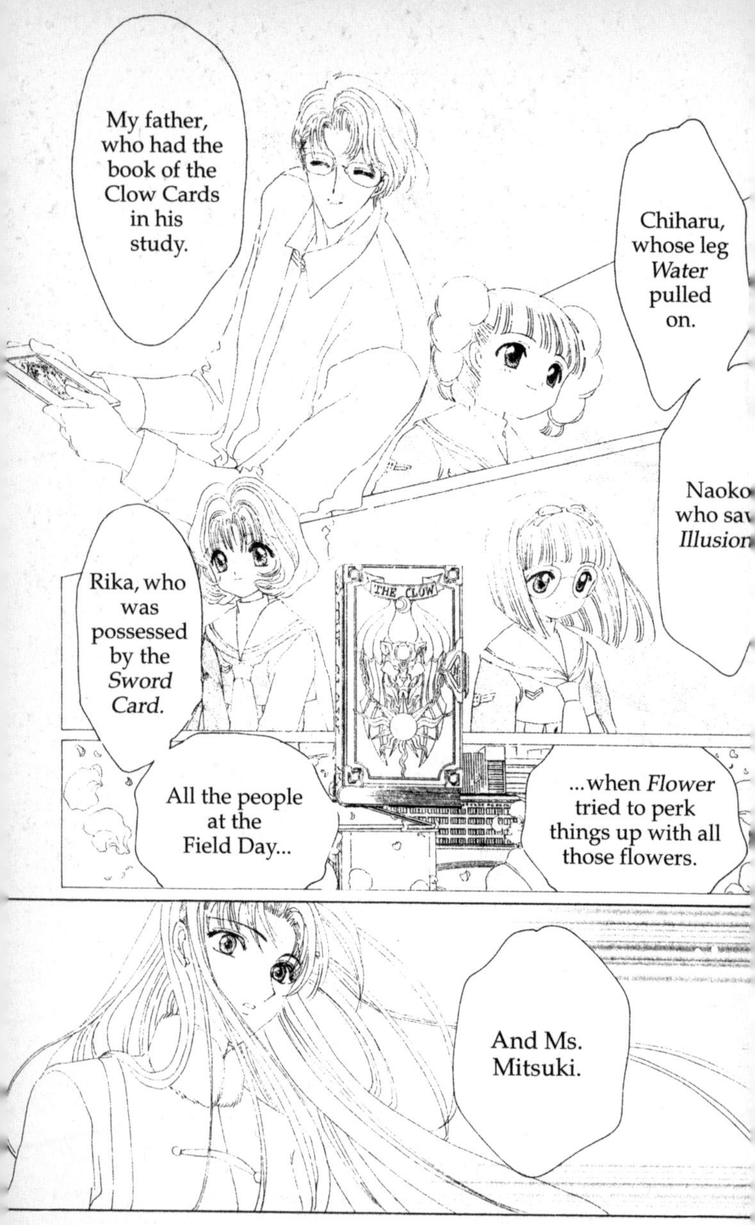
My father, who had the book of the Clow Cards in his study.
Chiharu, whose leg *Water* pulled on.
Rika, who was possessed by the *Sword Card*.
Naoko who sa *Illusion*
THE CLOW
All the people at the Field Day...
...when *Flower* tried to perk things up with all those flowers.
And Ms. Mitsuki.

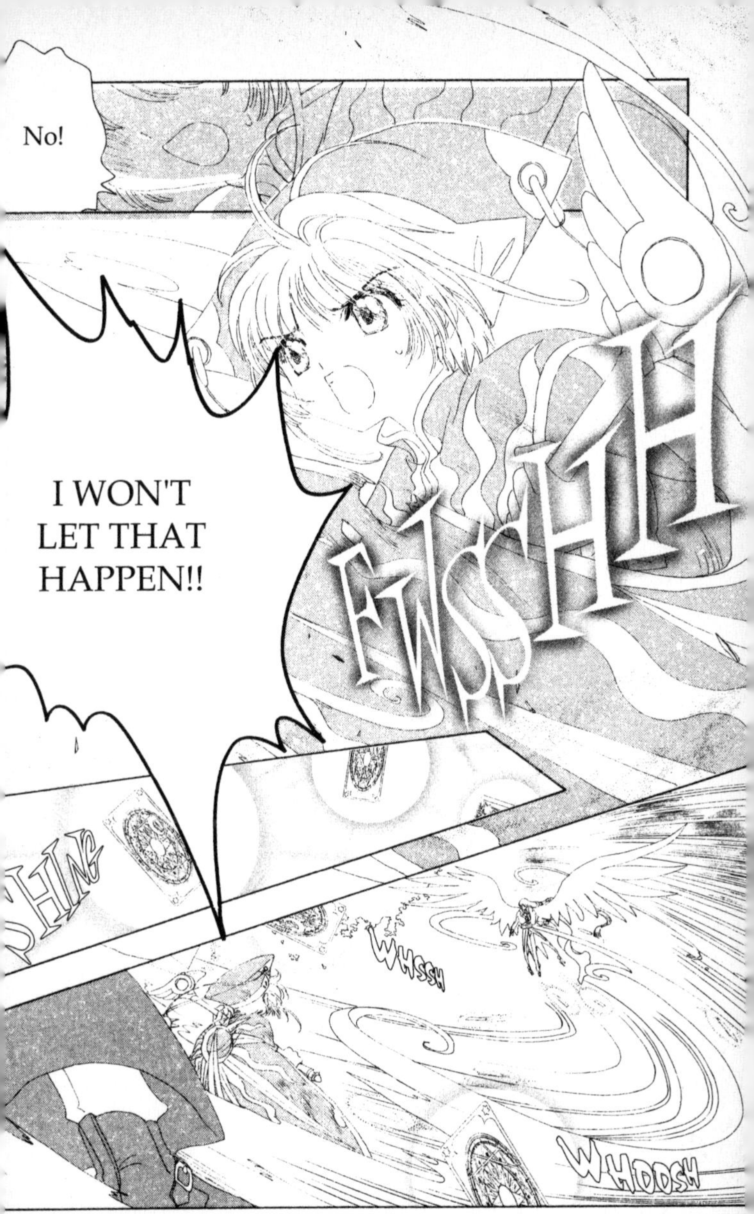
No!
I WON'T LET THAT HAPPEN!!
FWSSH
SHING
WHSSH
WHOOSH

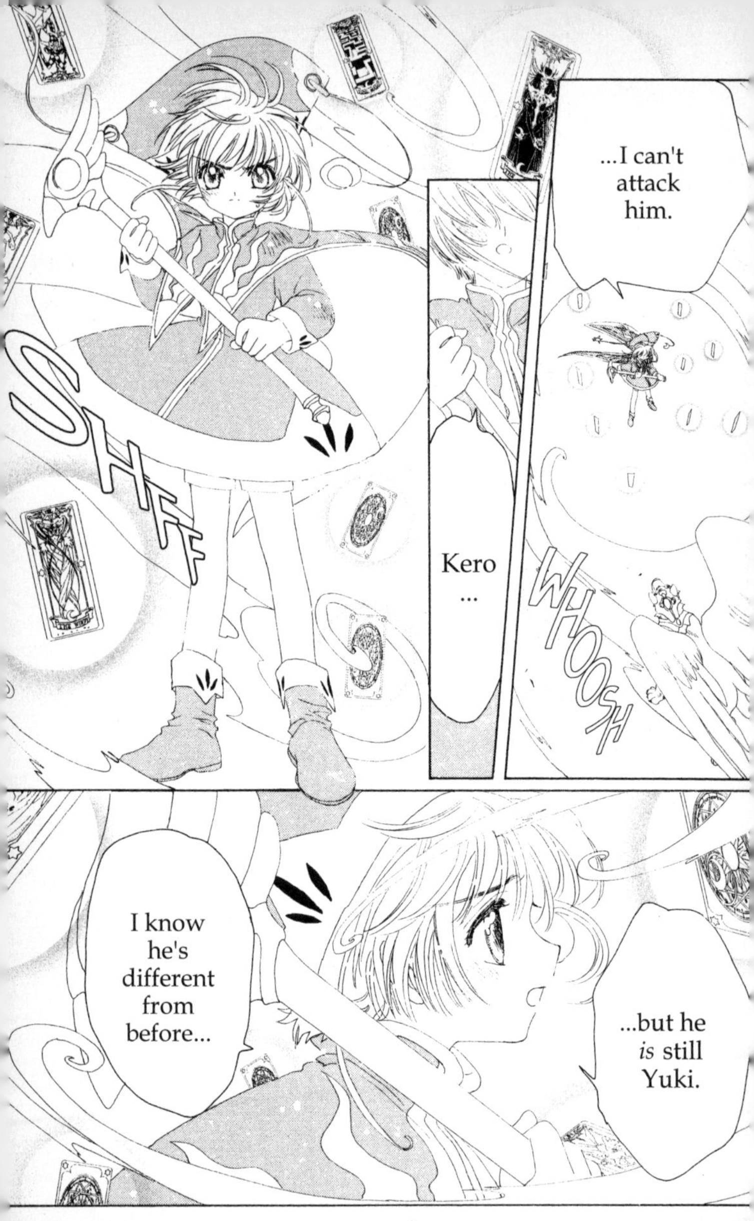
SHFF
Kero ...
...I can't attack him.
WHOOSH
I know he's different from before...
...but he *is* still Yuki.

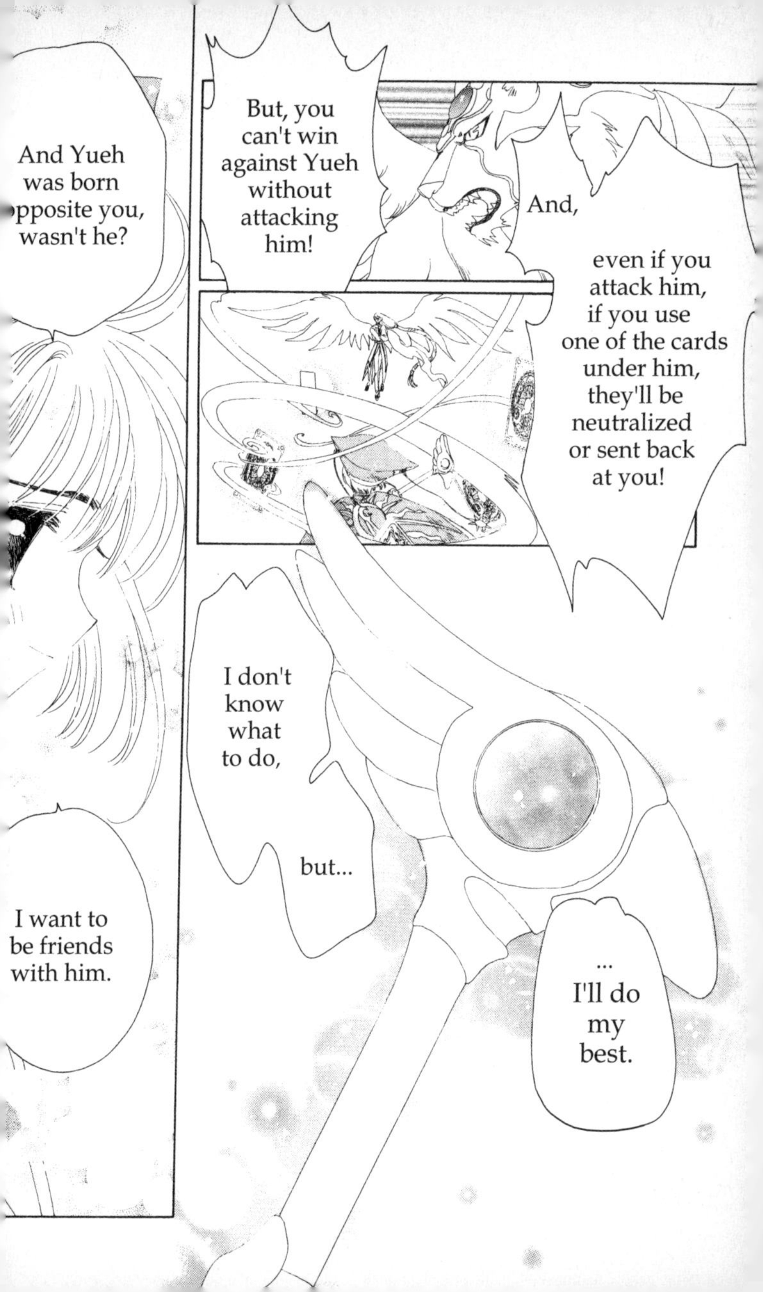
But, you can't win against Yueh without attacking him!
And,
even if you attack him, if you use one of the cards under him, they'll be neutralized or sent back at you!
I don't know what to do,
but...
... I'll do my best.
And Yueh was born opposite you, wasn't he?
I want to be friends with him.

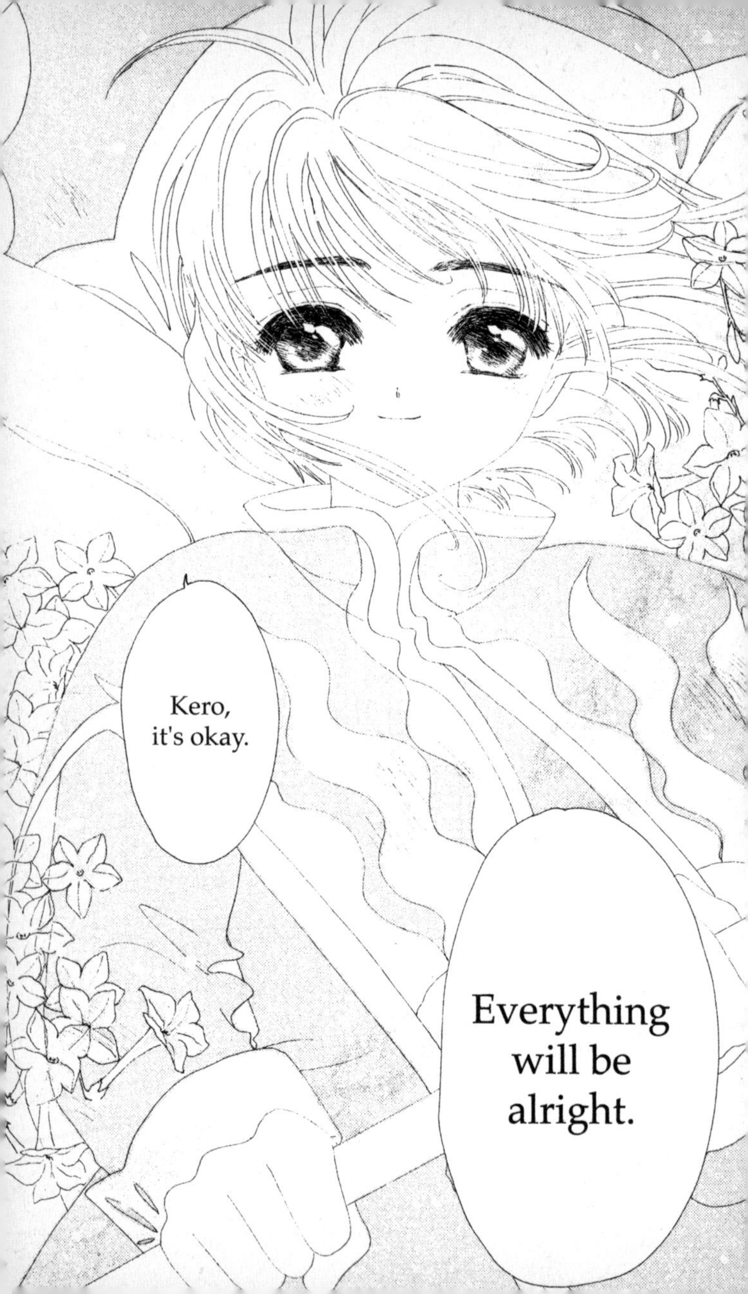
Kero, it's okay.
Everything will be alright.

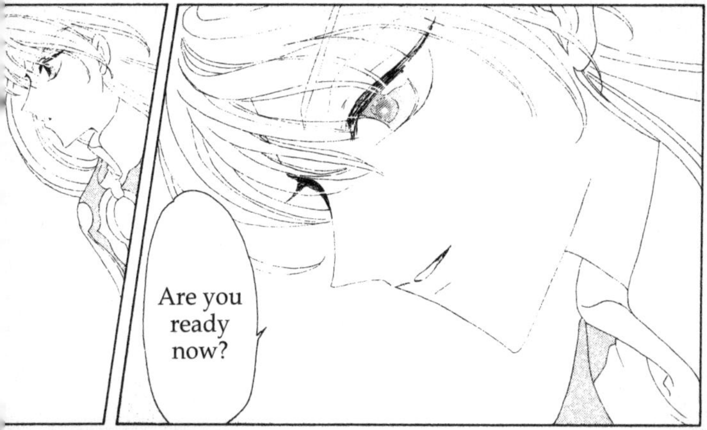
Are you ready now?
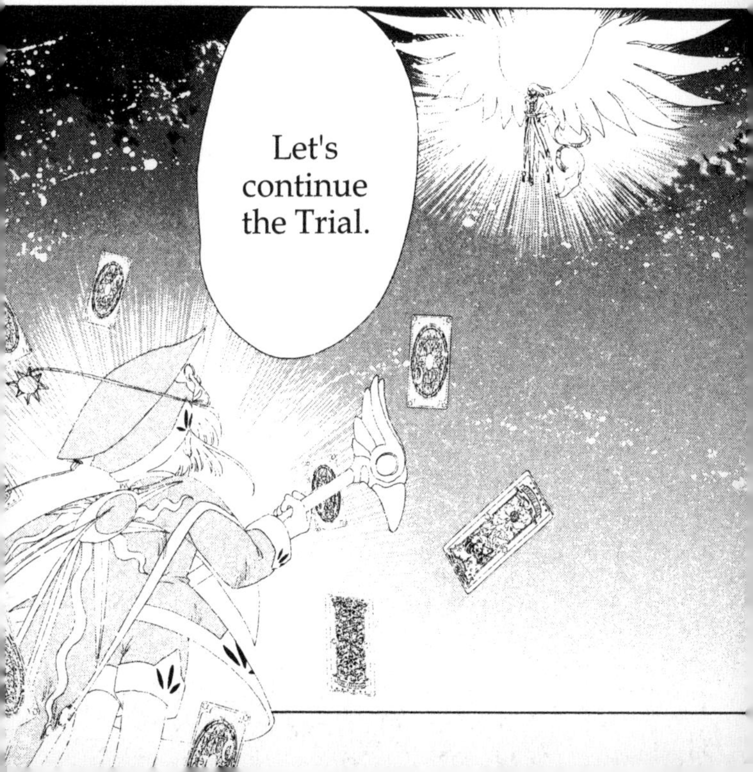
Let's continue the Trial.

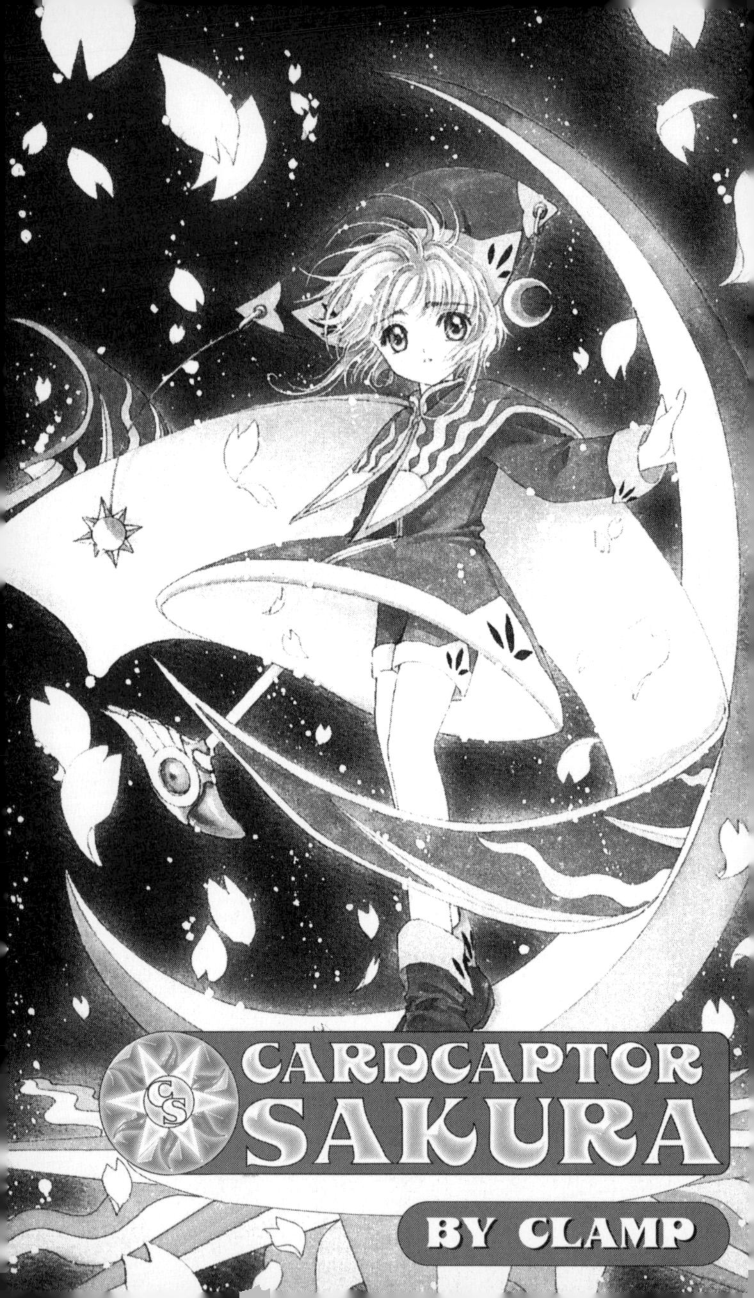
CARDCAPTOR
SAKURA
BY CLAMP

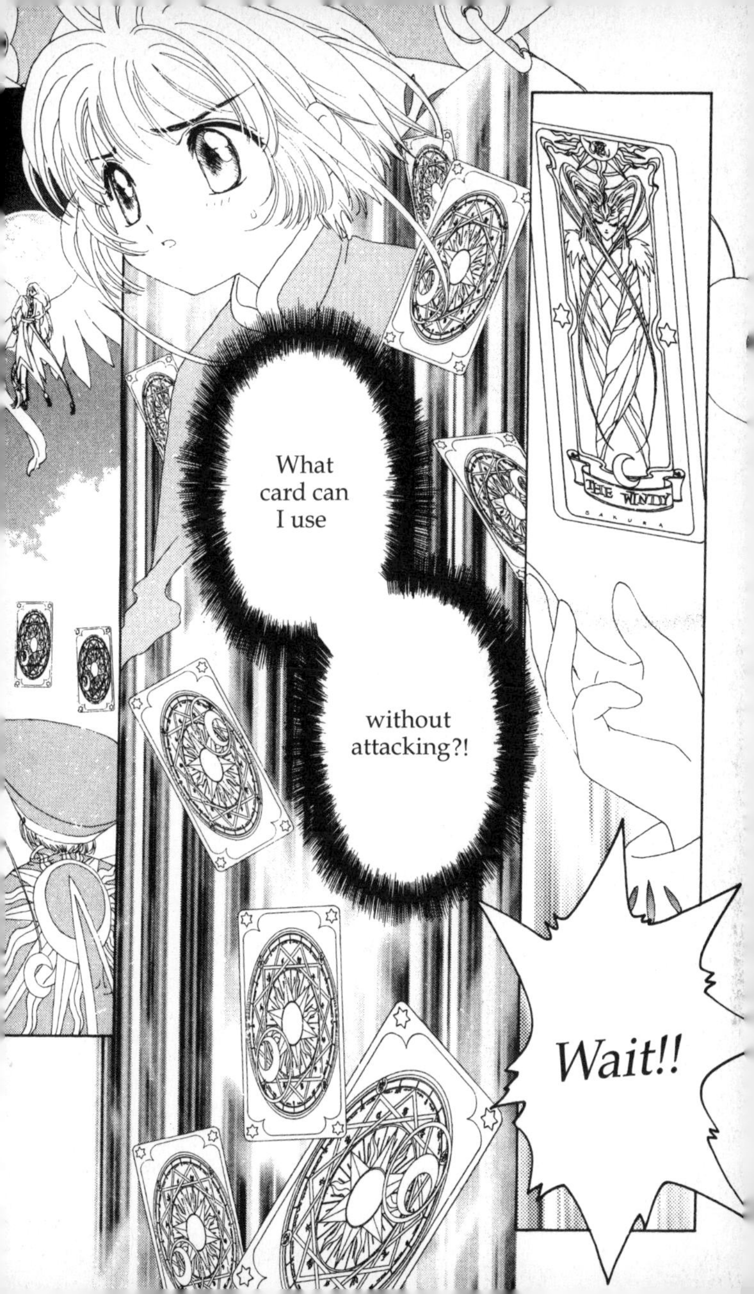
What card can I use
without attacking?!
THE WINDY
SAKURA
Wait!!

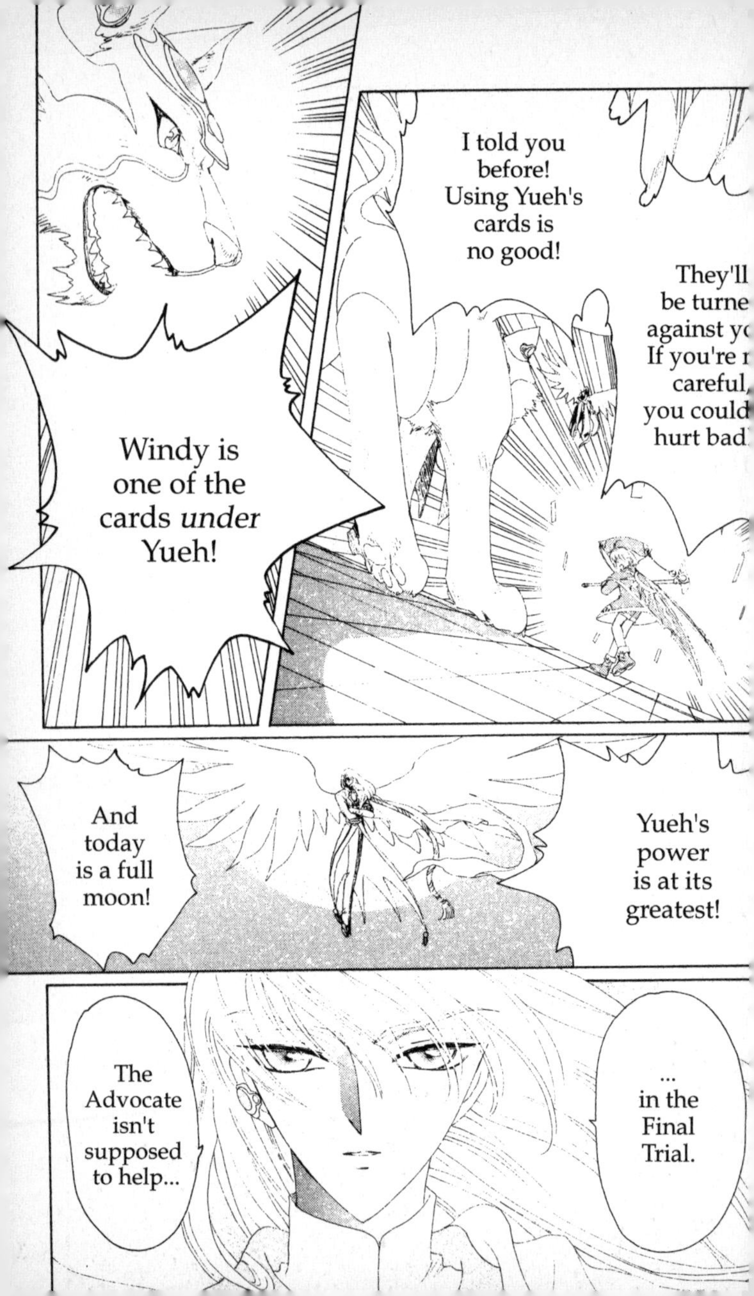

I told you before! Using Yueh's cards is no good!
They'll be turne against y If you're careful, you could hurt bad
Windy is one of the cards *under* Yueh!
And today is a full moon!
Yueh's power is at its greatest!
The Advocate isn't supposed to help...
... in the Final Trial.

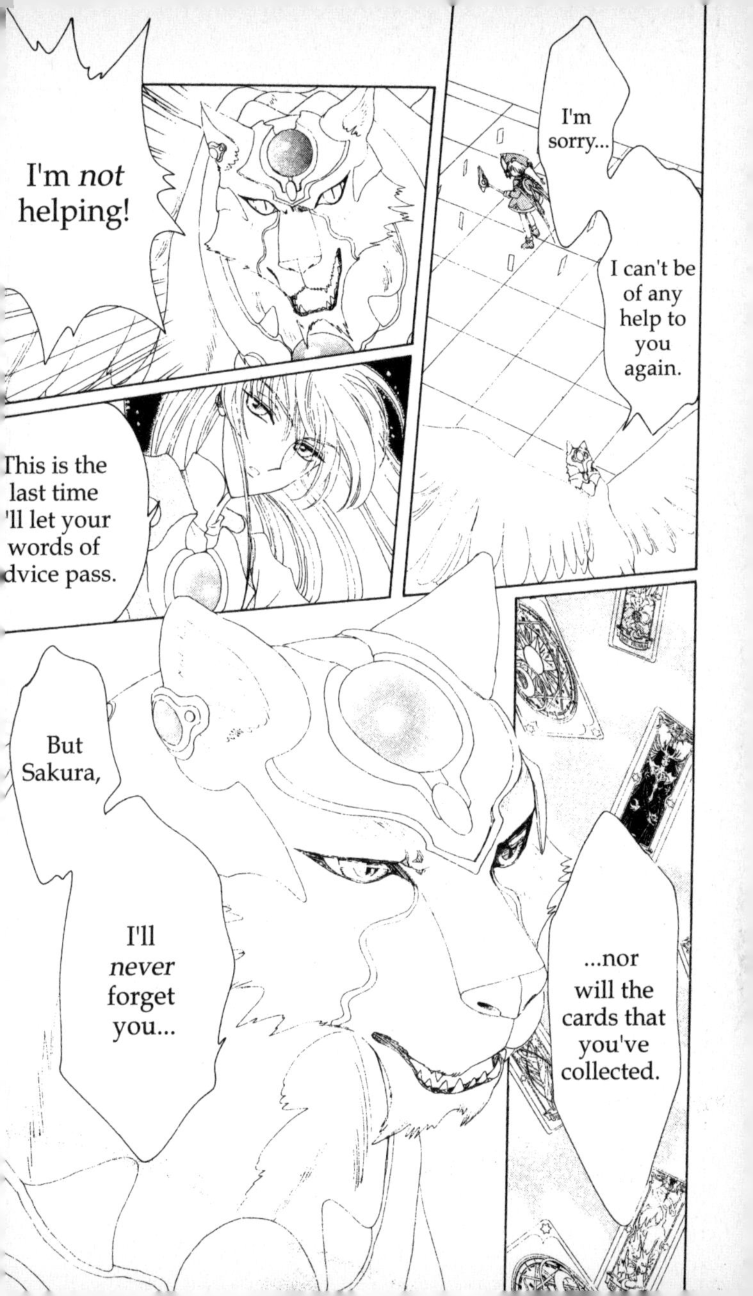
I'm *not* helping!
This is the last time 'll let your words of dvice pass.
I'm sorry...
I can't be of any help to you again.
But Sakura,
I'll *never* forget you...
...nor will the cards that you've collected.

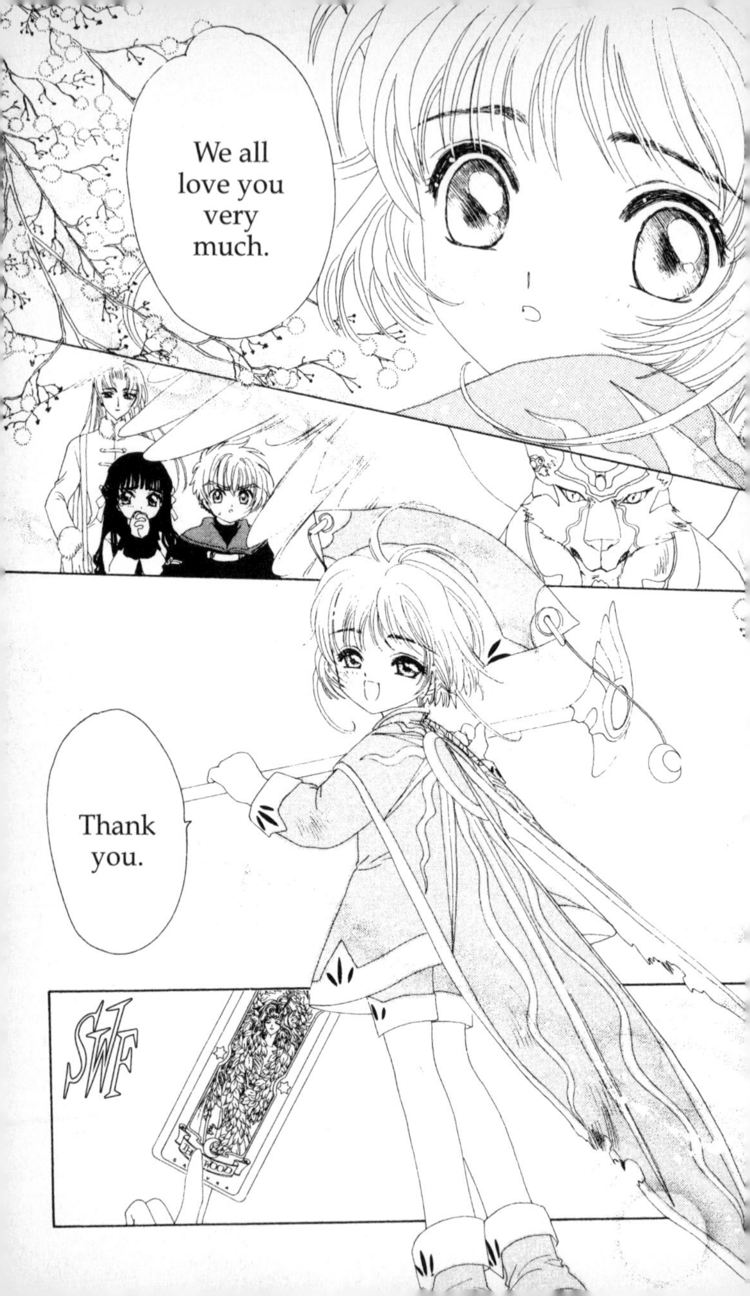
We all love you very much.
Thank you.
SWF

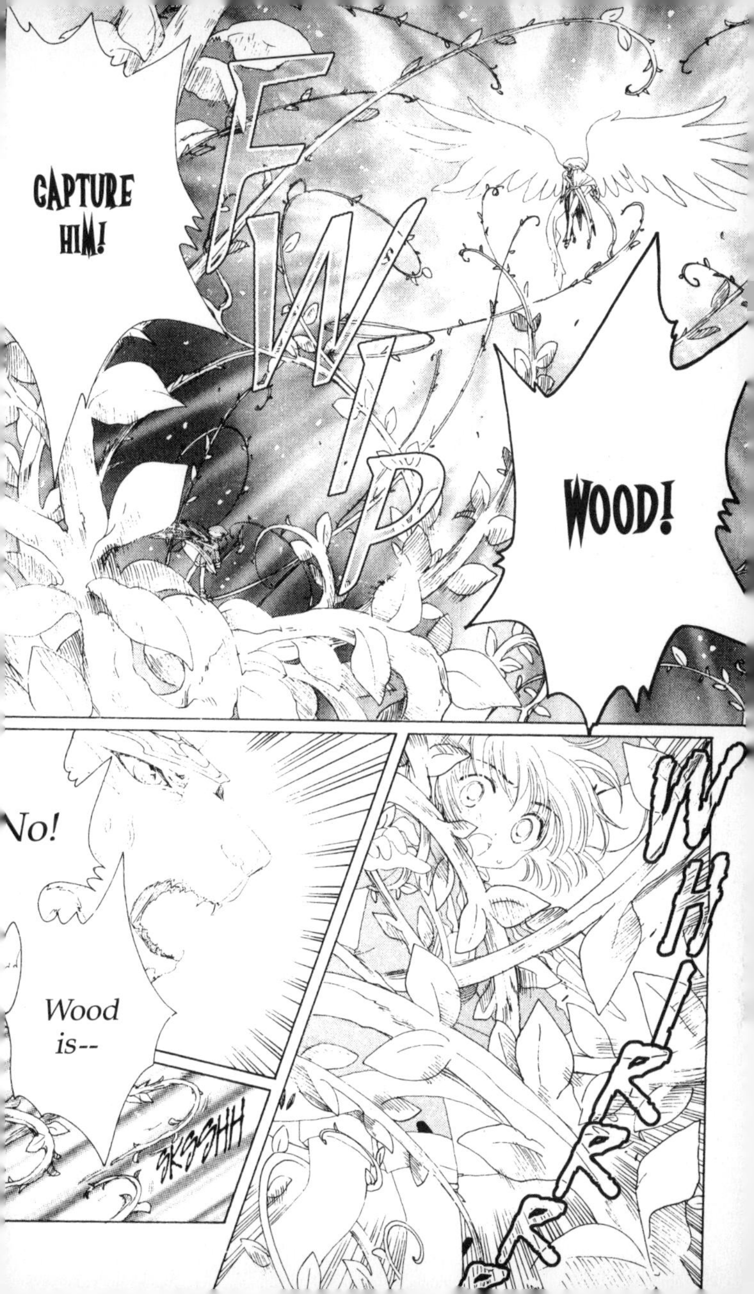
WOOD!
FWIP
CAPTURE HIM!
WHIRRR
No!
Wood is--
SKSHH

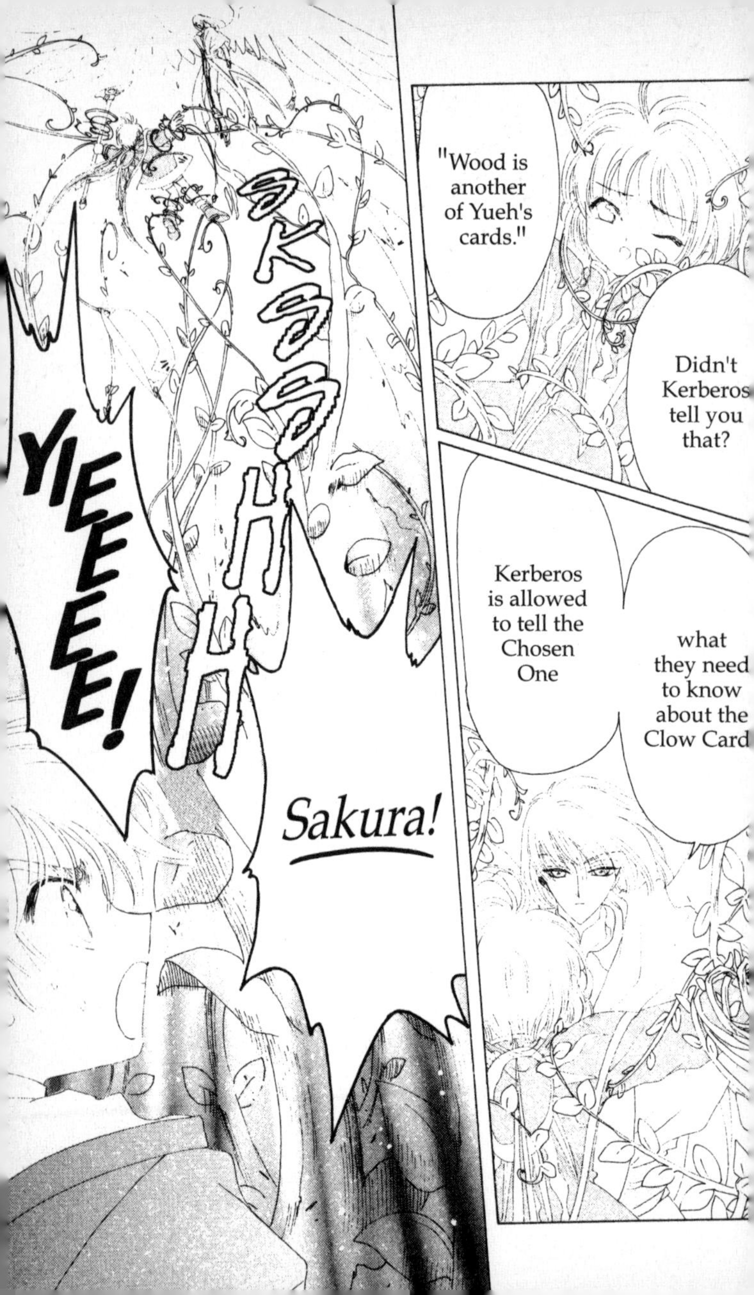
"Wood is another of Yueh's cards."
Didn't Kerberos tell you that?
Kerberos is allowed to tell the Chosen One
what they need to know about the Clow Card
YIEEEEE!
Sakura!

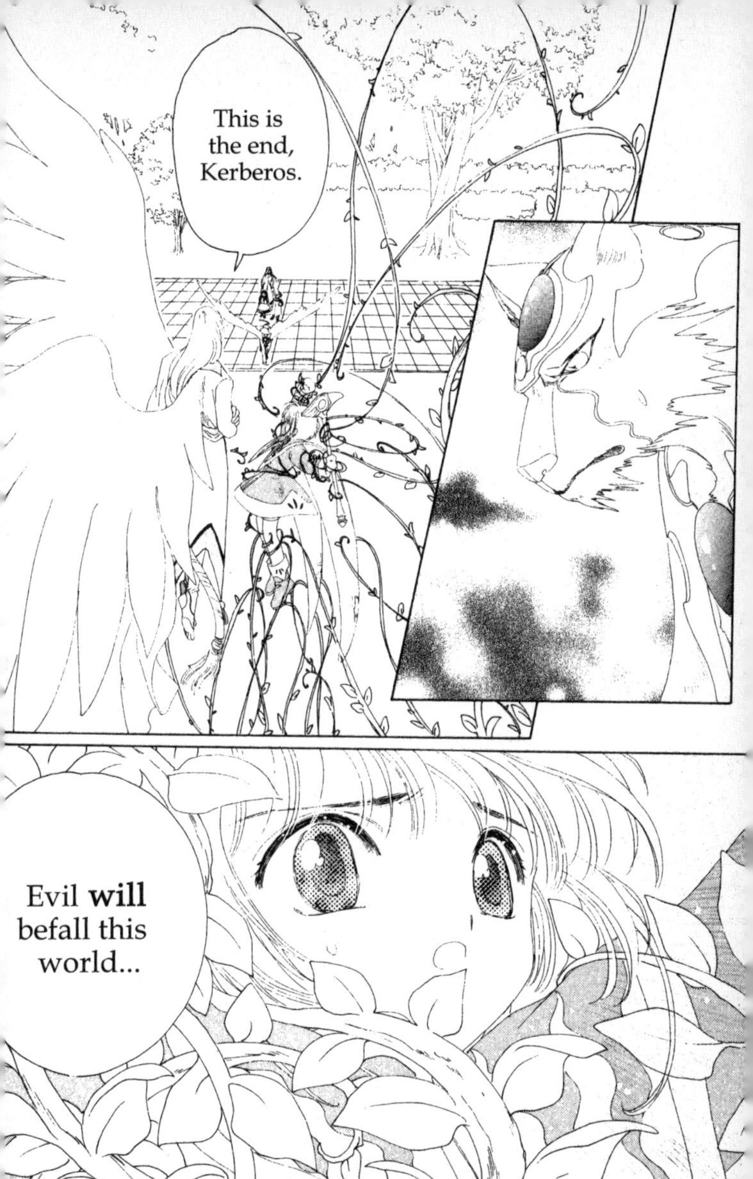
This is the end, Kerberos.
Evil **will** befall this world...

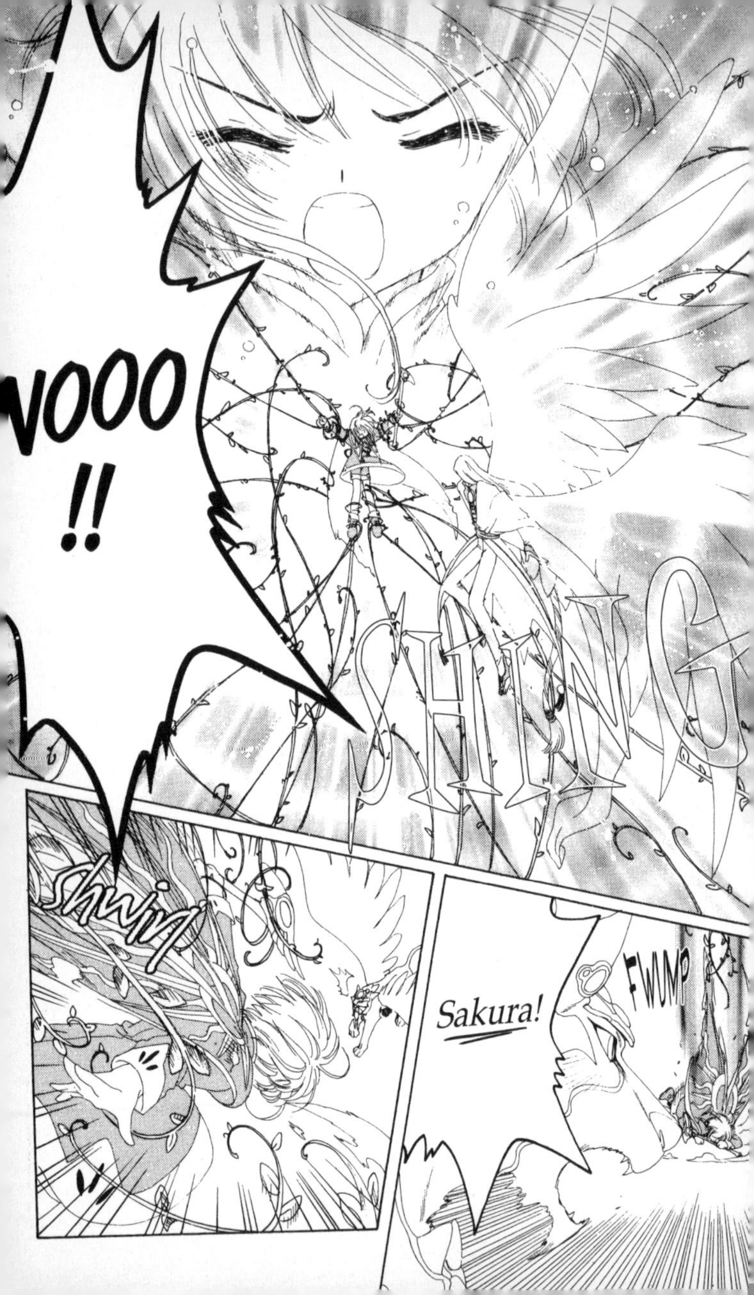
NOOO!!
SHING
Sakura!
FWUMP
shwing

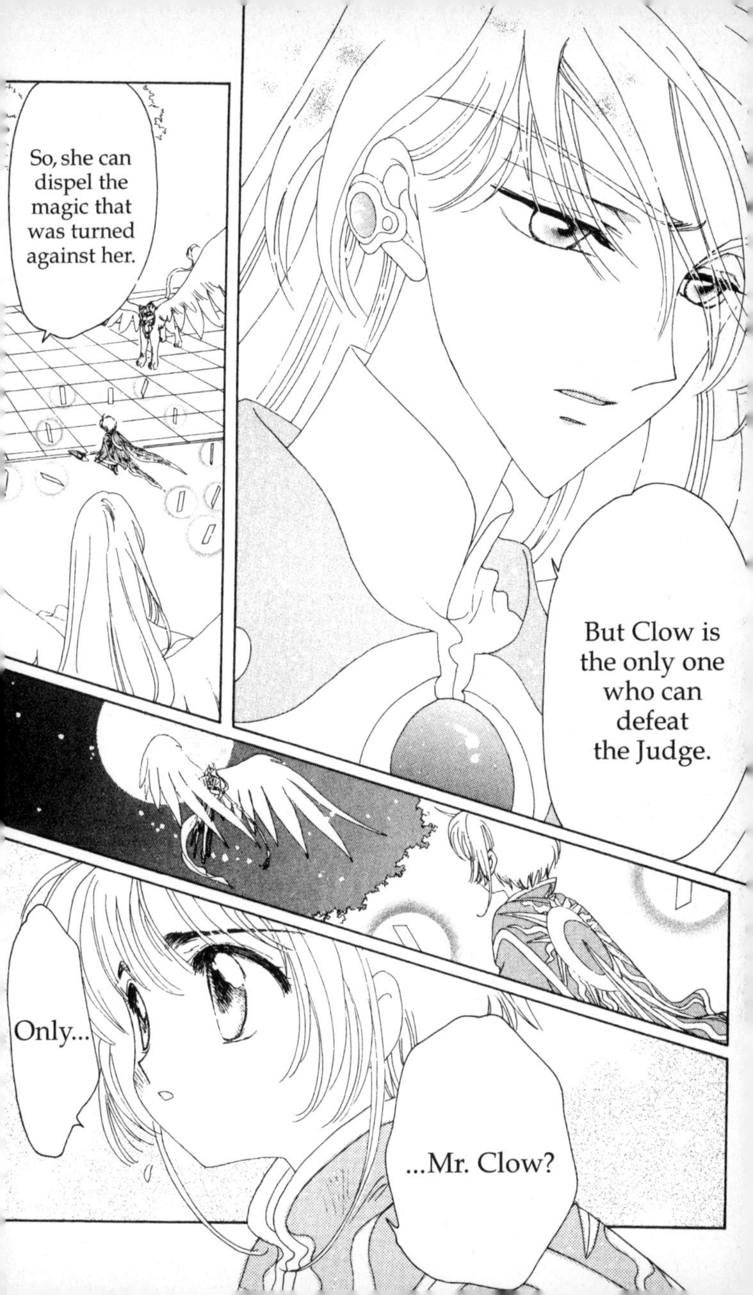
But Clow is the only one who can defeat the Judge.
So, she can dispel the magic that was turned against her.
...Mr. Clow?
Only...

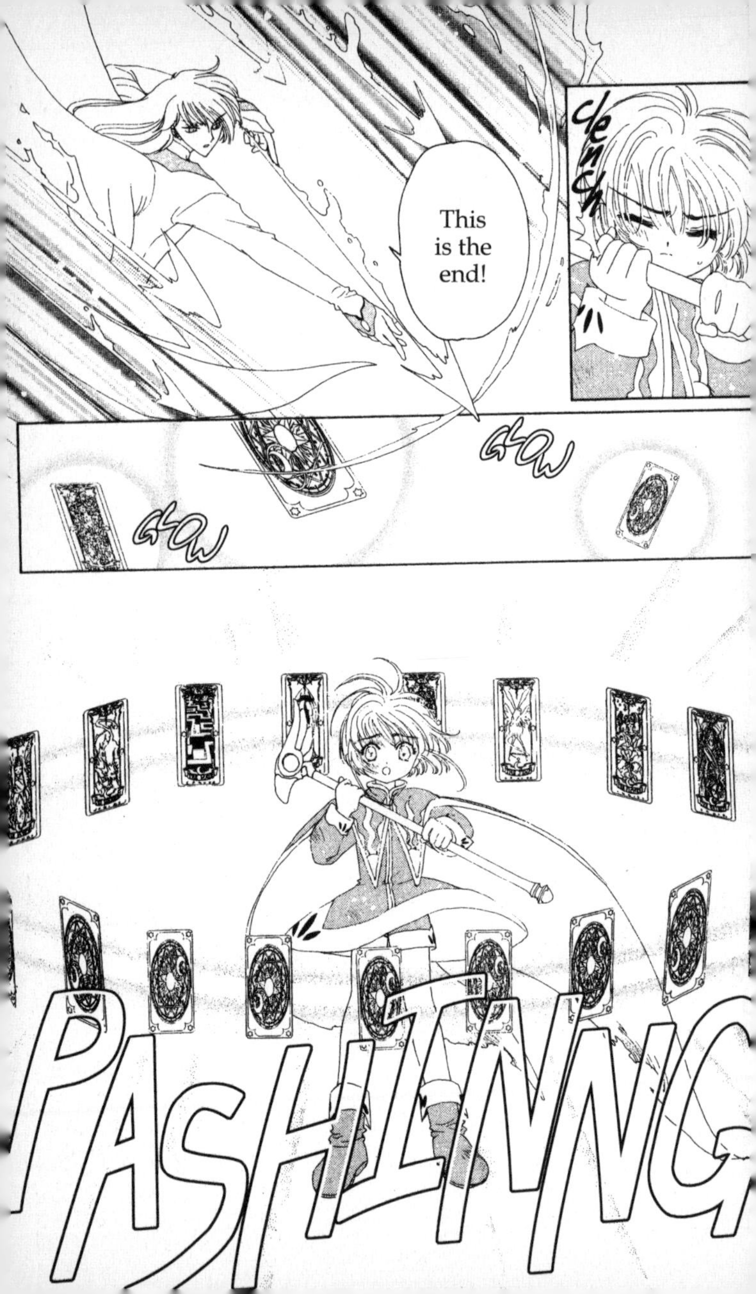
clench
This is the end!
glow
glow
PASHINNG

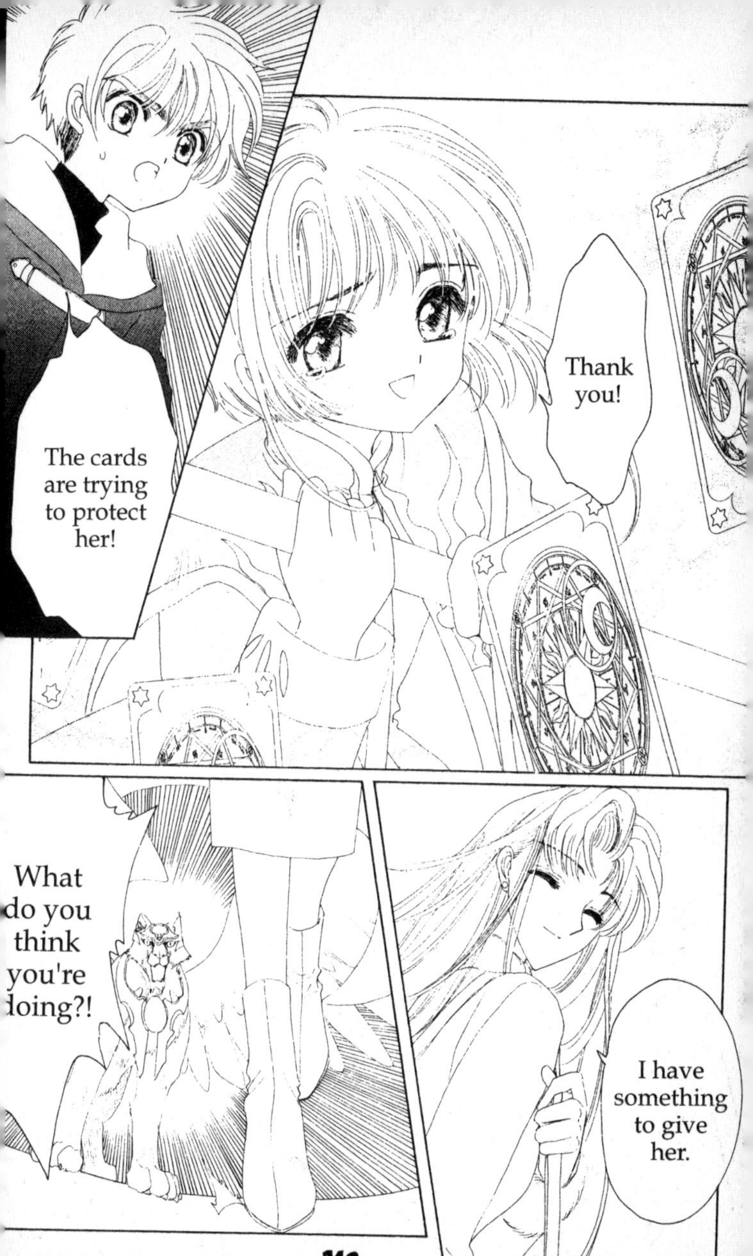

Thank you!
The cards are trying to protect her!
I have something to give her.
What do you think you're doing?!

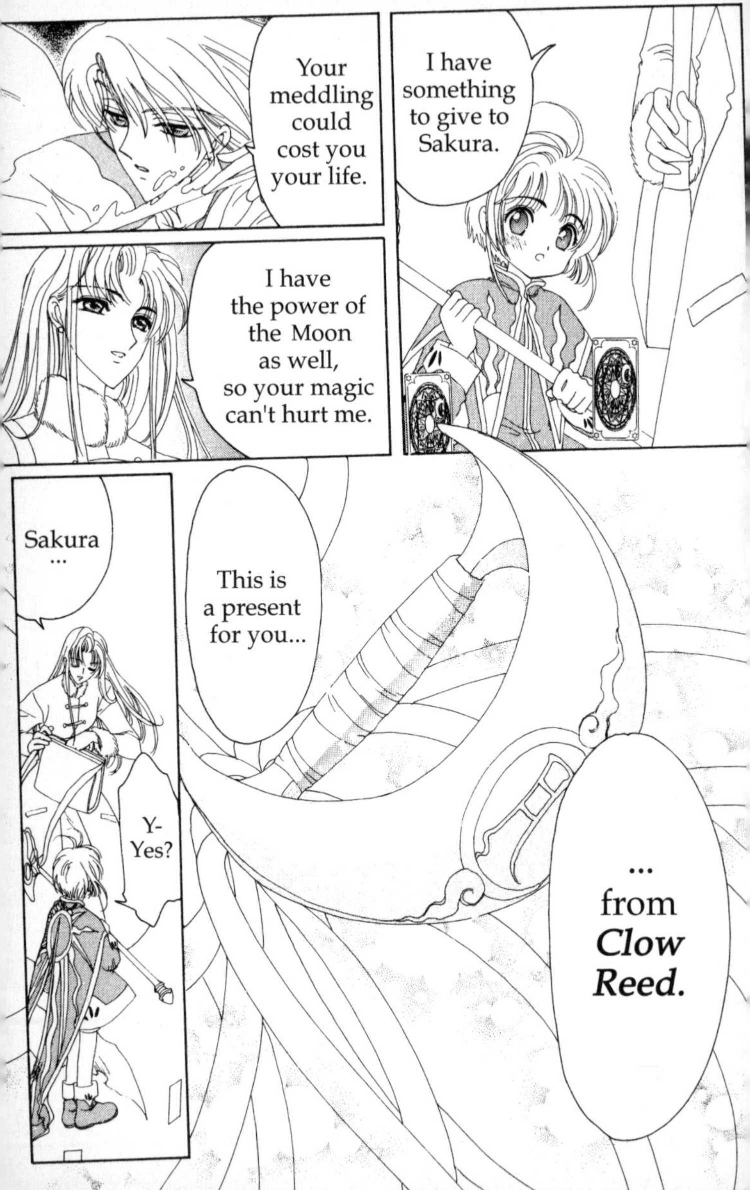
I have something to give to Sakura.
Your meddling could cost you your life.
I have the power of the Moon as well, so your magic can't hurt me.
This is a present for you...
... from *Clow Reed.*
Sakura ...
Y- Yes?

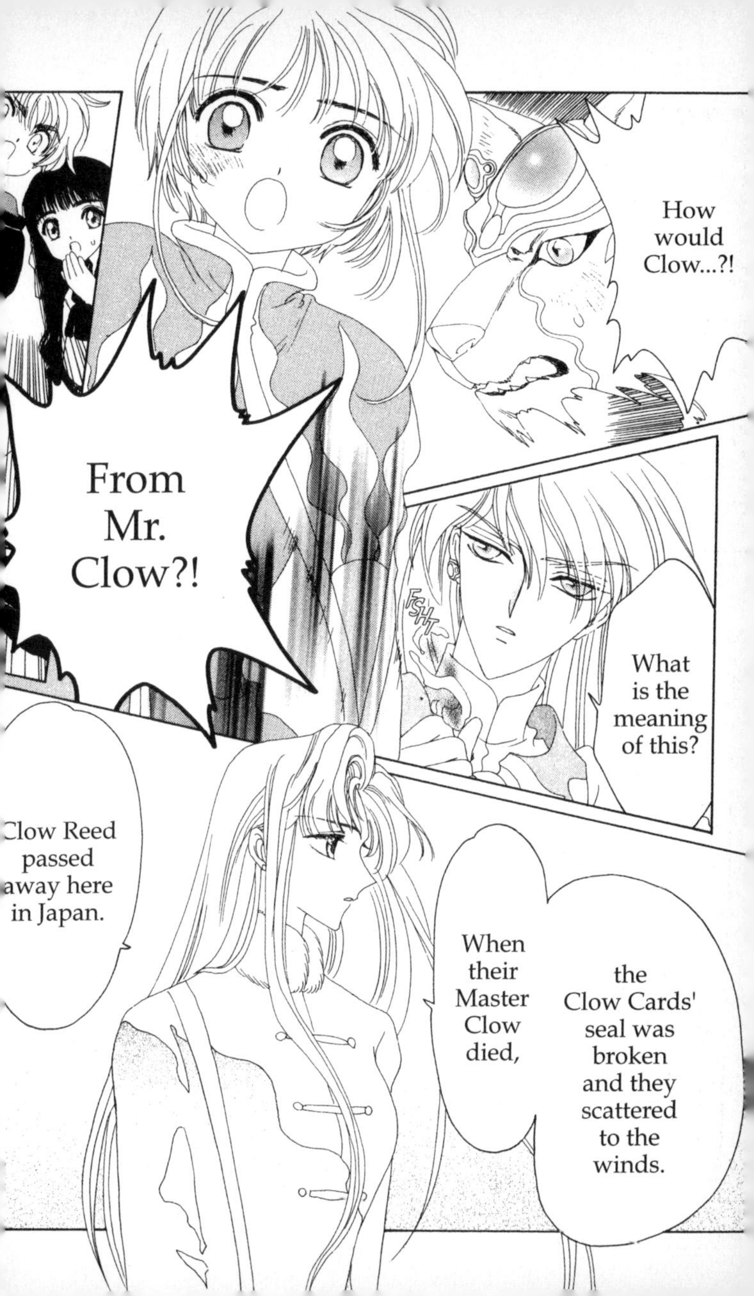
How would Clow...?!
From Mr. Clow?!
FSHT
What is the meaning of this?
When their Master Clow died,
the Clow Cards' seal was broken and they scattered to the winds.
Clow Reed passed away here in Japan.

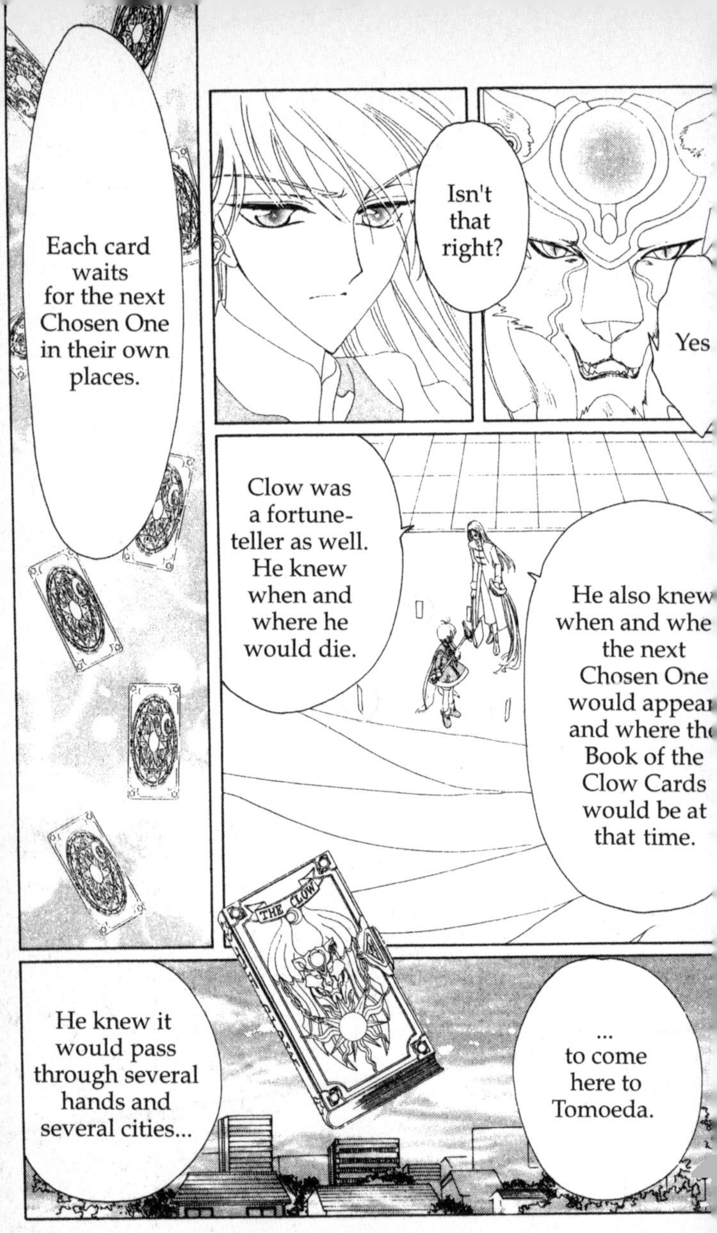
Each card waits for the next Chosen One in their own places.
Isn't that right?
Yes
Clow was a fortune-teller as well. He knew when and where he would die.
He also knew when and whe the next Chosen One would appea and where th Book of the Clow Cards would be at that time.
THE CLOW
He knew it would pass through several hands and several cities...
... to come here to Tomoeda.

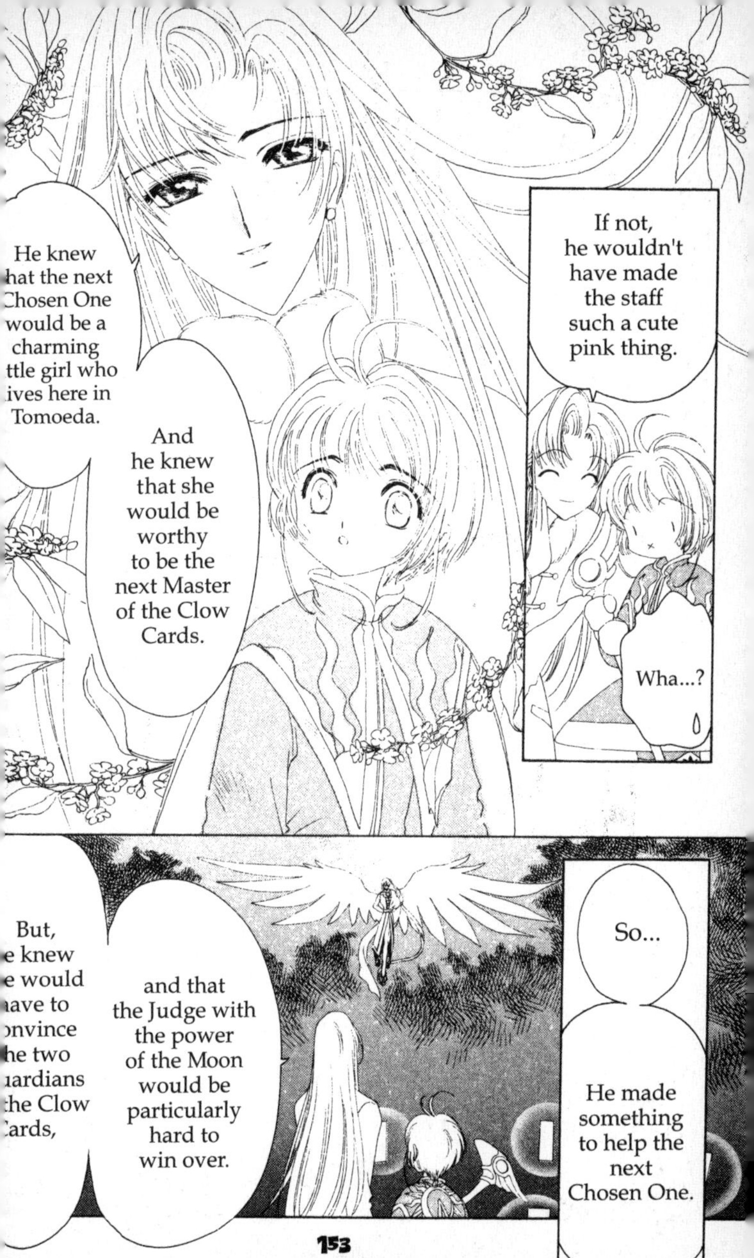
He knew
hat the next
Chosen One
would be a
charming
ttle girl who
ives here in
Tomoeda.
And he knew that she would be worthy to be the next Master of the Clow Cards.
If not, he wouldn't have made the staff such a cute pink thing.
Wha...?
But,
e knew
e would
ave to
onvince
he two
uardians
he Clow
ards,
and that the Judge with the power of the Moon would be particularly hard to win over.
So...
He made something to help the next Chosen One.

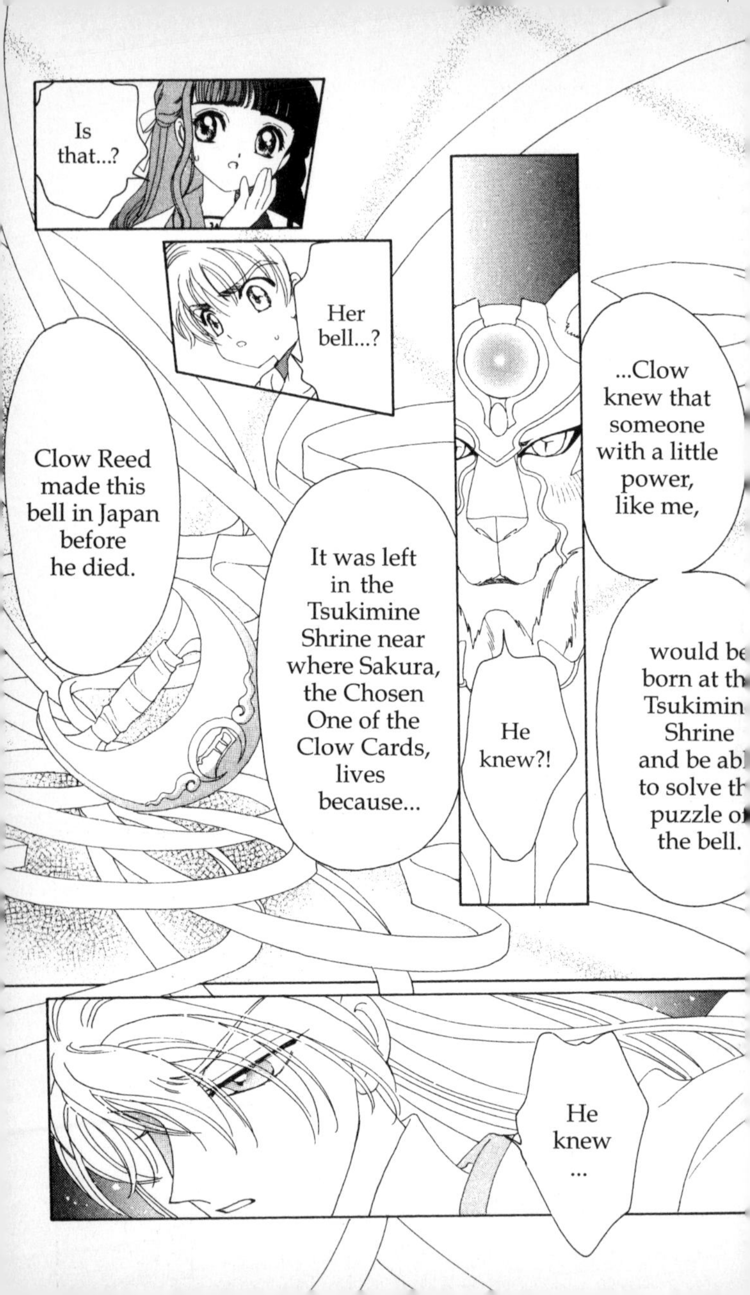
Is that...?
Her bell...?
Clow Reed made this bell in Japan before he died.
It was left in the Tsukimine Shrine near where Sakura, the Chosen One of the Clow Cards, lives because...
...Clow knew that someone with a little power, like me,
would be born at th Tsukimin Shrine and be ab to solve th puzzle o the bell.
He knew?!
He knew ...

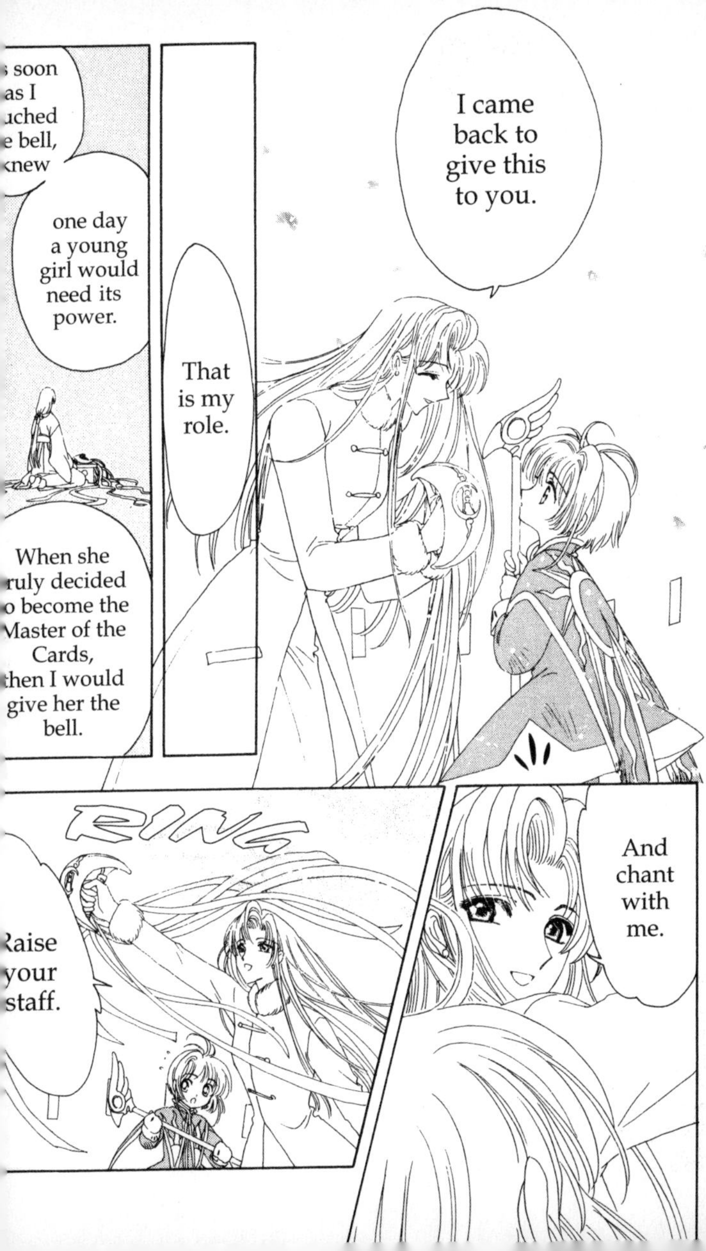
s soon as I uched e bell, knew
one day a young girl would need its power.
When she ruly decided o become the Master of the Cards, then I would give her the bell.
That is my role.
I came back to give this to you.
RING
Raise your staff.
And chant with me.

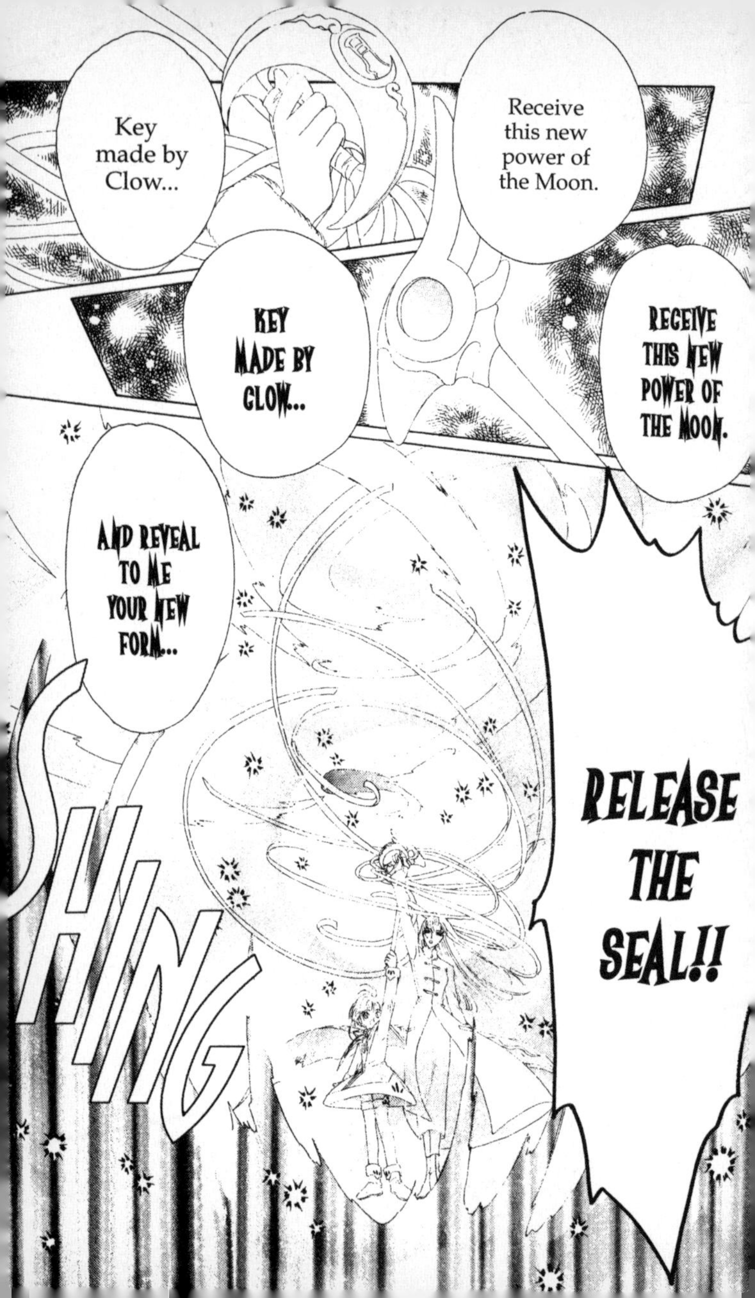
Key made by Clow...
Receive this new power of the Moon.
KEY MADE BY CLOW...
RECEIVE THIS NEW POWER OF THE MOON.
AND REVEAL TO ME YOUR NEW FORM...
SHING
RELEASE THE SEAL!!

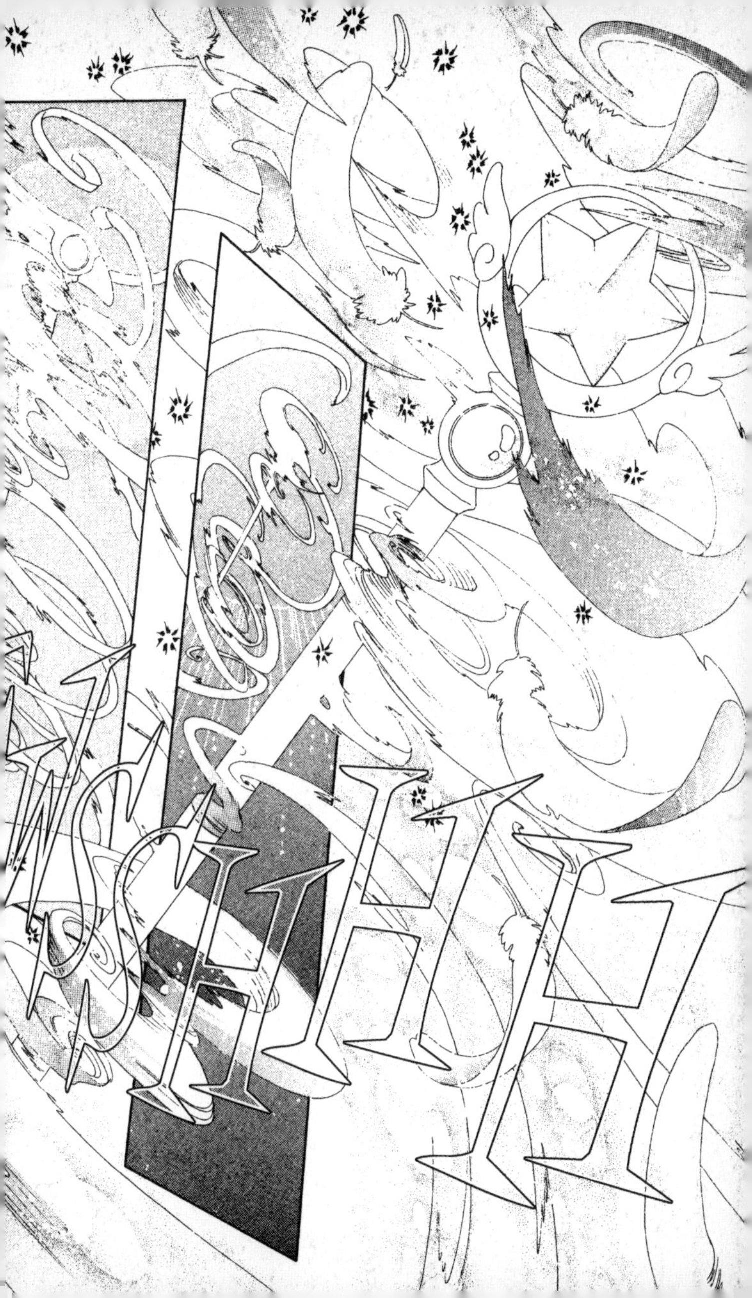
WSHHHH

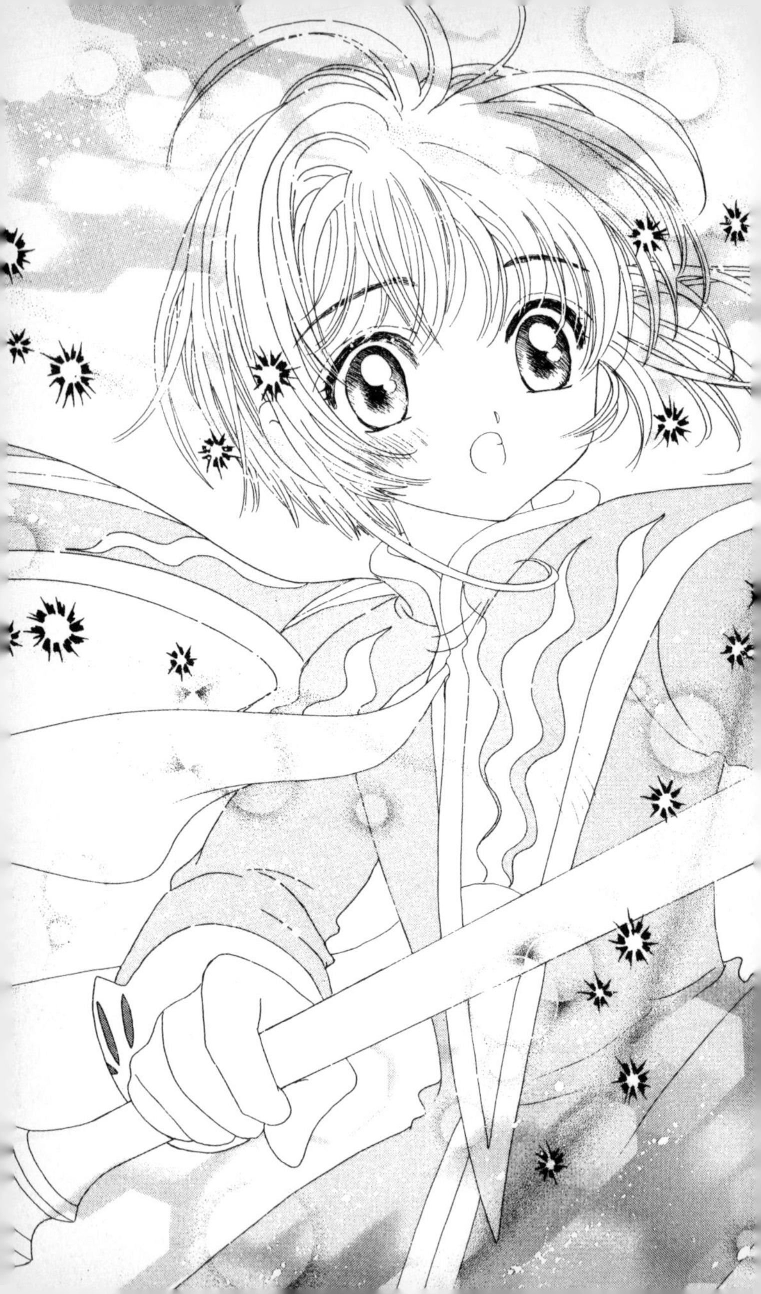

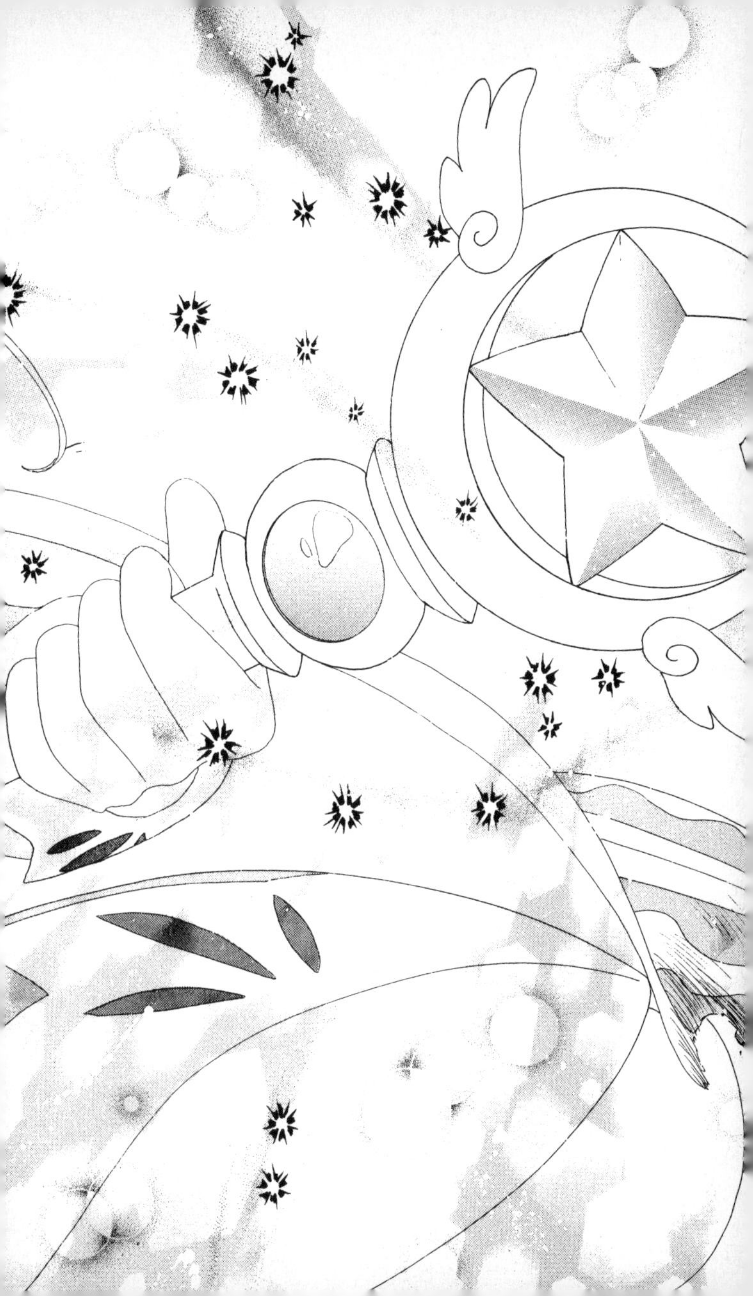

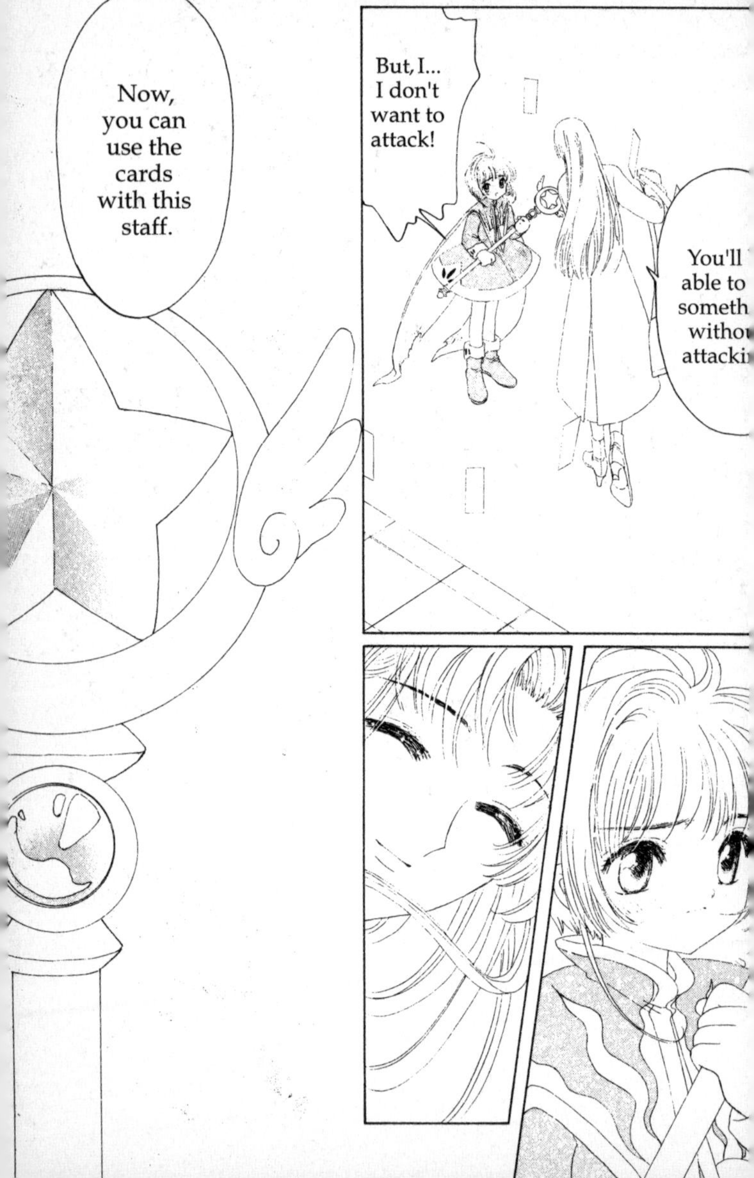
Now, you can use the cards with this staff.
But, I... I don't want to attack!
You'll able to someth withou attacki

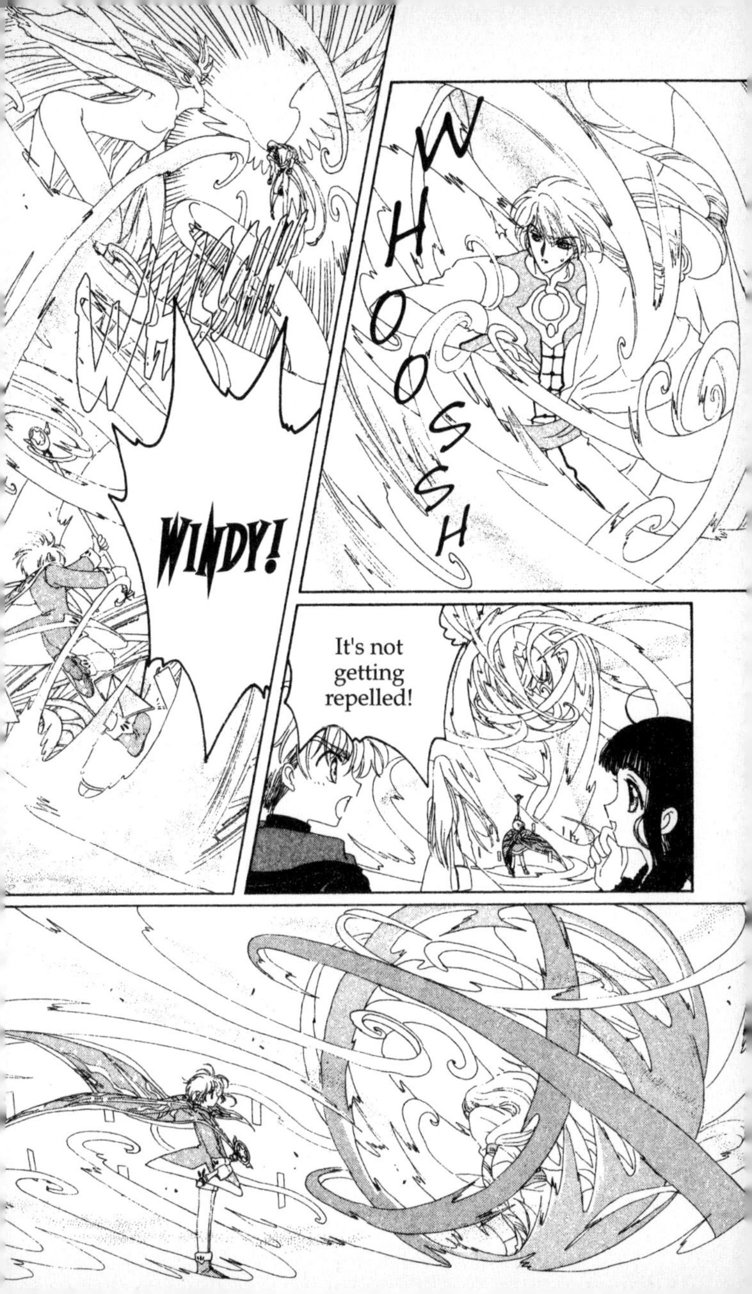
WHOOSH
It's not getting repelled!
WINDY!

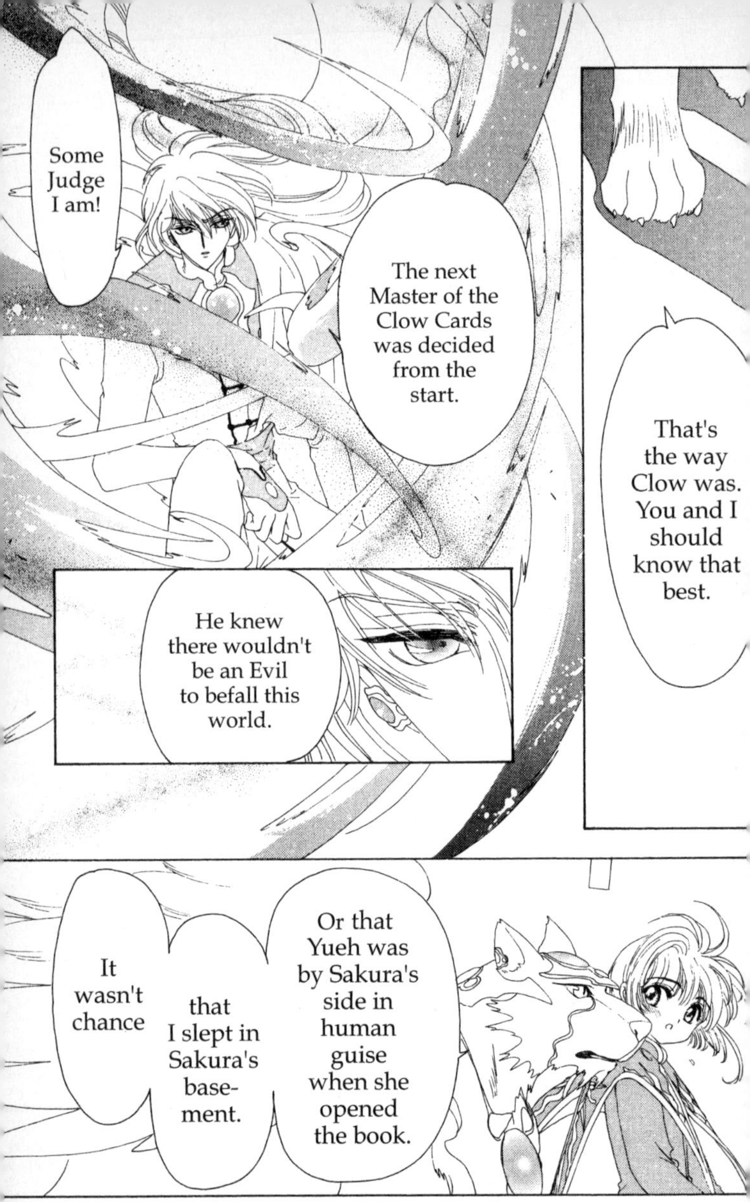
Some Judge I am!
The next Master of the Clow Cards was decided from the start.
He knew there wouldn't be an Evil to befall this world.
That's the way Clow was. You and I should know that best.
It wasn't chance
that I slept in Sakura's basement.
Or that Yueh was by Sakura's side in human guise when she opened the book.

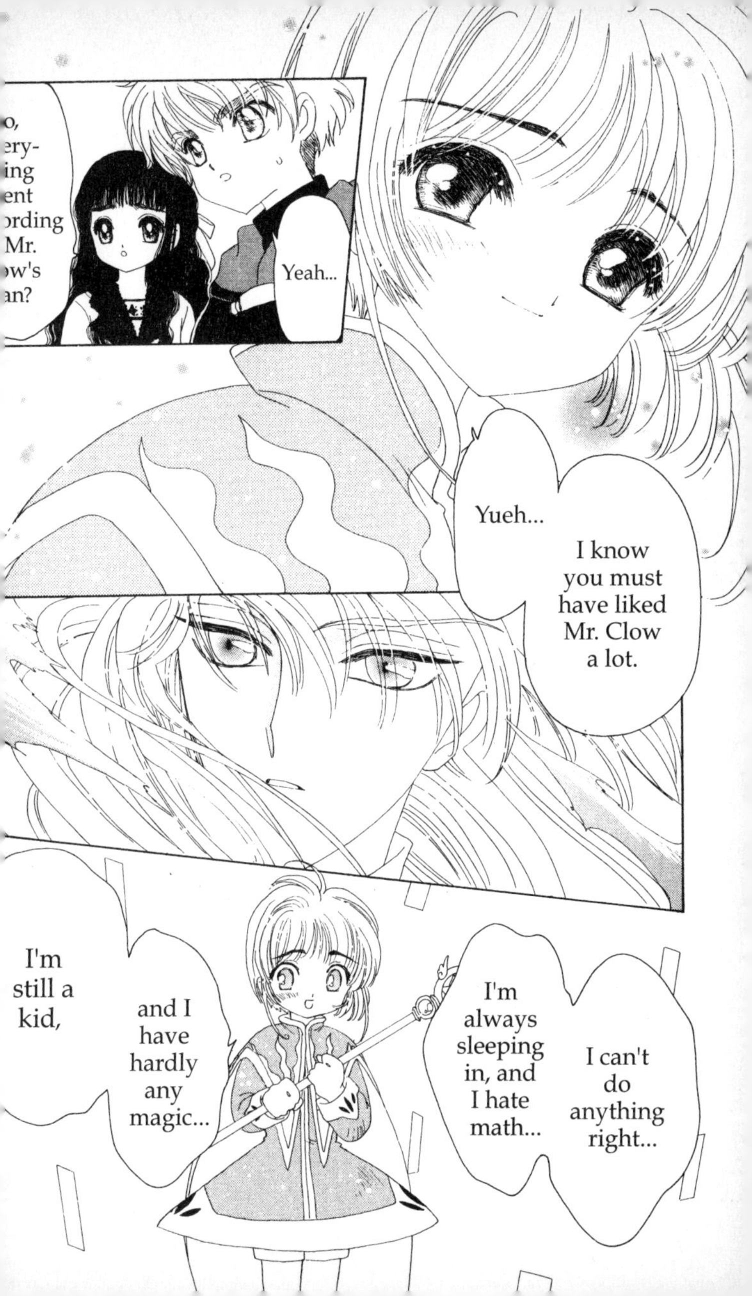
o, ery- ing ent ording Mr. ow's an?
Yeah...
Yueh...
I know you must have liked Mr. Clow a lot.
I'm still a kid,
and I have hardly any magic...
I'm always sleeping in, and I hate math...
I can't do anything right...

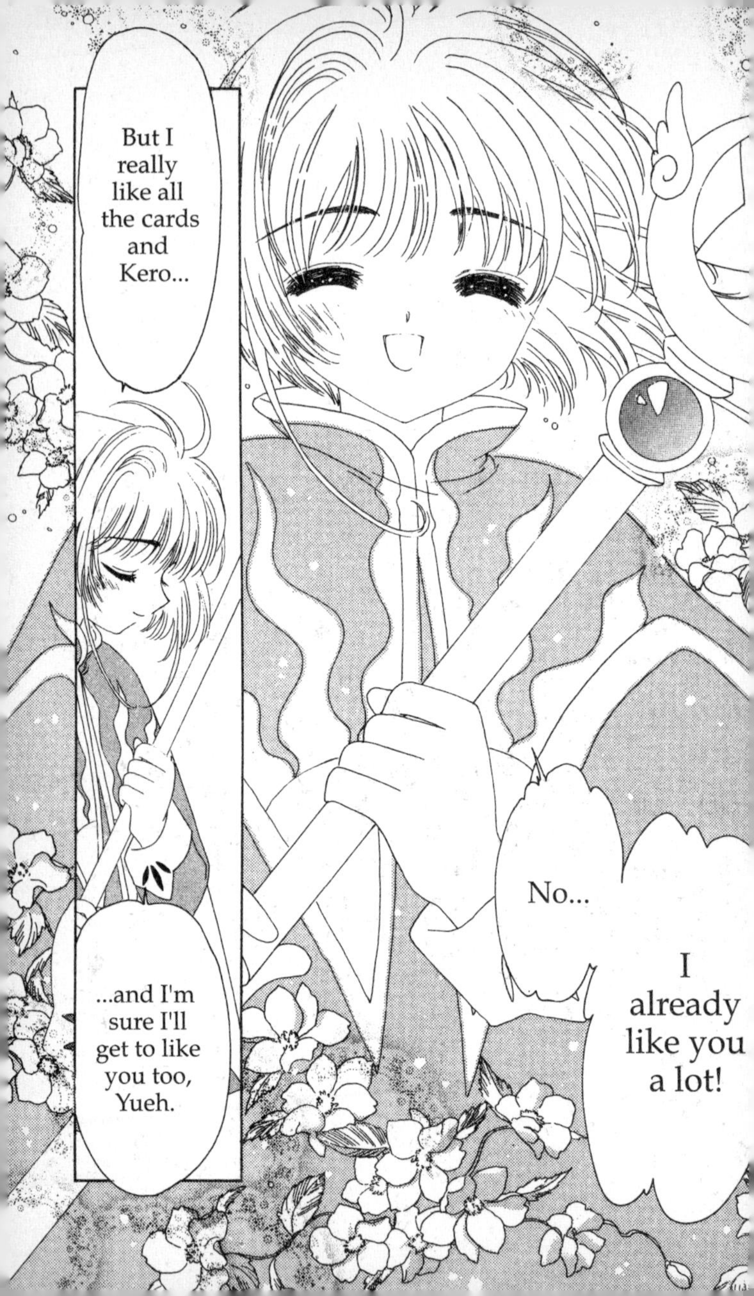
But I really like all the cards and Kero...
...and I'm sure I'll get to like you too, Yueh.
No...
I already like you a lot!

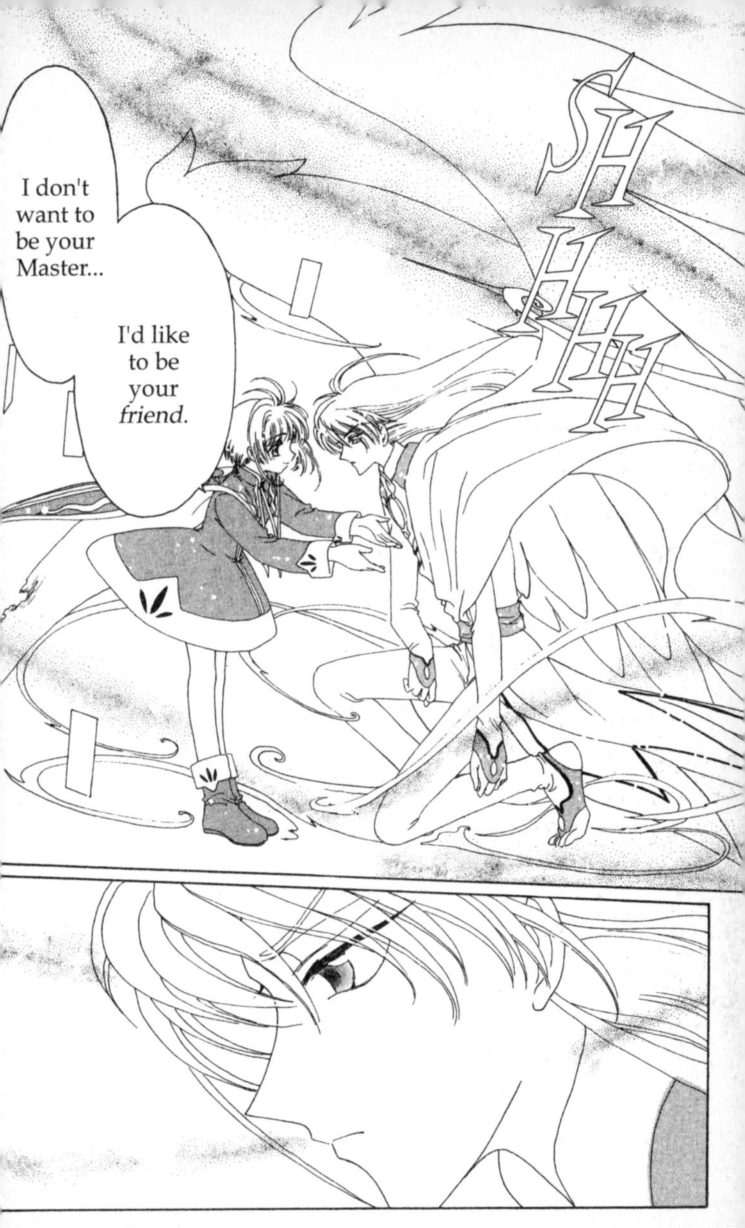

I don't want to be your Master...
I'd like to be your *friend*.
SHHHHH

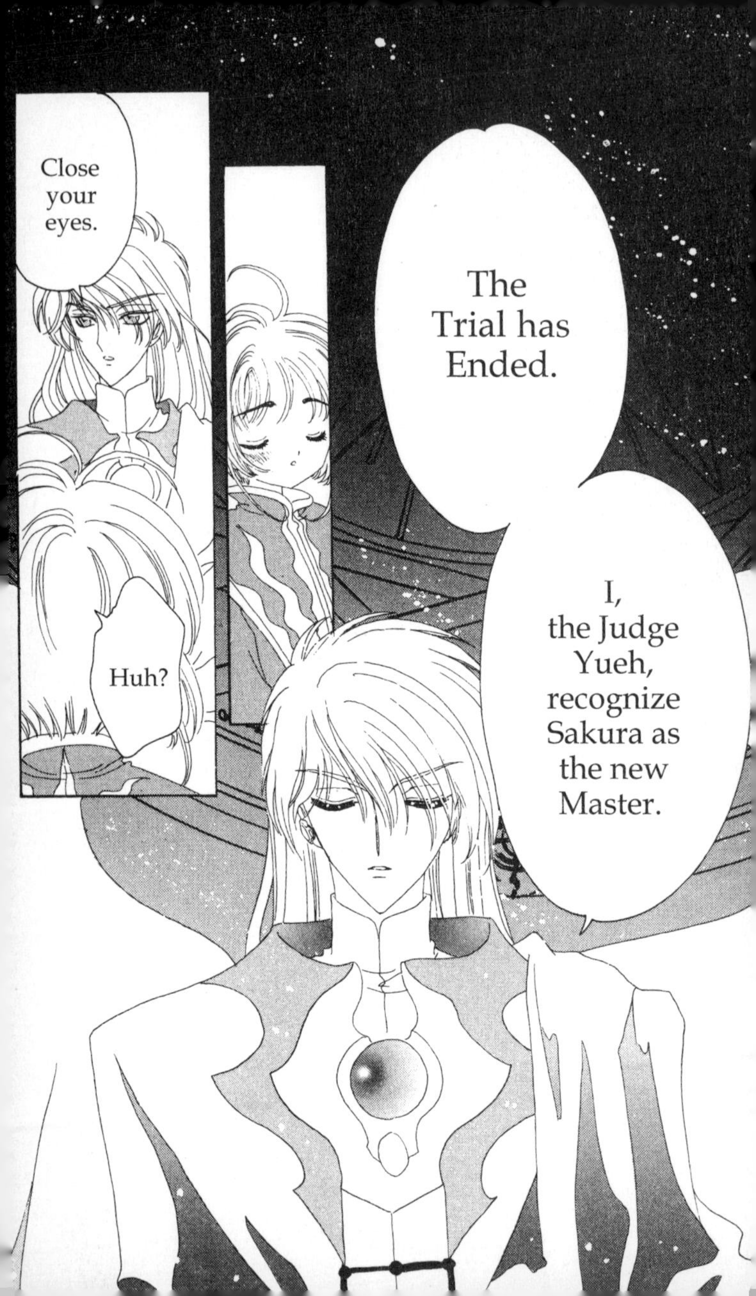
The Trial has Ended.
I, the Judge Yueh, recognize Sakura as the new Master.
Close your eyes.
Huh?

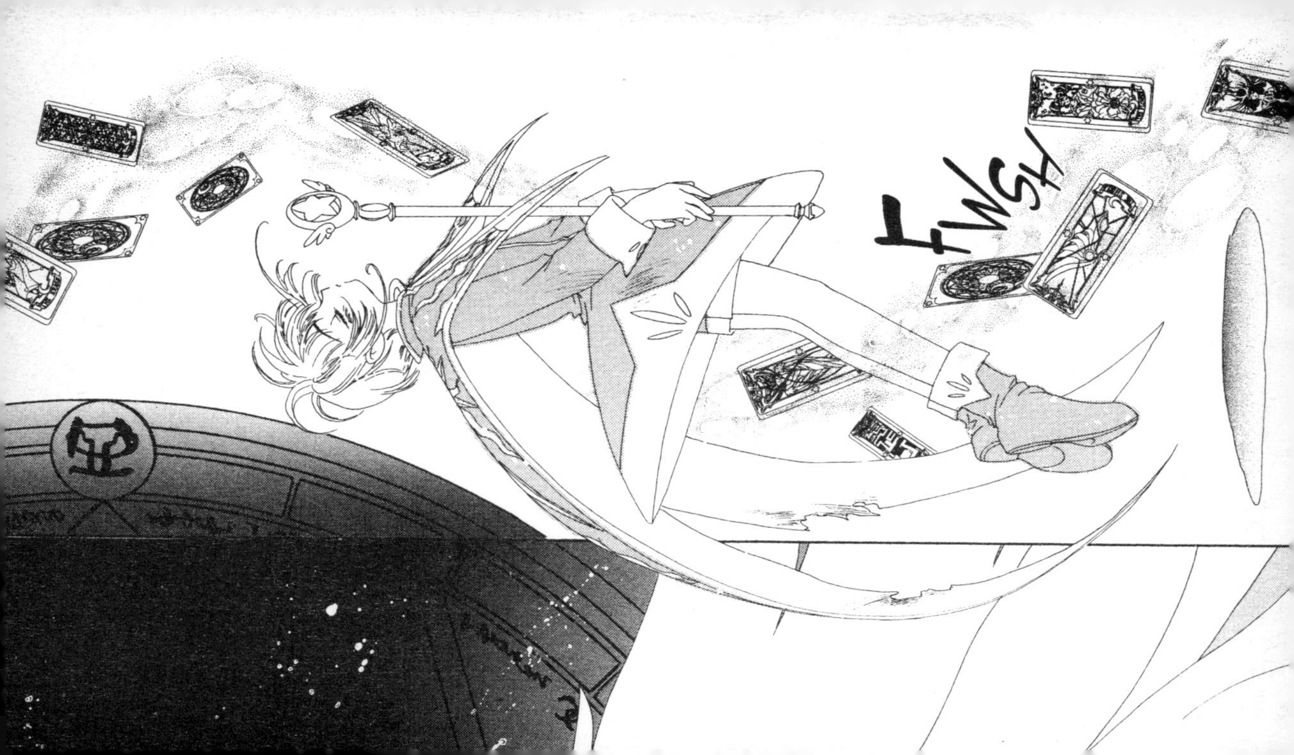
FWSH

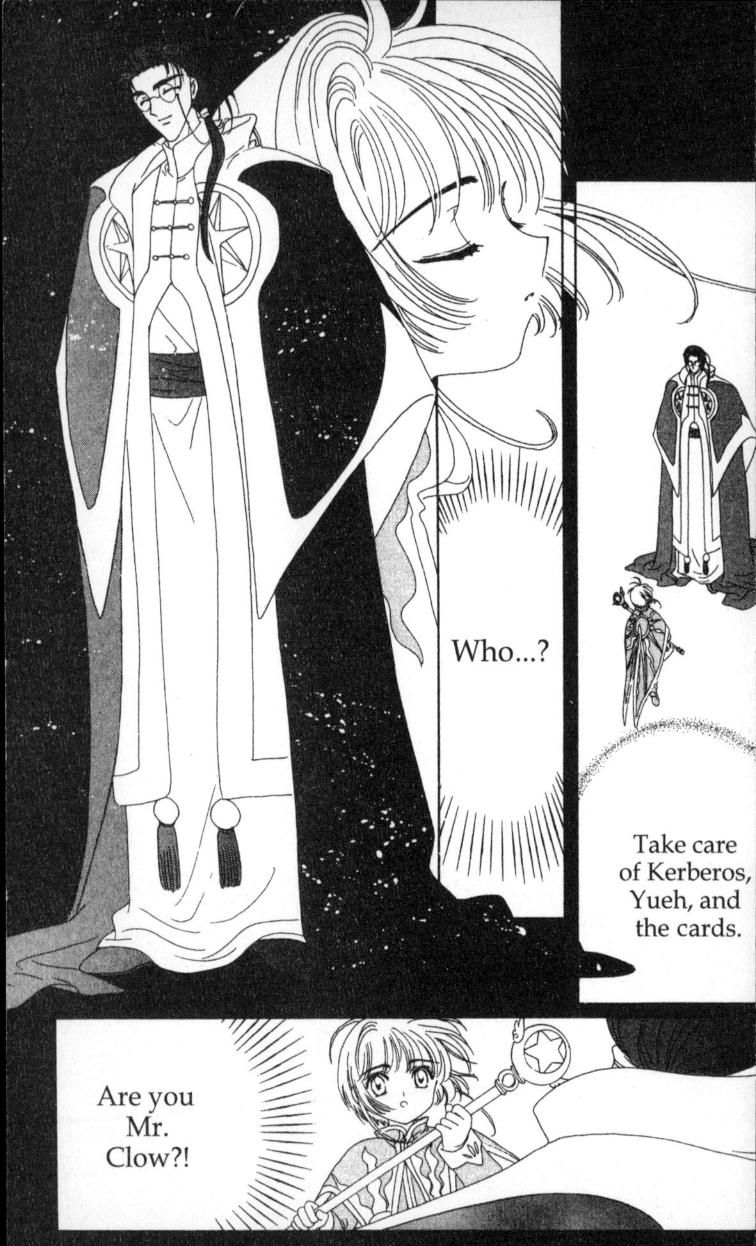
Take care of Kerberos, Yueh, and the cards.
Who...?
Are you Mr. Clow?!

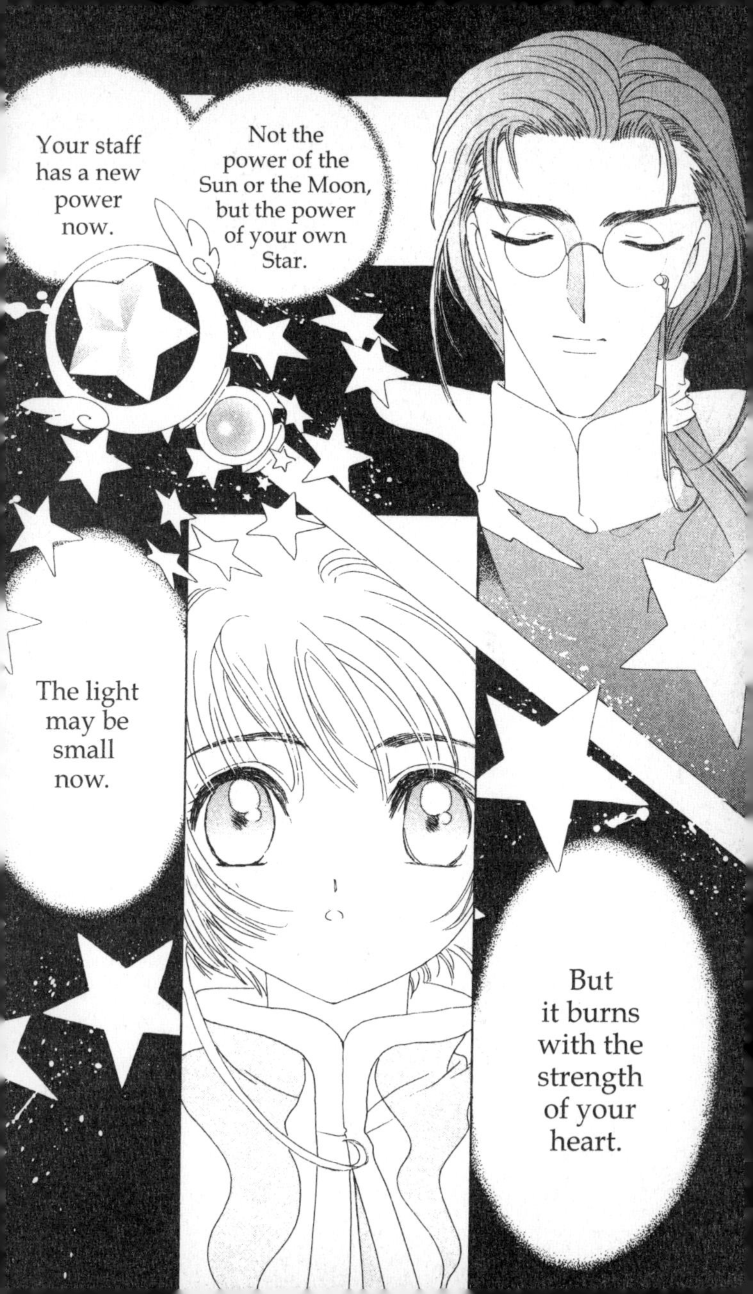

Your staff has a new power now.
Not the power of the Sun or the Moon, but the power of your own Star.
The light may be small now.
But it burns with the strength of your heart.

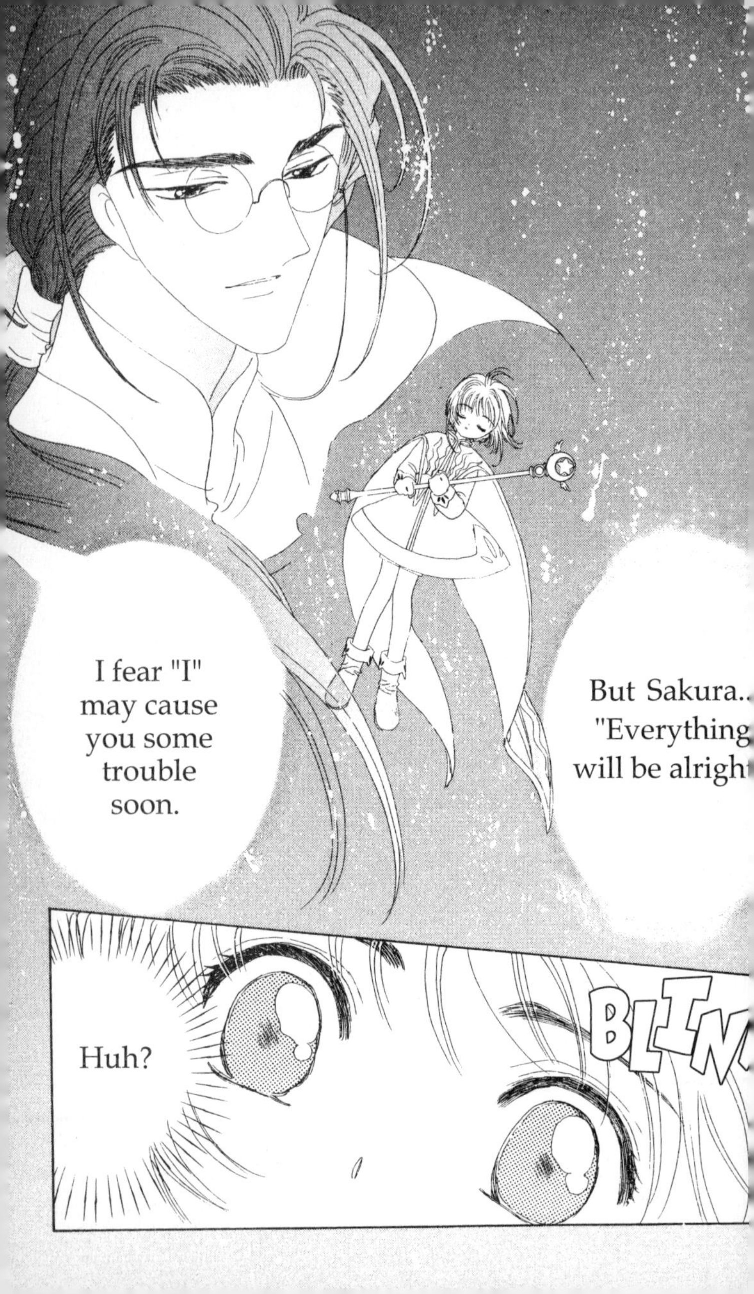
But Sakura.. "Everything will be alrigh
I fear "I" may cause you some trouble soon.
BLIN
Huh?

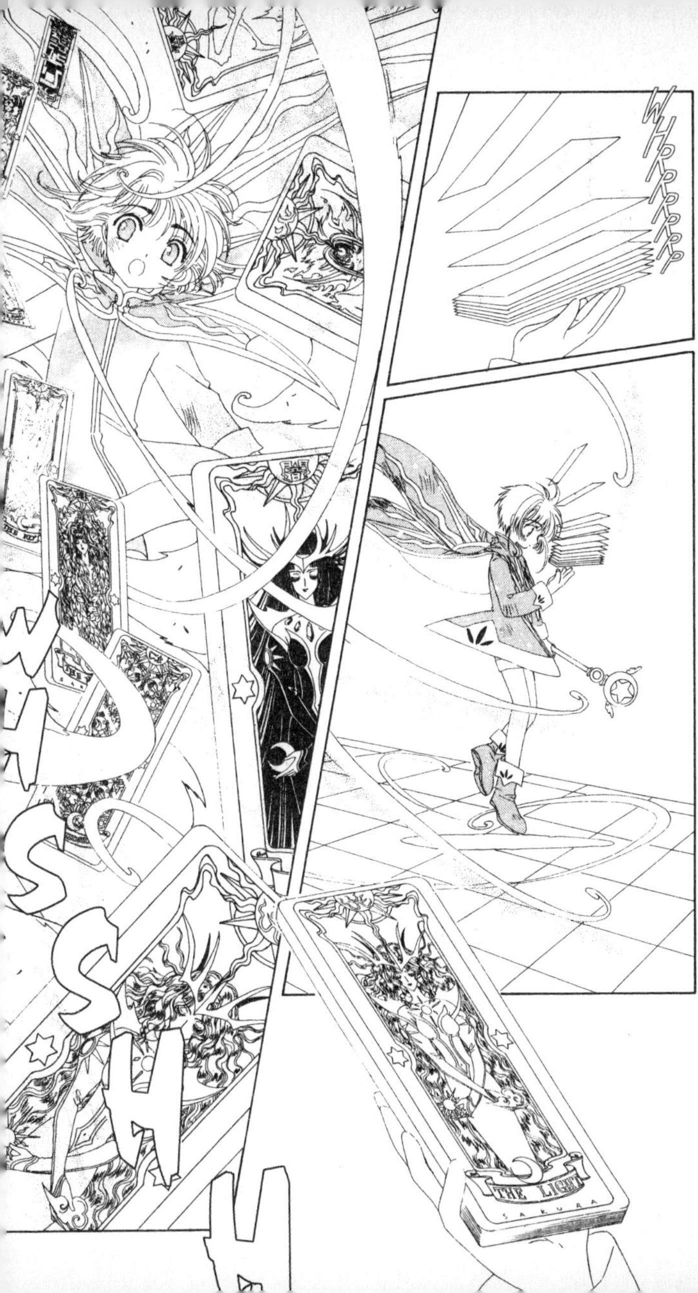
WHRRRRP
THE LIGHT
SAKURA
WHSSHH

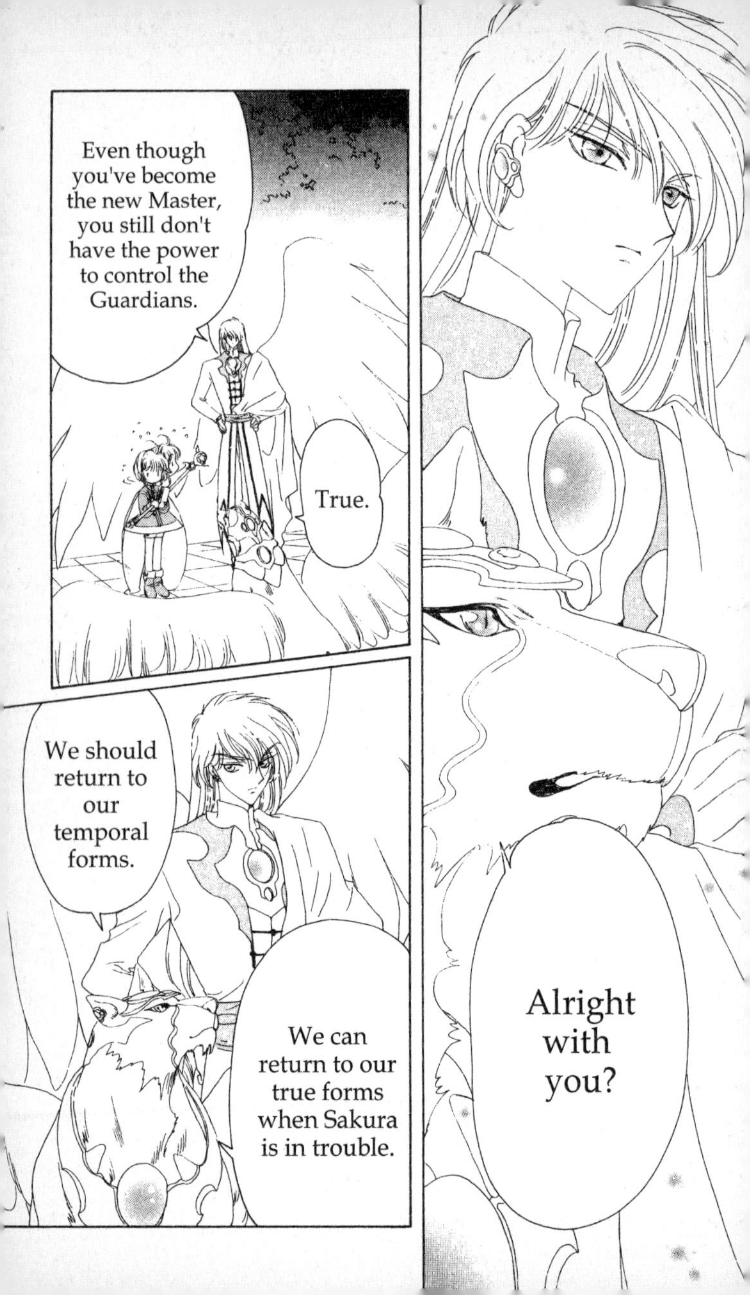
Even though you've become the new Master, you still don't have the power to control the Guardians.
True.
We should return to our temporal forms.
We can return to our true forms when Sakura is in trouble.
Alright with you?

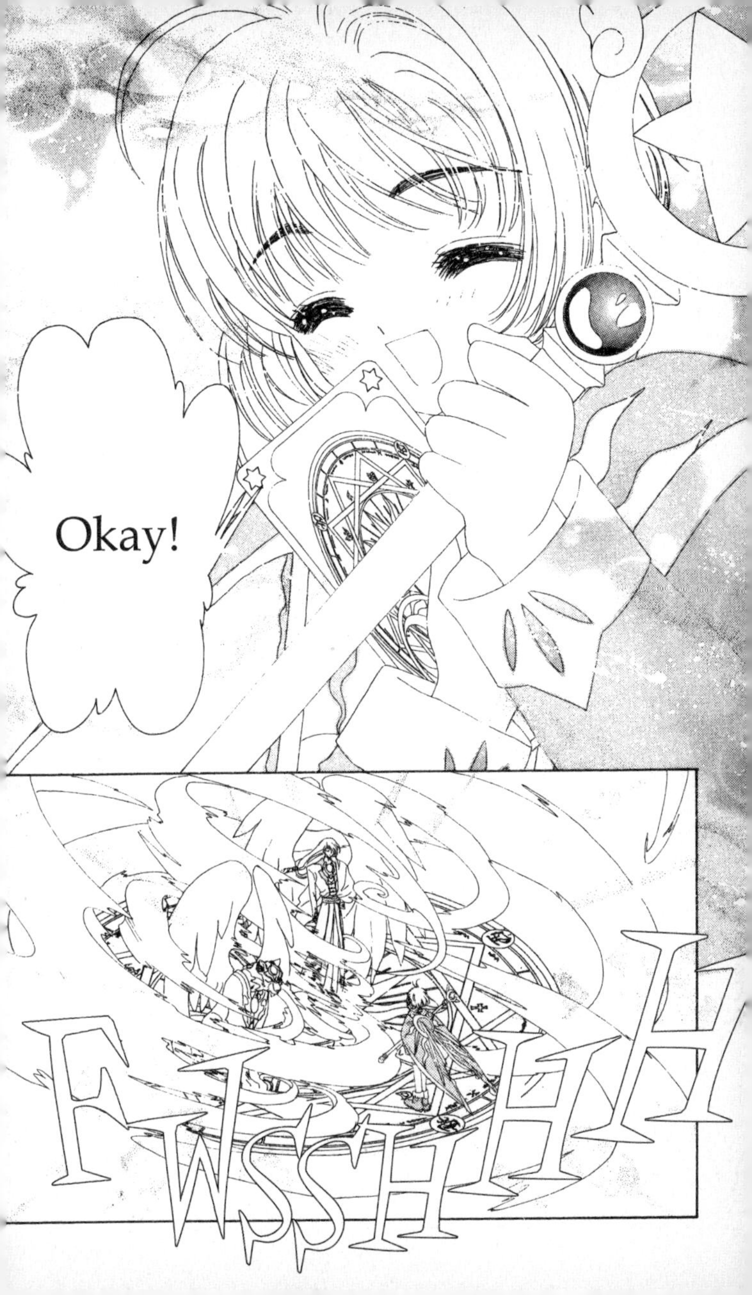
Okay!
FWSSHHHH

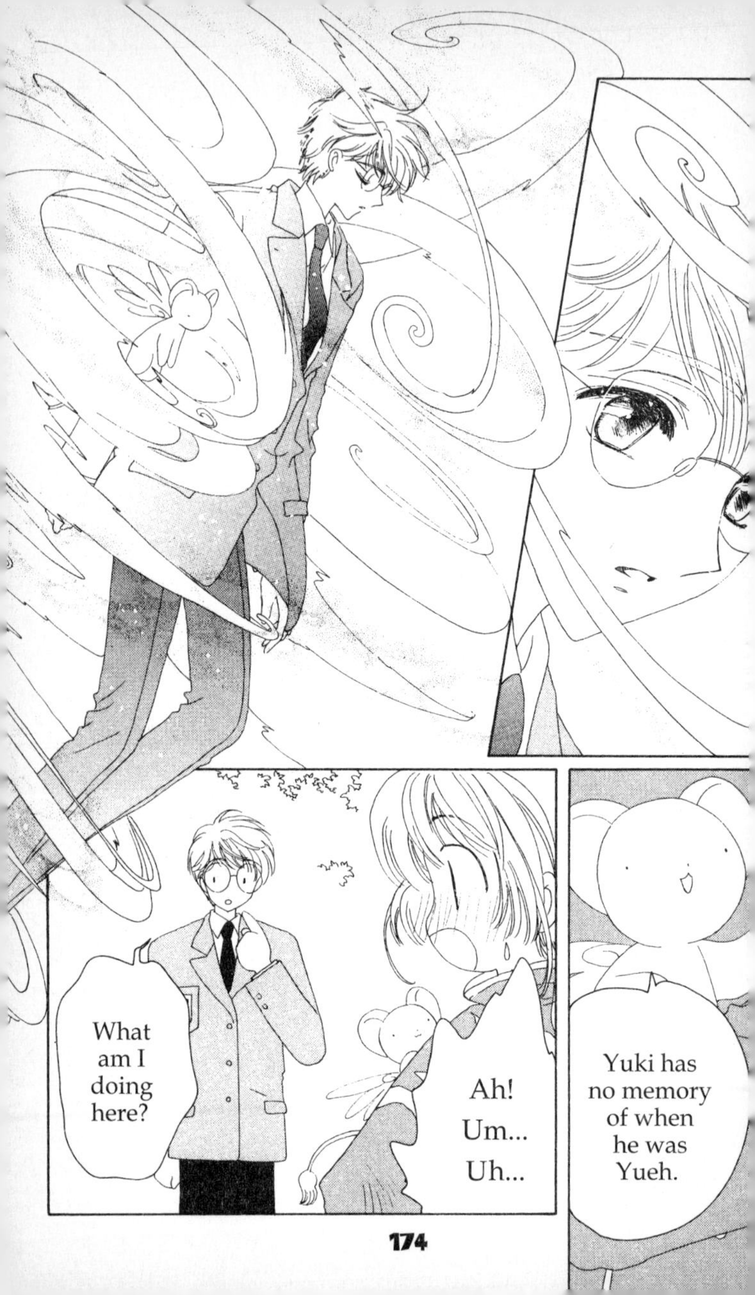
What am I doing here?
Ah! Um... Uh...
Yuki has no memory of when he was Yueh.

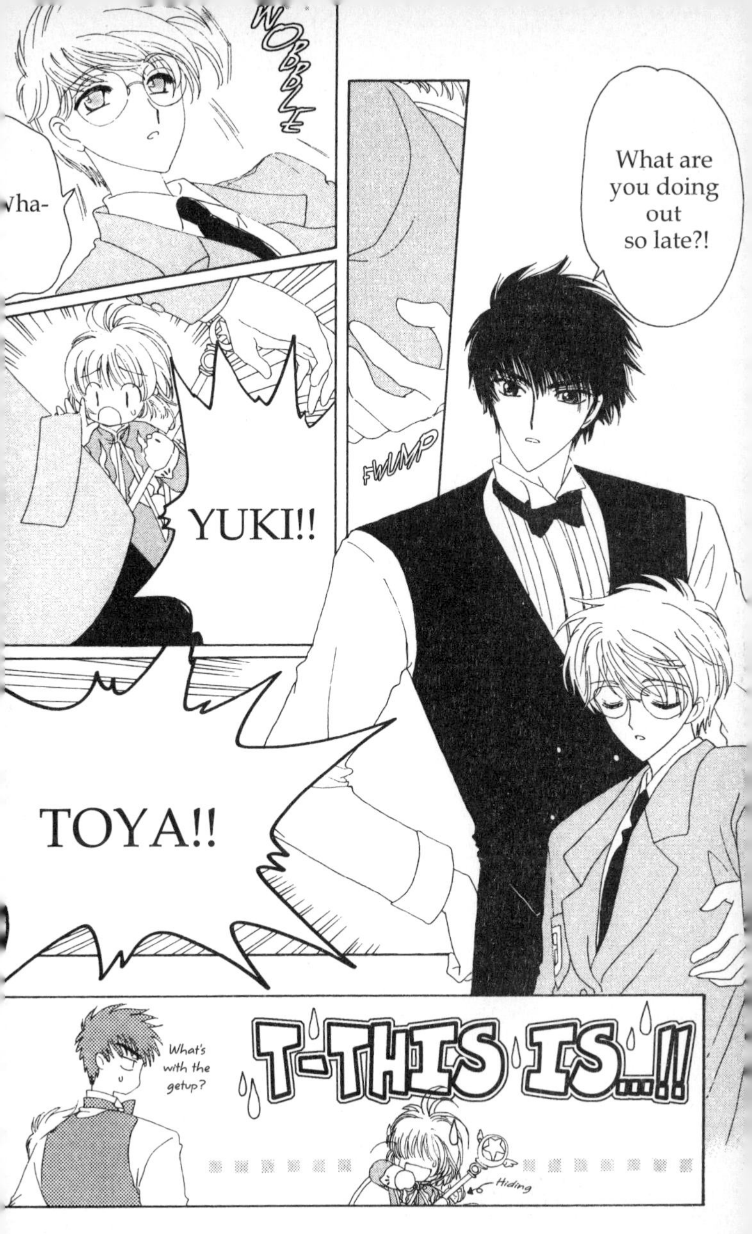
What are you doing out so late?!
FWUMP
WOBBLE
Wha-
YUKI!!
TOYA!!
T-THIS IS...!!
Hiding
What's with the getup?

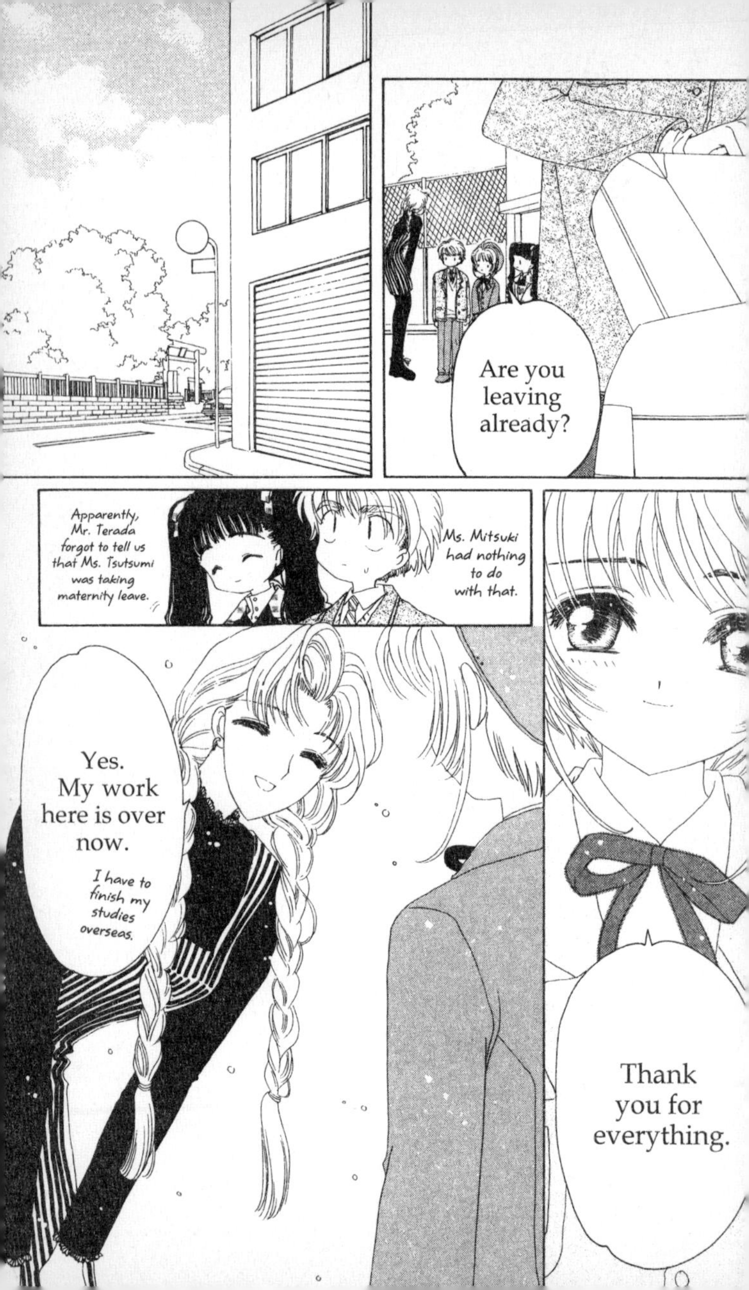

Are you leaving already?
Apparently, Mr. Terada forgot to tell us that Ms. Tsutsumi was taking maternity leave.
Ms. Mitsuki had nothing to do with that.
Yes. My work here is over now.
I have to finish my studies overseas.
Thank you for everything.

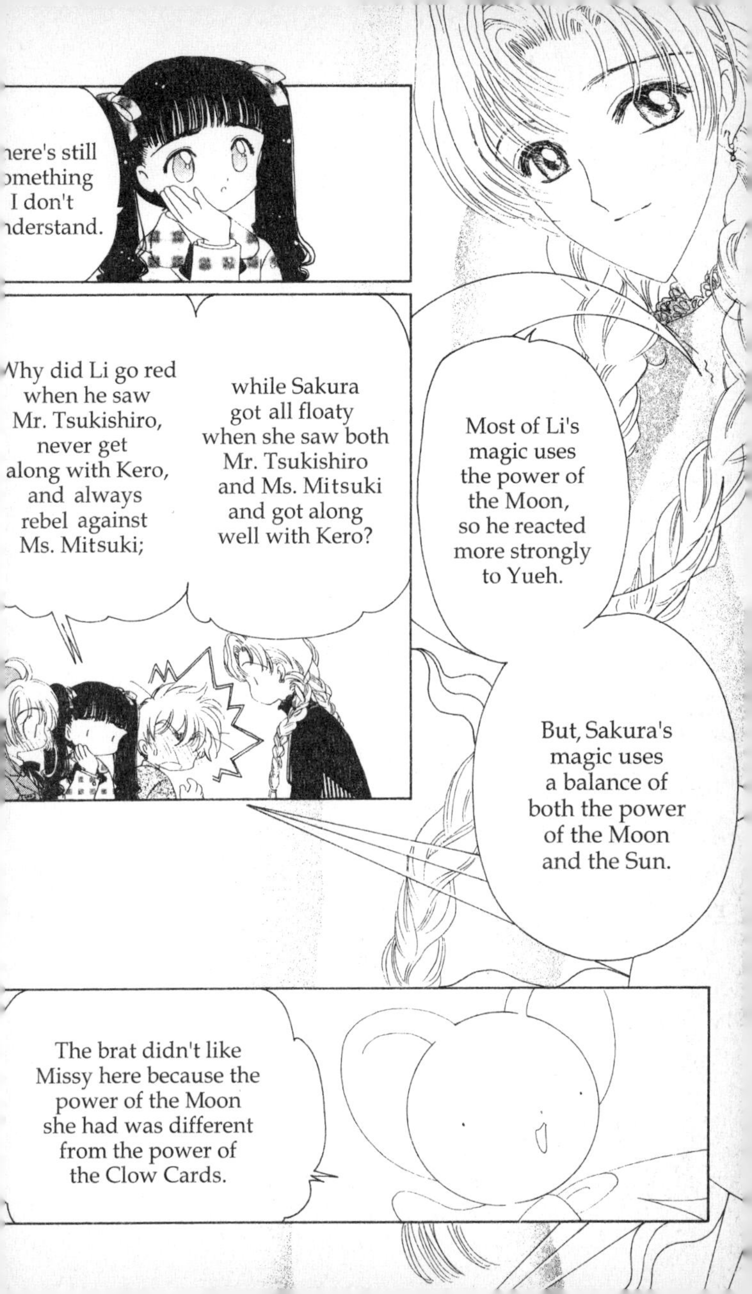

here's still omething I don't nderstand.
Why did Li go red when he saw Mr. Tsukishiro, never get along with Kero, and always rebel against Ms. Mitsuki;
while Sakura got all floaty when she saw both Mr. Tsukishiro and Ms. Mitsuki and got along well with Kero?
Most of Li's magic uses the power of the Moon, so he reacted more strongly to Yueh.
But, Sakura's magic uses a balance of both the power of the Moon and the Sun.
The brat didn't like Missy here because the power of the Moon she had was different from the power of the Clow Cards.

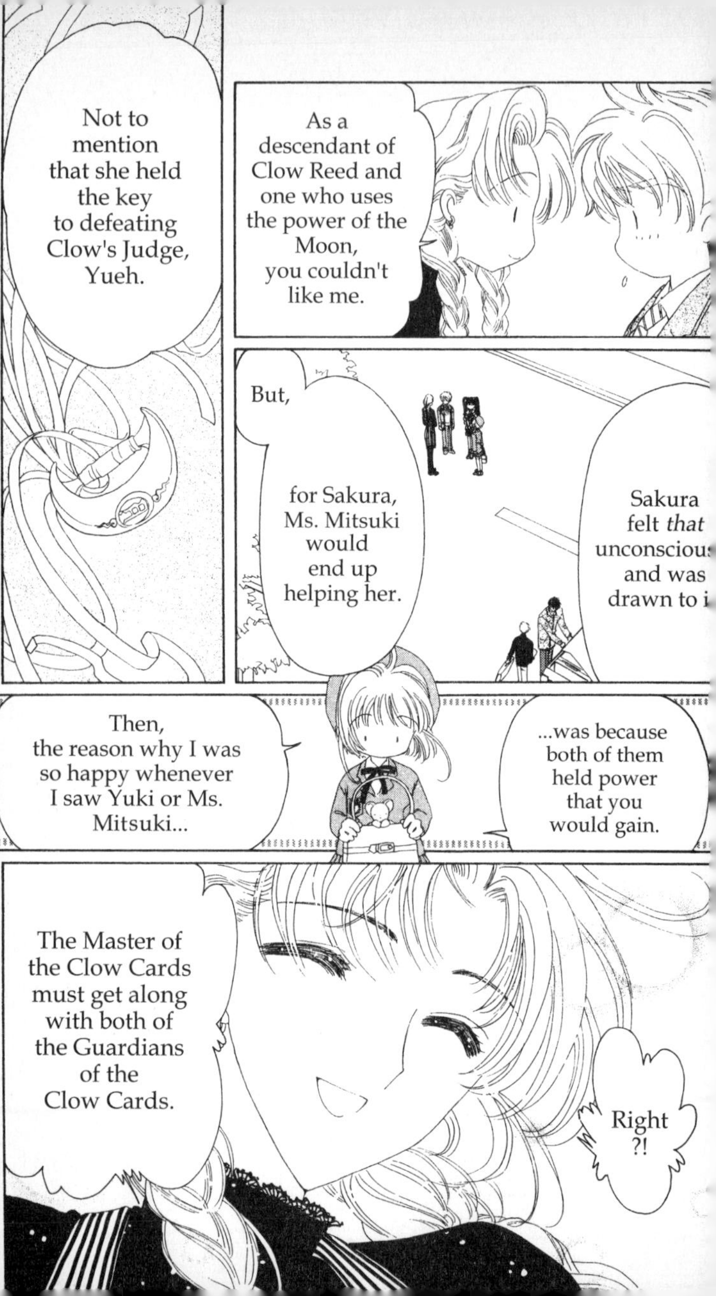

As a descendant of Clow Reed and one who uses the power of the Moon, you couldn't like me.
But,
for Sakura, Ms. Mitsuki would end up helping her.
Sakura felt *that* unconsciou and was drawn to i
Not to mention that she held the key to defeating Clow's Judge, Yueh.
Then, the reason why I was so happy whenever I saw Yuki or Ms. Mitsuki...
...was because both of them held power that you would gain.
The Master of the Clow Cards must get along with both of the Guardians of the Clow Cards.
Right ?!

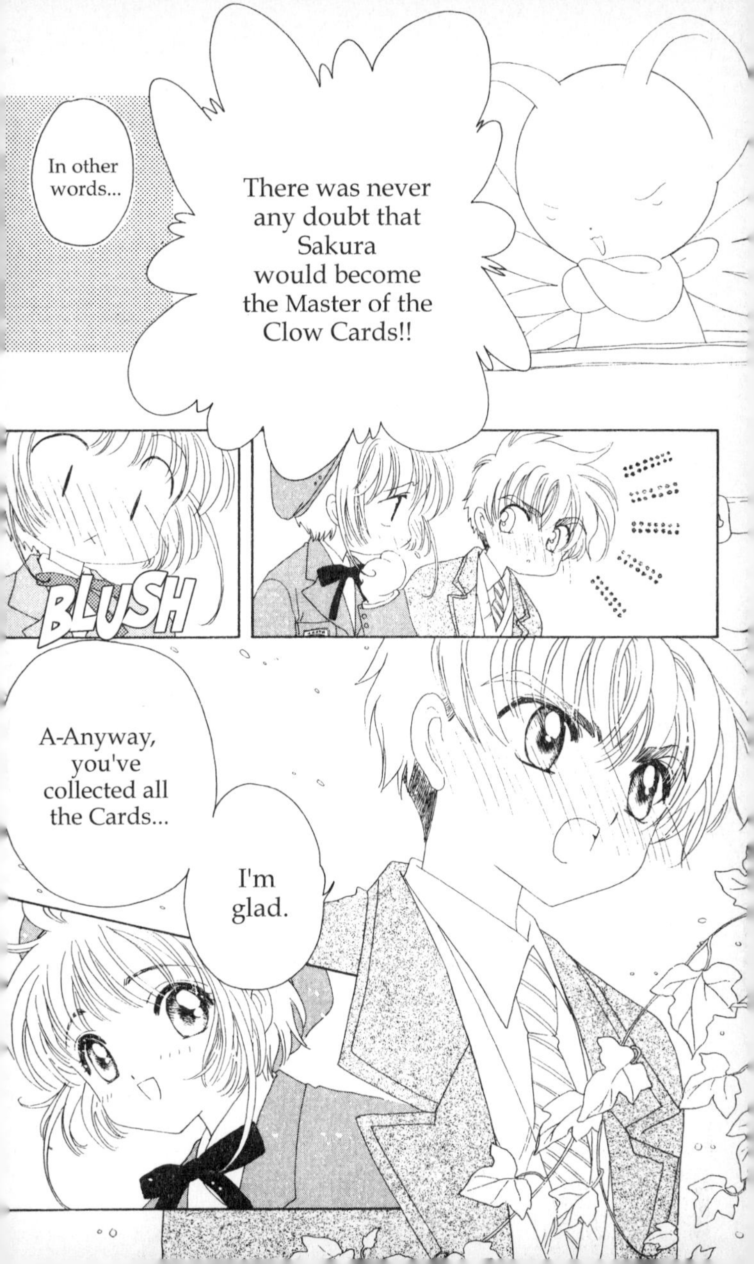
In other words...
There was never any doubt that Sakura would become the Master of the Clow Cards!!
BLUSH
A-Anyway, you've collected all the Cards...
I'm glad.

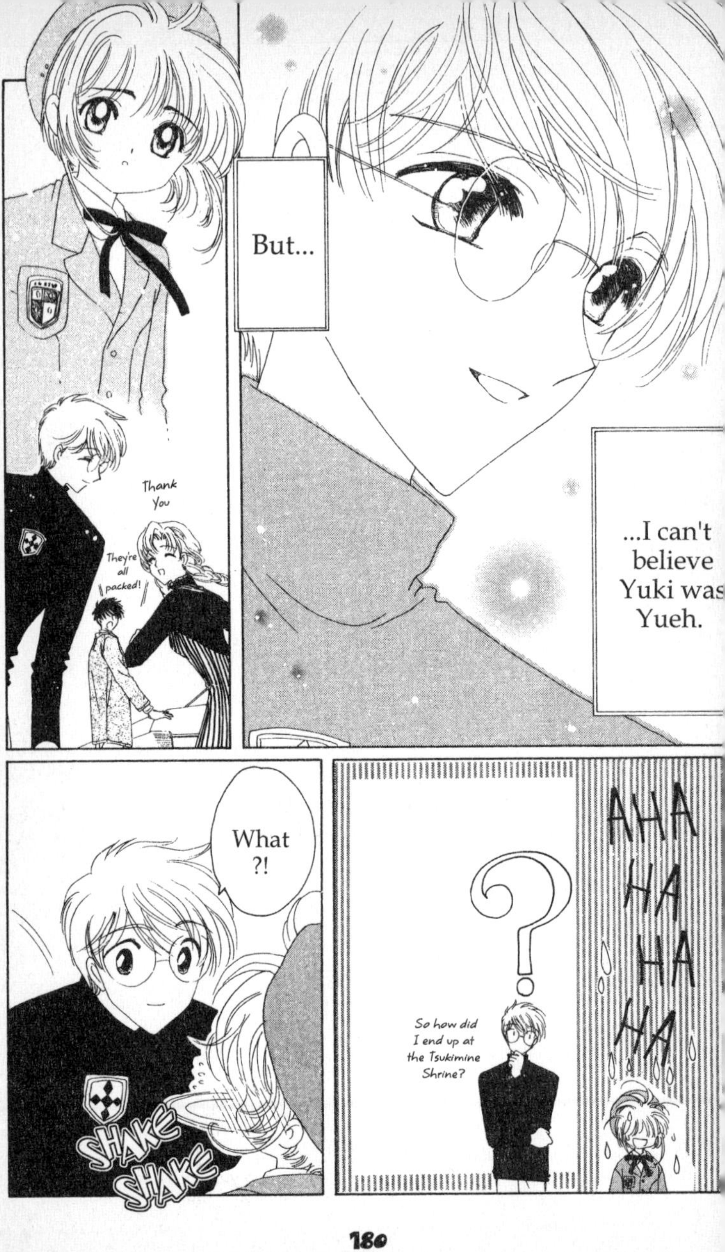
But...
...I can't believe Yuki was Yueh.
Thank You
They're all packed!
So how did I end up at the Tsukimine Shrine?
AHAHAHAHAHA
What?!
SHAKE SHAKE

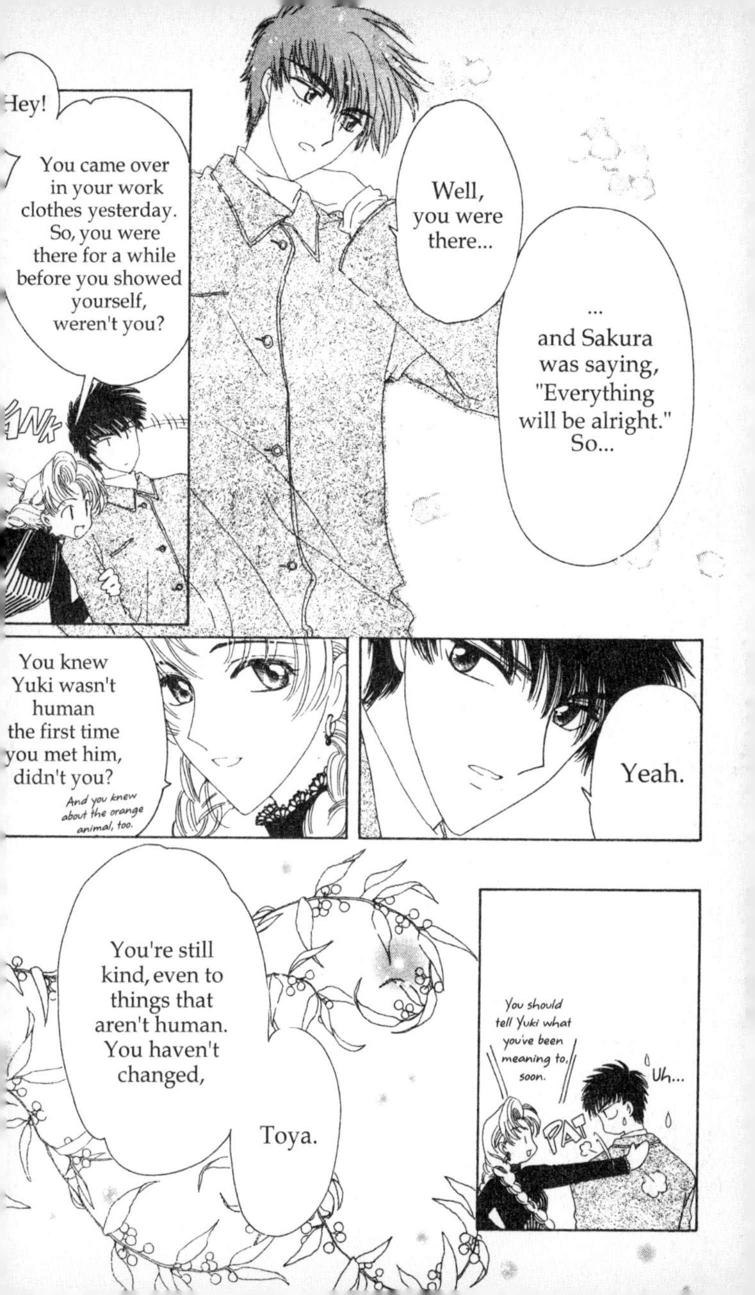
Hey!
You came over in your work clothes yesterday. So, you were there for a while before you showed yourself, weren't you?
Well, you were there...
... and Sakura was saying, "Everything will be alright." So...
You knew Yuki wasn't human the first time you met him, didn't you?
And you knew about the orange animal, too.
Yeah.
You're still kind, even to things that aren't human. You haven't changed,
Toya.
You should tell Yuki what you've been meaning to, soon.
PAT
Uh...

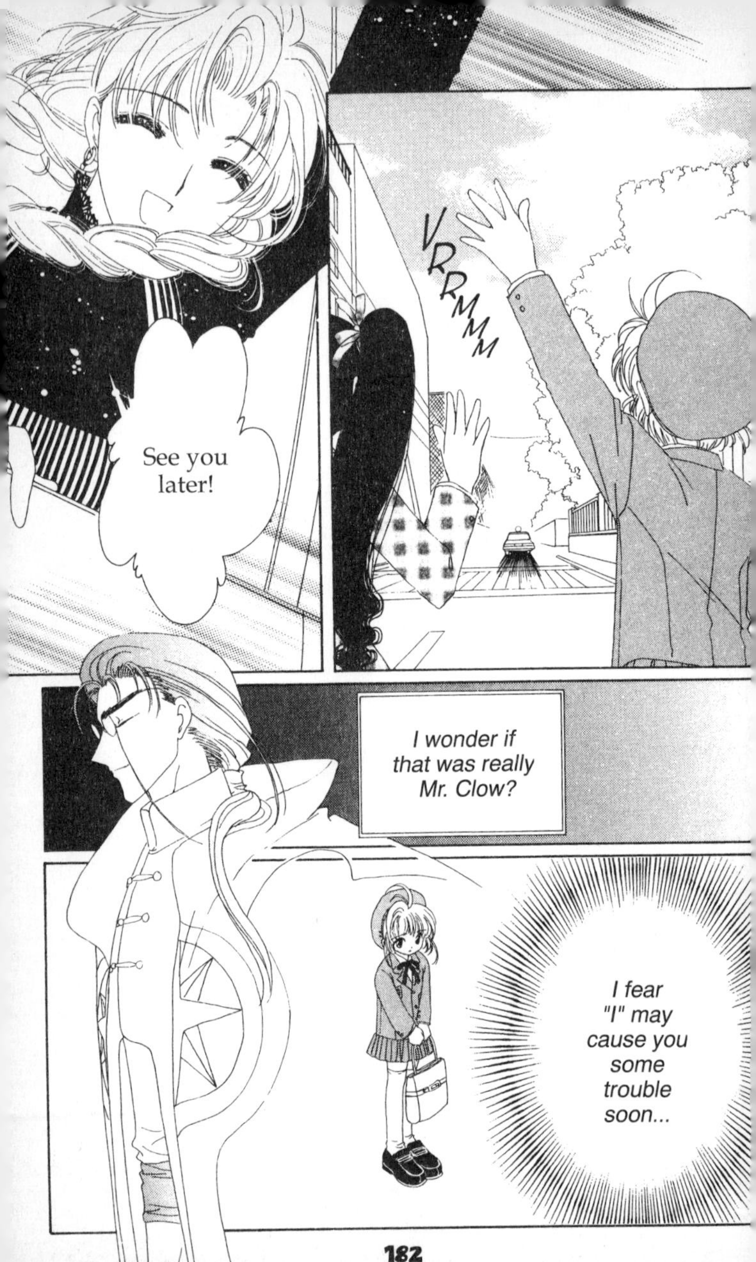
VRRMMM
See you later!
I wonder if that was really Mr. Clow?
I fear "I" may cause you some trouble soon...

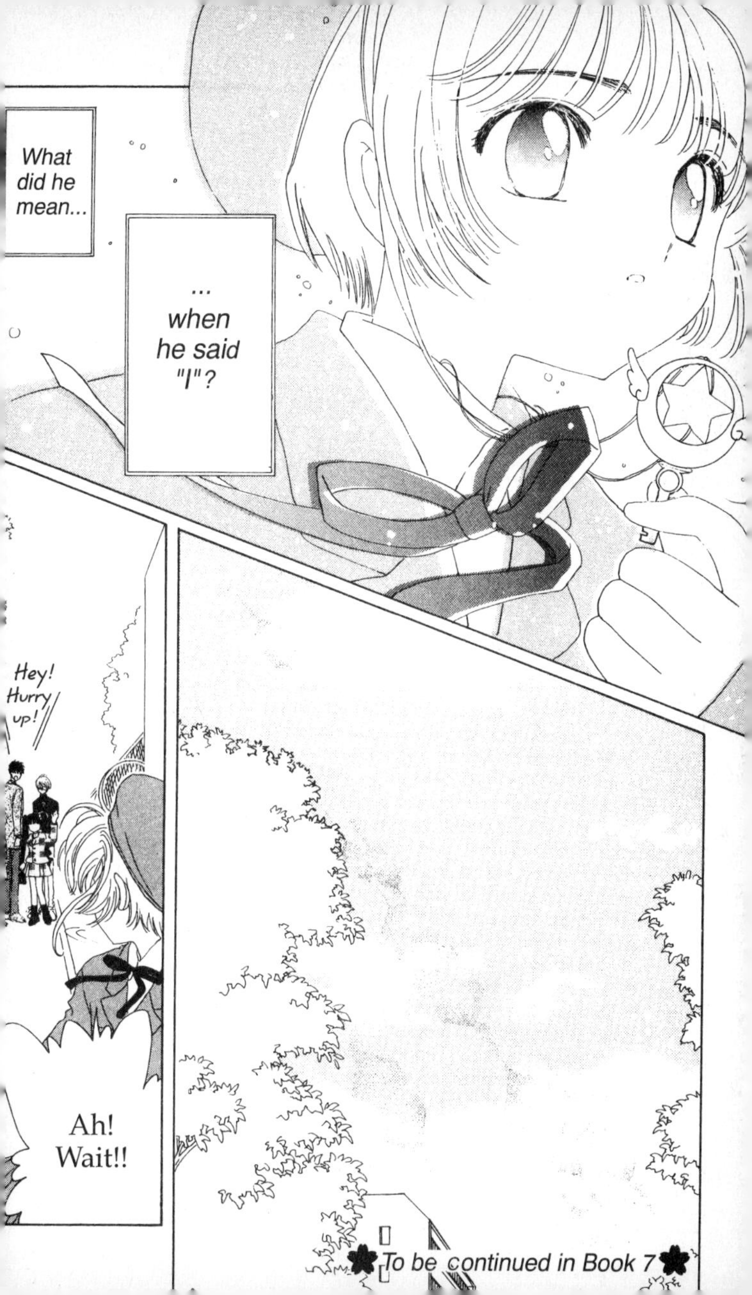
What did he mean...
... when he said "I"?
To be continued in Book 7
Hey! Hurry up!
Ah! Wait!!

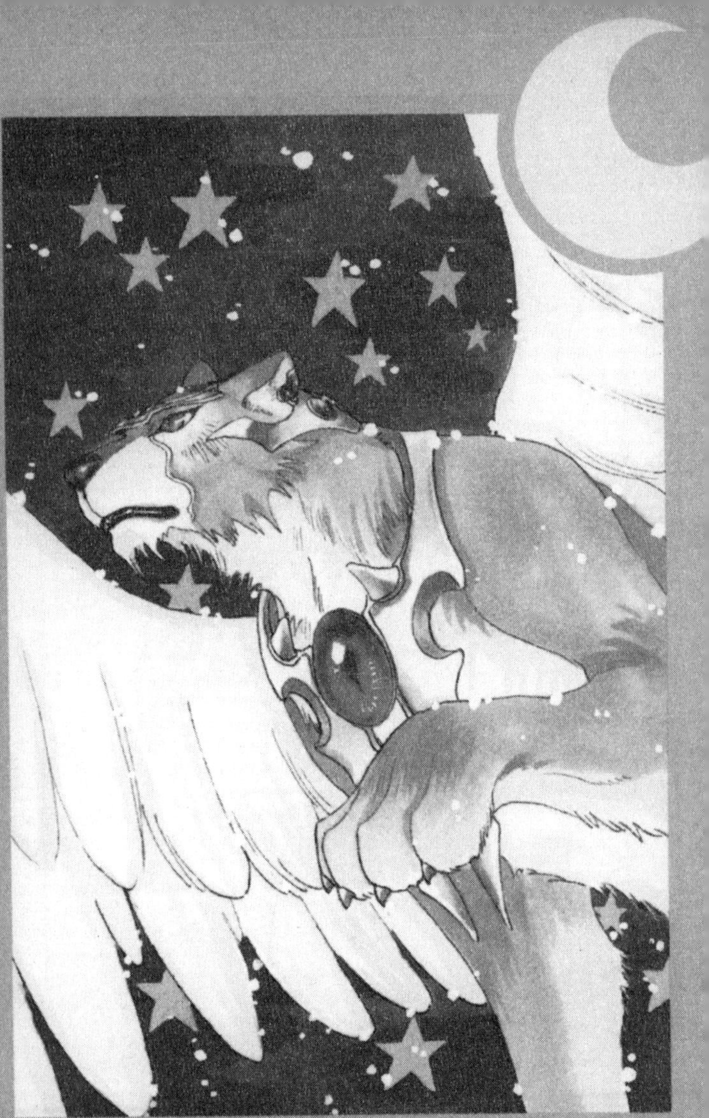

CLAMP

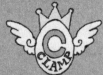